My congratulations to the
cartoonist.

Jawaharlal Nehru
29 . 7 . 1960

Bal Thackeray's tribute to Prime Minister Indira Gandhi (published in *Marmik*) after she was assassinated in October 1984.

BAL
THACKERAY
& THE RISE OF THE SHIV SENA

BAL
THACKERAY
& THE RISE OF THE SHIV SENA

VAIBHAV PURANDARE

Dear Ashoka Mody,

With Best Wishes &

The Warmest Regards,

VPurandare

Nov 2022

LOTUS COLLECTION
•
ROLI BOOKS

Lotus Collection

© Vaibhav Purandare, 2012

First published in 2012
The Lotus Collection
An imprint of
Roli Books Pvt. Ltd
M-75, Greater Kailash II Market
New Delhi 110 048
Phone: ++91 (011) 4068 2000
Fax: ++91 (011) 2921 7185
E-mail: info@rolibooks.com; Website: www.rolibooks.com

Also at
Bengaluru, Chennai & Mumbai

Editor: Padma Rao Sundarji
Cover picture © Getty Images
Cover design: Shrabani Dasgupta
Layout: Sanjeev Mathpal
Production: Shaji Sahadevan

ISBN: 978-81-7436-958-1

Frontispiece, i: A note of appreciation from Prime Minister Jawaharlal Nehru
for the young cartoonist Bal Thackeray, 1960.

Typeset in Bembo by Roli Books Pvt Ltd, and
printed at HT Media, India.

In memory of
Suryakant Chemburkar,
my grandfather.

CONTENTS

Acknowledgements   xi
Prologue   xii

1. The early years   1

2. The political cartoonist   7

3. Maharashtrians and migrants   16

4. Mobilising the Sena corps   28

5. Bal Thackeray: The person and the persona   39

6. Politics, promises and violence   48

7. The battle with the Communists   62

8. Greater Maharashtra and the first arrest   70

9. Bhiwandi burns   85

10. Murder and mandate   88

11. The tenets of *Thokshahi* and the success in Parel   94

12. Humbled at the hustings   98

13. The tiger's white collar   103

14. Sena stamp on Congress's employment directives:
    Locals first   108

15. Support for Congress, the Emergency and
    zero tolerance for artistic dissent   114

16. The surprise announcement   121

17. Textile tragedy leads to divorce   124

18. Swaying to the socialist song   129

19. Over to Hindutva and back to Bhiwandi   131

20. Joining hands with the BJP   138

21. Mumbai polls 1985: A fresh lease of life   141

22. Inroads into rural areas   145

23. Rolling out the saffron carpet   153

24. At the centre stage   165

25. Cross-voting and the ban on voting   173

26. Alliance with the BJP, again   176

27. Bhujbal sulks, quits Sena   184

28. The 1992-93 riots   193

29. The path to power   207

30. The Sena government   217

31. Raj versus Uddhav   228

32. Bal Thackeray = Shiv Sena   243

Notes   251
Bibliography   257
Index   259
Photo Credits   264

ACKNOWLEDGEMENTS

This book on Bal Thackeray and one of the most controversial political outfits of modern India would not have been possible without the help and encouragement of many.

I would first like to thank my publisher, Priya Kapoor, for the enthusiasm she showed for the project and for her efforts to make this book available to readers remarkably quickly. Priya also pushed me into putting in more biographical information on Bal Thackeray than I originally had; that has only made the book better.

A big thank you also to her father, Pramod Kapoor, the guiding force behind Roli Books, who has also published my biography of Sachin Tendulkar. Padma Rao Sundarji has been an outstanding editor. She went through the text in what must have been record time, and her intervention has made the text crisper and more readable.

Sanjay Raut, executive editor of the Shiv Sena mouthpiece *Saamna* helped me in every possible way he could, fulfilling the role of Bal Thackeray's alter ego which he has performed so well for close to two decades. Dilip Ghatpande and Vijay Gaonkar, among Thackeray's earliest associates, helped with their recollections, as did the Sena's counsel, Barrister Achyut Chafekar; Suresh Gothankar helped with the archival material he has painstakingly collected over the years; and K. Bala, Kishor Dhargalkar, Vasant Kher and Dr Satish Naik provided constant encouragement.

Some of the Sena's strongest opponents, Mrinal Gore, Ahilya Rangnekar (who are sadly no longer with us), Roza Deshpande and B.S. Dhume, opened up to me with candour.

The debt of gratitude I owe to my parents, Jyotsna and Jagdish Purandare, is incalculable. I would not like to repay it, because it is not money that you repay and forget. And thanks, as ever, to my brother Kunal, for his quiet and constant support. Finally, I would first like to thank Bal Thackeray himself, for being such an interesting subject, and for promptly agreeing to release the first edition of this book in 1999. The edition you hold in your hands is a revised and fully updated one. All these people are responsible for the good things in this book. For any errors, I alone am accountable.

Vaibhav Purandare
Mumbai
November 2012

PROLOGUE

'I'm 86 and tired… I have physically collapsed. Look after my son and grandson just as you looked after me all these years.'

Thousands of Bal Thackeray's followers had gathered at Shivaji Park, in north-central Mumbai, for the Shiv Sena's Dussehra rally on 24 October 2012. This was part of their annual ritual, the coming-together of party faithfuls for the annual address by their Senapati or chief. Thackeray had addressed his first Dussehra rally in 1966, the year in which the Shiv Sena was established, and had since held forth from the dais on this very ground every Dussehra, for 45 consecutive years, each time attracting a crowd of at least one lakh, a record of sorts.

There were some doubts about whether he'd attend this time. He had been ailing for a while and had just recently spent nine days in hospital for a gastro-intestinal ailment. Nevertheless, the Sainiks hoped he would come.

He did not.

Instead, after Thackeray's son Uddhav had spoken, there was a video-recorded message from the Sena chief which took the assembled crowd aback. The mood of the gathering turned sombre. They knew Balasaheb had been unwell, but this time, he looked utterly exhausted and even breathless. He admitted as much. 'I have physically collapsed… I'm 86 and tired. I can't even walk,' he told his followers, in whom he had bred such faith in his leadership over the past four decades, that they were willing to do anything for him.

'You looked after me all these years. Look after Uddhav and Aditya [the grandson],' he said. He expressed concern that the Shiv Sena had been broken into two in Dadar, the very part of Mumbai in which it had been formed, because of his nephew Raj's decision to break away and form his own party, the Maharashtra Navnirman Sena (MNS), in 2006. He said it was time to introspect why the split had happened, and urged Marathi-speaking people to unite to defeat the Congress and Sharad Pawar's Nationalist Congress Party (NCP) in Maharashtra. He also hit out at the Congress's leadership in New Delhi and the Nehru-Gandhi family in particular.

When the Shiv Sainiks quietly filed out of the park after his 25-minute talk, the overwhelming emotion was not about his politics but his health.

Bal Thackeray had always been the picture of defiance: he was always thin but never reticent, he had breathed fire even in his 70s and 80s, urging his men to violent upheavals all the time. And he abhorred showing any signs of weakness.

Now seeing him so frail and helpless moved many of them to tears. The Sena was built too closely around the personality of Bal Thackeray. What would it be without him, they wondered, even as they realised that evening that he was ready to hang up his boots. In their mind's eye, many of them pictured the Sena story that had unfolded with such drama over the decades, a story made possible by their astonishingly strong attachment to Bal Thackeray…

End of an era
On 17 November 2012 at 3:30 pm, just as this book was going to press, news broke that Bal Keshav Thackeray, the founder of the Shiv Sena and one of the most controversial and charismatic figures of Indian politics, had died of cardio-respiratory arrest. He had been suffering for months from ailments of the lungs and the pancreas.

It was the end of an era in Maharashtra politics. The turnout at his funeral was one of the largest seen in post-Independence India. Indeed, it was on the scale of those at the cremations of Mahatma Gandhi, Babasaheb Ambedkar, Jawaharlal Nehru, Vallabhai Patel and C.N. Annadurai. The size of the crowd demonstrated just how big an imprint Thackeray left upon the state and the country.

For more than four decades, lakhs had gathered at Shivaji Park, the historic maidan in central Mumbai, to hear the Shiv Sena leader's speeches. In death, he turned out to be an even bigger crowd-puller.

It ordinarily takes not more than 20 minutes to cover the 6 km distance from Matoshree, Thackeray's residence in Bandra East, to Shivaji Park, which had been chosen as the place for his cremation.

But the Shiv Sena leader's cortege took seven hours.

The garlanded truck carrying Thackeray's body draped in the Indian tricolour, which left his home just after 9 am, inched forward at an impossibly slow pace. The procession stretched out for more than 2 km and many more people had lined up on the streets and on balconies along the route.

Most Indian television channels focused almost exclusively on Bal Thackeray ever since the announcement of his death had been made, with many anchors airing their old interviews with him even though they had been among his strongest critics.

Estimates of the crowd ranged from five lakh to a million, and Thackeray, in keeping with his reputation, brought the whole of Mumbai to a halt. Theatres cancelled film screenings, the police commissioner of Mumbai put off his daughter's wedding reception, and film star Dilip Kumar, one of Thackeray's oldest friends, cancelled his 90th birthday celebrations.

But: there was none of the violence and disruption usually associated with the Shiv Sena.

Apart from followers of the Sena, the mourners included thousands of ordinary citizens of Mumbai. A quiet and controlled sense of grief hung over the metropolis. When the procession reached Mahim dargah, 2 km from Matoshree, Muslim religious leaders offered a garlanded chaddar over the casket as a mark of respect; and there was a shower of flowers at four points on the route. Thackeray's body was first taken to the Shiv Sena Bhavan, the Sena's headquarters at Dadar and kept there for half an hour before being taken to the maidan.

At the packed Shivaji Park, when police band struck up a tribute and a 21-gun salute, there was complete silence.

The who's who of Indian politics was present at the funeral. L.K. Advani, Sushma Swaraj, Arun Jaitley, Sharad Pawar, Pawar's daughter Supriya Sule, Nitin Gadkari, Praful Patel, Maneka Gandhi, Ram Jethmalani, Shahnawaz Hussain and Rajiv Shukla had flown down

(From left to right) Uddhav Thackeray, along with his cousin Raj, elder brother Jaidev and son Aditya performs the last rites of his father, Bal Thackeray, in Mumbai on 18 November 2012. Hundreds of thousands of people gathered in Mumbai to witness Thackeray's funeral procession from his residence Matoshree in Bandra to Shivaji Park and then for the funeral at the historic maidan.

from New Delhi; the Congress chief minister of Maharashtra, Prithviraj Chavan, brought a floral wreath; and chief minister of Madhya Pradesh Shivraj Singh Chauhan, Maharashtra Governor K. Sankaranarayanan, State Home Minister R.R. Patil, Maharashtra Assembly Speaker Dilip Walse-Patil, Gopinath Munde and Thackeray's one-time protégé, Chhagan Bhujbal were also there. Industrial magnate Anil Ambani also attended the cremation.

Bollywood did its bit. Actor Sanjay Dutt and his sister, Lok Sabha member Priya were present, as were Amitabh Bachchan, Nana Patekar, Shreyas Talpade and Riteish Deshmukh. The previous evening, Bachchan had tweeted with feeling about how Balasaheb had been a close friend and had supported him all through his career, coming to his rescue not only by dispatching a Sena ambulance to Mumbai airport after he was injured on the sets of *Coolie* in 1982, but also by backing him during the Bofors controversy.

Bachchan, who had rushed to visit Thackeray at his Matoshree residence when his condition turned critical on 14 November, also wrote about how, when he had visited the Thackeray home after his wedding to Jaya Bachchan, the Sena leader and his wife Meena-tai had welcomed her in exactly the way any daughter-in-law would be welcomed into a traditional Maharashtrian home.

Musical diva Lata Mangeshkar, who was close to Thackeray, reminisced: 'When Balasaheb was there, Maharashtra was there, when he's not there, there's nothing. No one can equal what he has done for Maharashtra. We needed him to be with us for many more years.'

I spoke to some women at the funeral who had been queued up for a 'darshan' of Balasaheb since 4 am. They had learnt that people would be allowed to pay their last respects to the departed leader at the maidan, and had come in very early. They said that their sense of loss was huge, as Balasaheb was a 'friend, philosopher, guide and protector'.

Talk around the maidan was of how Mumbai had seldom seen anything like this before. Lokmanya Tilak's was the only other funeral in the city that had been held, not in a crematorium, but in a public place (Girgaum Chowpatty) because of the huge following he had.

The Sena chief's estranged son, Jaidev, too accompanied the rest of the family: Uddhav and his wife Rashmi, their sons Aditya and Tejas; daughter-in-law Smita, Jaidev's estranged wife, and her two sons,

Rahul and Aishwarya; Raj Thackeray, his wife Sharmila and their son Amit; the two children of Thackeray's eldest son Bindumadhav, Nihar and Neha; and Bal Thackeray's sister Sanjeevani Karandikar.

Along with members of the family, Thackeray's doctor, pulmonologist Jalil Parkar a Muslim in whom Bal's theory of hardline Hindutva had reposed complete faith for years – was given pride of place at the funeral. So also was Thackeray's Man Friday for more than two decades, a young Nepali called Thapa. The pyre was placed beneath Shivaji's statue, at the exact spot from where Thackeray had addressed his rallies.

When Uddhav lit it, chants of '*Balasaheb Amar Rahe*' rent the air and both Uddhav and Raj, could not hold back their tears.

Separated by politics, grief had brought them together. Reportedly, the reunion was only temporary: there was speculation on why Raj was not on the garlanded truck bearing his uncle's body, and how he had decided to walk ahead of the cortege before taking his car home. He is said to have then watched the rest of the funeral procession on television at his home, situated next to Shivaji Park, before turning up for the cremation in the evening.

Bal Thackeray had never held any official position. And yet, he was honoured with a ceremonial state funeral. This bore testimony to the fact that even though his politics had been criticized as divisive since the Sena's inception in 1966, the state government acknowledged his status as a mass leader.

But controversy would not leave Bal Thackeray alone, even after his passing.

Two days before his death, rumours about his deteriorating condition had spread like wildfire. Mumbai had been on tenterhooks and had virtually shut down. Thousands of Shiv Sainiks had rushed to Matoshree to find out how he was, forcing the government to increase security and even call in the riot control police. And yet, there was no medical bulletin. Instead, the Sena leaders kept streaming in and out of Matoshree and reassuring the crowd outside that he was 'stable' and on the mend. Even the state government seemed to be in the dark.

At the funeral, the Sainiks recalled the agony of that week when they had no reliable information, and wondered whether anyone had considered how distressed they were by the uncertainty.

Just a day after the funeral and the remarkable composure displayed by them, some Sainiks seemingly returned to their old selves.

In Palghar, 87 km from Mumbai, two girls were arrested.

Their crime? Posting a comment on a social networking site criticizing the shutdown of Mumbai following Thackeray's death. A Sena functionary filed a complaint and the girls, barely out of college, were arrested on charges of 'hurting religious sentiments'.

Their arrest was promptly followed by the Sainiks vandalizing a clinic belonging to an uncle of one of the girls.

The social media erupted with outrage. Some prominent legal experts like the Press Council of India chief, Justice Markandey Katju, slammed the police for misusing the law on 'hurting religious sentiments', while others demanded that the section of the IT Act, under which the arrests were made, be revamped.

Even as this controversy raged, another one arose over the demand made by the Shiv Sena to build a memorial for Bal Thackeray at the cremation spot.

The Maharashtra government sounded positive, saying the demand would be hard to ignore given the 'unprecedented emotional outpouring', but there were legal hurdles. (The Bombay High Court had to decide on whether the Park was a recreation ground or a public playground, for it is only on the latter that constructions are allowed.) Local residents' associations meanwhile firmly opposed the idea.

Bal Thackeray's death also triggered speculation about how the Shiv Sena would fare without his imposing presence, what shape it would take and whether the warring cousins would come together, or would they drift further apart.

To lakhs of Shiv Sainiks, all of this only served to reinforce the image of the departed leader. In life, he had been their hero. In their grief-stricken eyes, death lent Thackeray a near-mythical stature.

1

The Early Years

Barely two months after the Samyukta Maharashtra movement under writer-activist and the reigning badshah of lampoonery, 'Acharya' P.K. Atre, one of the struggle's stalwarts succeeded in getting the state of Maharashtra with India's financial nerve-centre Mumbai as its capital approved by the Central government, a new moon rose in the solar system of Mumbai.

In a freshly-launched Marathi cartoon weekly called *Marmik* (literally meaning satirical), readers began to encounter humorous non-episodes from ordinary life in the evocative brush strokes of the magazine's editor, cartoonist Bal Thackeray. In this endeavour of bringing out the weekly, Bal had the support of his father 'Prabodhankar' Keshav Thackeray who, with his pen, contributed in large measure to the humorous prose content. His brother Srikant, with his involvement in the world of music and his knowledge of the arts, took care of feature-writing.

But given the rapid closure of several Marathi publications at the time, it was yet to be seen whether the new moon's trajectory would be wayward and wobbly or remain on a steady ascent.

Marmik was born after Bal Thackeray quit his job as a staff cartoonist at the *Free Press Journal*. There is a theory propounded by some Mumbai journalists of that period that A.B. Nair, the then managing editor of *Free Press Journal*, was instrumental in the creation of Bal Thackeray, the fire-breathing Shiv Sena chief.

Their story: When Thackeray was working as a staff cartoonist along with R.K. Laxman at the daily, three of his cartoons had been chosen to be published in a world anthology of cartoons on Winston Churchill. But Nair stalled the handing over of the cheque – worth 70 pounds – sent by the publishers of the anthology for Thackeray, and he left dismayed.

Thackeray dismisses the story. 'I had not done the cartoons for money. Besides, I was not even aware if the cheque had come, so where does the question of complaining arise?'[1]

According to him, this is what happened:

> When the Katnanis from Calcutta took over *Free Press Journal*, A.B. Nair became managing editor of the paper. [S.] Sadanand had asked me to rejoin the daily in 1952, saying I was a pillar of his institution. So my second stint at the paper began in '52, two years after the end of the first one.

> One day, a pencil-sketch of mine on M.R. Masani went to A.B. Nair for approval. He had a look at it and summoned me to his cabin. "Do you know Mr M.R. Masani?" he asked me. When I told him I didn't, he said: "He is a good man." I said, maybe. Then came the advice: "Try and avoid drawing cartoons on Masani." I came out of the cabin in disgust.

> Sometime later, when I drew a caricature of (then Congress heavyweight) S.K. Patil, I was summoned again. And was asked the same question: "Do you know Mr S.K. Patil?" I replied: "I don't know these people. They are my models, and I use them as and when I think fit." I got the same suggestion – that I should avoid Mr S.K. Patil as far as possible.[2]

Nair had a long list of holy cows, Thackeray said, and would not allow him to poke fun at some powerful political figures in Maharashtra. 'If you take away my models by imposing such restrictions, how can I continue?' an angry Thackeray asked the managing editor and submitted his resignation.

'My editor Hariharan then called me and asked me if I had gone mad. I told him it was impossible for me to work with a person who had A.B. as his initials but did not know the A and B of journalism, leave aside cartooning.'[3]

Thackeray also points to the role of Hariharan in the Churchill cartoons episode. 'When I received the letter from Cassell & Co., which was to publish *Churchill's Autobiography in Pictures*, I showed it to him and asked him for permission to send my cartoons. But he brusquely turned down the request. This created a lot of rage in my mind. Later, one of my friends Nadkarni helped me send my cartoons.'[4]

The journey on which the young Thackeray, apparently miffed by the attitude of Nair and Hariharan, set out after walking away from the *Free Press Journal* took a curious turn in the form of *Marmik*.

But why was *Marmik* launched at all?

Thackeray said: 'Those days, the Sunday supplements of newspapers carried stories like "Causes of polio" and "Ill-effects of diabetes". Why explain the ill-effects of diabetes to those already suffering from it? That too, on a day like Sunday, when people want something other than the run-of-the-mill, customary staple to read? I felt the readers needed something crisp, heart-warming and refreshing to read on weekends. *Marmik* was launched to fulfil this need.'[5]

When Thackeray was with the *Free Press Journal*, he had become recognised as one of the most gifted cartoonists in India. This reputation – of a Paper Tiger of the stinging kind – was bound to work in favour of his fledgling magazine. The reputation of his father, 'Prabodhankar' as an uncompromisingly strident social reformer, was another asset; and there was also the fact that a cartoon weekly was then a novel thing in Marathi.

The march of the magazine in the first three years took place through Thackeray's desired hallway: light, lilting fun, comic burlesque and satire. And it proved to be a success with readers who lapped up the young cartoonist's rib-tickling humour and acerbic wit that laid bare the follies and foibles of the mighty and the not-so-mighty of the land. It represented colour and a certain brand of fun, as against a dreary, muffled environment that had come to exist soon after the creation of a separate linguistic state. This environment formed a dark backdrop to the sour, slow-moving lives of Mumbai's Marathi-speaking people.

As the landscape grew darker, Thackeray peered into the Marathi soul and created humour tinged with the dejection that now occupied a prominent place in the local people's existence. As a sensitive observer tuned to the various frequencies of Maharashtra's life, he mirrored the daily deprivations of the Marathi populace with his strokes.

In 1963, some Marathi people approached Thackeray with their grievances, saying no matter where they went, they were being discriminated against and denied job opportunities. Soon after, Shrikant Gadkari, a friend of Thackeray, met him and, showed him the telephone directory, pointing to the number of non-Maharashtrians occupying top positions in various companies. 'This is where the first spark went off,'[6] Thackeray recalled. 'Mumbai was included in Maharashtra, but the Marathi *manoos* counted for nothing. Since outsiders had all the top slots, only their people got a look-in. I started publishing entire lists of all these names in *Marmik* under the columnhead *"Vacha ani Thanda Basa"* (Read and Sit Silent). After a month had passed, people started sending more lists. But the Marathi *manoos* does not get roused unless he is bitten. So I renamed the column *"Vacha ani Utha"* (Read and Rise).'

The response to it was prompt: youngsters flocked in large numbers to Prabodhankar Thackeray's 77-A, Ranade Road, Dadar residence, which also then served as the *Marmik* office. Bal's espousal of the sons-of-the-soil cause had struck a chord among Mumbai's middle- and working-class Maharashtrians, and a voiceless constituency of youngsters had found expression.

Discontent had been simmering for quite a while; it had found a release.

From 1963, *Marmik* began to be known as much for its regular reproduction of the listings of Nairs, Menons, Shahs and Patels from Mumbai's telephone directory as for its satire. And for its editorials and polemical articles as well. Of course, not much importance was attached to intellectual analysis in the edits and the polemical pieces, as high-brow terminology has all along been anathema to Thackeray ('My father taught me to speak and write in a language that the common man would understand,' he says), but *Marmik* was so effective in highlighting alleged discrimination that its circulation nearly doubled in 1966: from 20,000 in the previous year, it leaped to 40,000.

Mary Fainsod Katzenstein, in her book *Ethnicity and Equality: The Shiv Sena Party and Preferential Policies in Bombay*, draws a parallel between widespread literacy in Mumbai in the 1960s and the success of the Sena. Terming the role of literacy as 'readily apparent' in the spreading of the Sena appeal, she writes: 'In Bombay, as distinct from many other rural or even urban localities, widespread literacy opened the possibilities of using the media to elicit public interest and support.'

The city had undoubtedly reached a high level of literacy by the beginning of the 1960s. According to census figures, the decade-wise growth of literacy in Mumbai from 1921 took place as follows: that year, the literate percentage of Mumbai's population was 23.3;

in 1931, it rose to 23.8, in 1941 to 40.8, in 1951 to 49.3, and in 1961, the percentage went up to 58.6. Katzenstein notes: 'By 1961, the level of literacy in Bombay was twice as high as the average for Maharashtra State.'

Significantly, at the core of the Shiv Sena's genesis was the printed word, something the party has often scorned and despised in its more than four decades of existence. *Marmik* played a key role in focusing the attention of Mumbai's Marathi populace on the declared injustices inflicted on locals and in preparing the ground for the Sena organisation.

With the publication of the ingeniously compiled lists, the cartoons, hard-hitting editorials and articles, the magazine reached out to a cross-section of the Maharashtrian multitude, and the fact that the news medium was in Marathi helped Thackeray disseminate his ideas to a much more wider readership in the community. Had it been in English, it would have missed its intended target.

The sometimes simple, sometimes sophisticated, but 'never heavy' language of *Marmik*'s articles went down well with readers. Mostly there were short, funny censures made in humorous sketches and accounts of current social and political events, and there was the occasional sprinkling of historical pieces.

Given below is an excerpt from one of the articles of *Marmik* published in the 15 August issue of 1965. A classic example of the kind of satirical pieces the magazine carried, it's a tongue-in-cheek portrayal of what Mumbai would be like when the southerners had taken over the state. A special day is celebrated in Madra Matungam in AD 2065, and the writer has been given the job of interviewing the chief guest:

> In the calm and quiet of night, I went to the house of Ganapati Maratham, and greeted him with Namaskar, informing him that I had come to take his interview. Ganapati looked at me with surprise and said: "Oh, after so many years the old Marathi language is again spoken today. How do you know this language?" "I took the subject 'Old Marathi language' for my Ph.D.," – I replied. He said, smiling, "Nowadays this language is never heard. In my childhood, Marathi was spoken in pure form; now that pure language is heard only in a small habitation of Chambal valley. A hundred years ago in Mumbai, Madrasi governors, mayors and sheriffs were appointed.

The Marathi people of that time used to call these people outsiders. Then, the Madrasi lungi was a topic for fun. Today, everyone wears a lungi." "Yes," I said, "Recently in a fancy dress competition, one man wearing a dhoti received a prize from the Governor... What a strange garment."[7]

Thanks to such pungent prose, the rage and resentment of Maharashtrians grew increasingly demonstrative in the form of letters sent to *Marmik* and actual dialogue sought with Thackeray.

Pramod Navalkar, a regular visitor to the Thackeray home those days, has cited an incident that took place in March 1966. 'A few activists from Lalbaug [in central Mumbai] had come to meet Balasaheb. One of them was speaking intensely about something when I entered the house. Seeing me, Balasaheb asked him to halt for a moment and told me about the topic under discussion. The activists had come to him to say that there was a need for an organisation of Maharashtrians that would work as a line of defence against large-scale migration and fight the injustice meted out to sons of the soil. Various such groups used to meet him around that time and request that he form an organisation.'[8]

2

THE POLITICAL CARTOONIST

A politician and a cartoonist have contrasting aims. The politician seeks to cover up, obfuscate, and muddle things. This, at least, is the truth in contemporary India and in many other parts of the world, though it does not meet the classical description of the politician as someone involved in public affairs; who engages with issues in keeping with the contract between the people and the state and, through this, seeks resolution of issues, means of better governance, and solutions to conflicts and methods of conciliation and reconciliation. The cartoonist seeks the opposite. He tries to show cracks in the image the politician portrays in public, to find the little defects that cannot be detected on the surface, and to expose pretence and duplicity, all by using the gift of sardonic expression. Bal Thackeray has been both, a cartoonist and politician. But he does not like to be called a politician. He prefers the term political cartoonist – in order to stress how he has candour in a way that is not permissible in a conventional politician, in order to explain how he is liveliest on the attack and in order to highlight how he does not want his sense of humour and perspective to be partially diluted by a hypocritical political strain. The fact also is that when he started out as a cartoonist, Thackeray would have hardly seen himself as a political leader. Bal Keshav Thackeray was born on 23 January 1927. Though his birthplace was Pune, his parents, Keshav Sitaram Thackeray, popularly known as Prabodhankar, and Ramabai, soon shifted to Bhiwandi, a handloom town in the Thane district neighbouring Mumbai. The Thackerays have close familial links to Thane. This was where Bal Thackeray's great-grandfather, Krishnaji Madhav, known as Appasaheb, practised law and was given a seat next to the district magistrate's chair. Krishnaji was a rebel. He had given up his claim to ancestral property in the former Bhor principality in Pune district, the place to which the Thackerays trace their roots (though their earliest known ancestor, they say, was a soldier who guarded the fort of Dhodpe near Nashik, 180 km from Mumbai), and had decided to practice law in Thane. Thackeray's great-grandmother, Ramabai, was also a dissenter. She was a mid-wife who charged nothing for her service, and she detested caste and class distinctions, the Sena chief says. Thackeray's grandfather, Sitaram, died young, but Sitaram's son and Bal's father, Keshav, inherited the rebellious streak. He became associated with the Satya Shodhak movement founded by the social reformer Mahatma Phule to eliminate caste distinctions, protested against ritual and superstition, and fought Brahminical supremacy by writing pamphlets, plays, treatises and film scripts. The Thackerays themselves belong to the Chandraseniya Kayastha Prabhu (CKP) caste, which claims prominence in the caste hierarchy after the Brahmins, but Keshav would have none of the old social order. He edited and published a periodical called *Prabodhan*, which means renaissance, and soon became known as Prabodhankar. Prabodhankar was multi-faceted: he was an editor, stage artiste, screenplay-dialogue writer, historian and reformer. But he had to face hardships, the family says, as he often had to switch jobs and start his entrepreneurial activities afresh because of his refusal to part with principles.[9] The father, whom Thackeray refers to as Dada, has been the biggest influence in the Sena chief's life. From Bhiwandi, the Thackerays moved for a while to Thane, where a theatre company – Deccan Spark – founded by Prabodhankar was based, and from there to 77-A, Ranade Road, Dadar, very close to the historic Shivaji Park maidan (Bal Thackeray moved to Matoshree bungalow in Bandra East, Mumbai, in the late 1960s, that is, soon after the formation of the Shiv Sena). There were only three rooms in this Dadar home: the drawing room, where Prabodhankar would sit, a bedroom and a kitchen. There was some space in the backyard where Thackeray would later sit to draw cartoons, but he stopped sitting there after a while and started sitting on the floor in the drawing room for his work. In the house, Prabodhankar's presence was imposing even though he was out for work most of the time. Early in Bal's childhood, Prabodhankar wanted to train him to be a music composer. Bal took up the brush instead. Thackeray describes his beginnings as a cartoonist thus:

When we were in Bhiwandi, Dada got me a *bulbul* (a string instrument). But I found it hard to synchronise my hand-movements; if one worked on the instrument, the other would not. Once, Dada tried to teach me by placing his hands upon mine, and I cut my finger and started crying. Then, one day, when he returned home, he heard the bulbul being played. He asked my mother who was playing it. Shri, she said, meaning my brother, Shrikant. Shri was summoned and went up to Dada slowly, scared. He thought he'd be scolded for using the bulbul that had been brought for my use and training. Dada asked him, "Were you playing the bulbul?" Yes, he said, sounding guilty. "Bring it here," father said. And then he sat and played some notes to show him how it was meant to be played. While that settled matters for Shrikant, I had, by this time, developed a habit of scribbling and drawing things on the walls of our home. The walls of the Dadar home that we had moved to were especially clean, so I loved drawing on these. Dada saw this and realised that while Shrikant would be the music composer in the family, I would be the artist.[10]

Thackeray says art was in his blood because Prabodhankar himself drew well. 'What couldn't he do? He played the harmonium, the sitar and the *dilruba*; he painted, he drew portraits, and he also did number-plates for *tongas* (horse carriages) in old Mumbai. I am just a chip of the old block.'[11] Thackeray attended the Oriental High School in north-central Mumbai up to Class 6 but had to abandon studies that year as the family could not afford the fees. 'The accumulated arrears came to ₹ 60, and we could not pay,' he says.[12] Bal's interest in art, meanwhile, was growing. He loved to see the works of contemporary masters such as Dinanath Dalal and S.M. Pandit, and he especially liked cartoons. He would doodle on the walls and look closely at cartoon strips in the *Times of India*, and he saw the Walt Disney film *Bambi* six times in a cinema hall in south-central Mumbai, entranced. He soon bought colours and canvases, for ₹ 60, and began practising. Prabodhankar was keen that his son develop this interest further. For, the one thing he did not want Bal to be was a 'government servant'. Most Maharashtrians with a middle-class or lower-middle-class background then ended up in government service, and Prabodhankar made it clear to his son that he did not want him to go down that route. So he began to help Bal in his training:

As he was himself an artist, Dada used to hold my hands, when I was very young, and help me draw. He used to ask me to draw the cartoon strip in the *Times of India* that I liked and to put in colours. He'd look at it when he came back from work and tell me where I'd gone wrong. He would compare the lines, show me the difference between what I had drawn and the original, and make suggestions. He'd show me, for example, the difference between the eyes of a character that I had sketched and the way they'd been originally sketched. When I came to the stage where I could sketch on my own, father got me an ink bottle and a brush. Thus I started inking and emerged as a cartoonist.[13]

We have independent confirmation of the Thackeray siblings' talent in childhood. The famous Marathi writer, Pu La Deshpande, wrote in a letter sent to Bal and Shrikant on the occasion of *Marmik*'s fourth anniversary in 1964 that he remembered how both had been precocious: 'Bal's sketches would adorn the school magazine and enhance its look, and Shrikant would win applause for playing the violin at functions.'[14] We can rely upon the late Pu La's words because he was not used to praising the Thackerays under duress. When he was awarded the Maharashtra Bhushan (Pride of Maharashtra) award by the Shiv Sena government in 1996, Pu La hit out at the Sena's tactics at the awards function, saying he did not approve of its concept of *Thokshahi*, that is, rule by force, but in *Lokshahi* (democracy). Thackeray then attacked the literary icon, saying that if he disapproved of the Sena so much, he should not have accepted the award given to him by the Sena government. When Bal reached the age at which a student normally goes to college, he decided to join the Sir JJ School of Art, a premier institution in south Mumbai. But that too did not happen:

Once, Baburao Painter, the famous artist, had come to our house. He saw on the wall a portrait I had drawn. "Who has done this?" he asked. When my father said I had, I was summoned. "Do you know him? He's Baburao Painter," my father told me. "Yes, I've seen his works," I said. Baburao told my father, "The boy's got a good hand," and asked me what I was doing. When I told him I was going to join the JJ School of Art, he told my father not to send me there. "He will lose what talent he has. Send him to Kolhapur (where Painter was based), I will train him," he said. Though I never went to Kolhapur, I never went to JJ either, and continued practising at home. During those days, I would draw whatever came to my mind. But what I would do was fine art, not applied art.[15]

In 1947, Bal Thackeray, then just 20, joined the *Free Press Journal* (FPJ) as a cartoonist, on a monthly salary of ₹ 75. We have, in the previous chapter, seen how Thackeray left the job the second time because he was told not to touch certain 'holy cows', but he did not leave *FPJ* twice but thrice. When he quit for the first time in 1952, he says, S. Sadanand, the paper's editor and an institution in Indian journalism, visited his home to persuade him to come back. Thackeray explains why he had quit and how Sadanand got him to rejoin:

There was a troublesome guy at the paper, called Mitra. He gave me a chair next to the telephone operator. The phones would ring constantly, and there would be constant conversation happening. And while the operator always kept saying "hold on", I used to be forced to hold on to my brush because of the disturbance. I was angry and sent in my resignation and left. Soon after, Sadanand knocked on the door of our Dadar home and asked my father if I could come out to meet him (he couldn't come in because of his illness). He sat me down in his car and said, "What is this? I've become old, my health is not good, why don't you join me again?" I said I don't mind, but there are certain things... "Don't worry about those things, leave them to me. I'll take care of all that," he said, and asked how much money I wanted. I said, "Sir, this is not a bargain, nor am I going to discuss money with you. I have respect for you, and as you have come to my house to request me, I will join again."[16]

In the early 1950s, the agitation for a linguistic state for Maharashtrians began to gain momentum. Thackeray, with his family background and the influences on him, could hardly stay out of it. His home was a centre for meetings for the Samyukta Maharashtra core group, and his father was among the leading advocates for the state of Maharashtra with Mumbai as its capital. Among the others were writer–journalist–activist Acharya Atre, the editor of *Prabhat*, B.R. Kothari, Madhavrao Bagal and Appa Pendse. Atre was to eventually be among the top faces of the movement, along with socialist leader S.M. Joshi, Communist leader S.A. Dange, social worker Senapati

Bapat and Prabodhankar himself. As Thackeray was then working with the *FPJ*, he could not draw cartoons for other publications. But as the Samyukta Maharashtra agitation intensified, he began contributing cartoons to eight magazines under the pseudonym Mavla (an inhabitant of the Maval region of Maharashtra to which Shivaji's core supporters belonged). One cartoon he drew in a magazine called *Bombay* in 1954 got him into trouble. He had shown Congress leader Morarji Desai, who was strongly opposed to the creation of Samyukta Maharashtra, sitting atop a heap of human skulls and had described him as a *Nar-Rakshas*, a human demon. A case was registered, and Thackeray, for a while, was forced to go 'underground' – that is, he would come home for lunch and dinner but would stay at the house of his sister. Eventually, the arrest never happened. One day, Thackeray says, while a meeting of the agitators was on at their home, his father called him to the door and pointed to the footwear kept there. 'What is this?' he asked Bal. 'Chappals,' he answered, baffled. 'No, this is our glory, this is all we have. Preserve this. Always,' he was told.

Thackeray's involvement in his cartooning, nevertheless, was total during this period, and senior journalist M.V. Kamath, who worked at the *FPJ* at the same time as Thackeray, says Bal was such a quiet man, it was impossible to think he would in future lead a militant organisation. A character called Chachaji – a bald man with a walrus-like moustache – drawn by Thackeray appeared on the front page of *FPJ* every day during those days and became quite popular. Here it must be mentioned that although Thackeray is best known for his cartoons on the political situation in Mumbai, Maharashtra and the rest of India, some of his earliest cartoons published in the *FPJ* are about international affairs: he drew cartoons featuring the likes of Stalin, Marshal Tito of Yugoslavia, Nasser of Egypt and the then top political leaders of the UK and the US, although, even in these cartoons as in those on Indian politics, Pandit Nehru seems to have been one of his favourite characters, depicted without his Gandhi topi, with a solitary strand of hair on his head but with a charismatic face and personality. Later, Indira Gandhi emerged as one of his favourite characters, and the last interesting character he found for cartooning, he says, was P.V. Narasimha Rao. While the second exit from *FPJ* was prompted by the 'holy cows' episode, Thackeray left the paper the third time along with an entire group of journalists, who had decided to come together and launch a newspaper called *News Day*. Thackeray left that place in just a couple of months. He explains why:

> The place was full of South Indians, and I got fed up of the atmosphere. Initially *News Day* ran well, but it went downhill soon because people who were part of it began misuse of the paper for air travel, junkets, and even for ordering food in the name of the paper. Fiscal indiscipline, in short. Then we heard that some Shah was going to buy the paper. I said, why did we leave Sadanand if we weren't going to be independent? And I quit.[17]

Thackeray thereafter started sketching cartoons for Marathi periodicals and papers such as *Maratha*, *Kesri* and *Dhanurdhari* and also did show-cards for a movie company called Famous Pictures. Besides, he drew the picture of Sant Gadge Baba for the cover of a biography of the social worker that Prabodhankar wrote. The decision to launch a light cartoon weekly was made in 1960, but Thackeray needed funds for the launch:

> The main concern was the newsprint costs, which constitute the major part of costs in publishing. I needed ₹ 5,000. One newspaper agent I went to promised me the money but never gave it. Then I approached the Bank of Maharashtra, where I met Mr Varde, then called the Bank Maharshi. He gave me and my brother a lecture on why we shouldn't be getting into this. We left. One true gentleman then stood behind us – Bua Dangat, the newspaper agent. He gave us ₹ 5,000, and we started *Marmik*.[18]

Significantly, this was an era in which Marathi magazines and periodicals were shutting one after the other. *Vividh Vrutta* and *Navyug* were among those that had shut, and one of Acharya Atre's periodicals had had to fold up too. The initial cost of *Marmik* was Re 1; it was brought down to 50 paise later. Initially, Prabodhankar wrote the editorials for it, but soon D.P. Khambete joined as executive editor and took over the responsibility (later, Bal Thackeray started writing the editorials). It is important to mention here the famous feud the Thackerays had with Atre at the time, because both were among the chief proponents of the Samyukta Maharashtra movement and were on good terms even after the movement had ended. Atre, in fact, was a hero for all of Maharashtra, so how the Thackerays, who also purport to represent the state and sons of the soil, feuded with him is necessary for us to examine. Thackeray says their ties were so strong that Atre would come to their house for Diwali every year, along with Hu. Ba. Hurlikar, a teacher of German Krupa Kulkarni and the writer Anant Kanekar. He would especially love the *anarse*, a food item prepared by Thackeray's wife Meenatai. What was more, Prabodhankar would do the rounds of the house till late every night, that is, till he got a phone call from Atre, and go off to sleep only after he had spoken to him. So what went wrong? According to Thackeray:

> Once D.P. Khambete, executive editor of *Marmik*, had come home with Bhole Nath Baba, a Maharaj or godman that Khambete believed in. Atre had also come to our place at the same time, and Khambete introduced him to the godman. Atre responded cursorily and almost ignored the Baba, which Khambete did not like. The Baba was a fraud in any case – once, when my sister was unwell, she had gone to meet him and was told he was busy; when she peeped inside his room, she saw him playing cards and smoking. Now, Atre and the poet Vasant Bapat were friends who had worked together on the award-winning film *Shyam Chi Aai*. Somehow, their relations soured, and Atre wrote a nasty piece on him, calling him *Bin Bapacha Bapat* (Bapat the bastard). We obviously felt no need to respond to Atre because the verbal assault was on Bapat, not on us. But Khambete wanted to respond to it and to criticise Atre for having hit out at Bapat. So we said go ahead, you are executive editor, write what you feel like. Atre did not like what was written, and put out a box on the front page of his paper *Maratha* casting aspersions on my father's character. That angered us, and Prabodhankar then wrote a series of articles against Atre, and I drew cartoons lampooning him. After quite a few exchanges, Atre put an end to the conflict himself, saying he was drawing the curtains on the feud.[19]

Atre later dubbed the Shiv Sena as 'Vasant Sena', to highlight Thackeray's alleged closeness to the then Congress Chief Minister Vasantrao Naik, and 'Sadashiv Sena', to indicate that the Sena had links with another Congress strongman, S.K. Patil. Thackeray says that though Vasantrao Naik was his friend, he never did what Vasantrao wanted him to, and he disliked S.K. Patil. And though he had excellent relations with Y.B. Chavan, the state's first chief minister, who launched the inaugural issue of *Marmik*, he did not appreciate Chavan's stance during the Samyukta Maharashtra movement (Chavan had said Nehru was greater than Maharashtra and had called the demand for a linguistic state regional imperialism).Thackeray has always refuted allegations that the Sena was a Congress product, intended to fight the Communists and reduce their influence in Mumbai. For all the feuding with Atre, Thackeray says he remains a hero for him. He is among the three orators – the other two being Prabodhankar and Dange – whom he admires. 'Dange had such oratory, you'd just feel like listening to him. He spoke in simple terms but had a nice touch of humour. Atre was very powerful. But again, here too, the path I have followed is that of my father. He told me, don't give a speech, just talk to people. Have a direct dialogue with them. That explains my style of speaking. I never learnt anything by heart, and have never taken notes I could refer to.' Even before he had turned into an accomplished orator, that Thackeray was an effective communicator had become clear from the responses he drew to the lists of non-Maharashtrian names taken from the phone directories that he published in *Marmik*.

3

MAHARASHTRIANS AND MIGRANTS

It is plain that Thackeray succeeded in articulating the core concerns in the deepest recesses of the Marathi mind through *Marmik*. But did these concerns arise due to heavy migration into Mumbai during the 1950s and 1960s? Was there a sudden change in the demographic profile of the city during the decade that troubled the Marathi-speaking people? Or were other factors, like inter-ethnic group relations and economic inequality, responsible for the Shiv Sena's emergence?

The Sena certainly was not an offshoot or a splinter group of any political party. What were the conditions, then, that contributed to *Marmik's* appeal and Sena's birth? The organisation could not have sprung up out of nothing. But was only emotionalism the founding basis of the Sena, or was Thackeray's declaration of injustice and inequality rooted in reality? Or was it empowerment of one kind that led to the questioning of another kind of dependence? Was the Sena an overnight development, or a result of a long drawn-out historical process? We shall see.

Between 1941 and 1951, Mumbai witnessed a total increase of 950,000 migrants, but the figure dropped to 600,000 in the following decade.[20] Thus, the incursion of migrants between 1951–61, the period before the Sena's establishment, was less rapid than in the earlier decade. In 1951, migrants constituted 72.1 per cent of Mumbai's population,[21] and in 1961, they formed 64.5 per cent.[22] So although the percentage of migrants in Mumbai remained high, and the rate of migration more significant than in other cities in India, no abrupt cityward flow was noticed.

The linguistic composition of the city's population calls for examination as well, for the number of people born outside Mumbai cannot be the sole applicable statistic here. Did the percentage of Marathi speakers suddenly slope or that of 'outsiders' shoot up during the period preceding the Sena's founding? Marathi-speaking people comprised 43.6 per cent of Mumbai's population in 1951. In 1961, the percentage of people born outside Maharashtra but staying in Mumbai was 33.8 and that of Marathi speakers went down to 42.8, but the decline was not dramatic. The percentage of South Indians, the first targets of Sena ire, during the decade 1951–61 also did not register any phenomenal increase: in 1951, they accounted for 7.8 per cent of the city's population; in 1961, they formed 8.4 per cent.[23]

The absence of weighty shifts nothwithstanding, the non-native population of Mumbai remained large, considering both birth-place and mother-tongue figures.

Marathi-speaking people living in other areas of Maharashtra too had Mumbai as the favoured destination. Not surprisingly, the rate of out-migration of Maharashtrians to other places in India was also low: 2.3 per cent.[24]

But the Marathi-speaking population in Mumbai was, even in 1881, only in a thin majority – 50.2 per cent. By 1961, it had dwindled to 42.8 per cent.

The drought in 1965-66, which had dried up agricultural and industrial production, had proved detrimental to the Marathi labour class and created an atmosphere for rebellion. In Maharashtra, the foodgrains output had dipped from 6.75 million tonnes to 4.70 million tonnes that year. Thus, there was a fall in employment in Mumbai's labour-intensive industries, and demand for factory workers dropped distinctly. The slump was especially severe in the already crisis-ridden textile industries, where Maharashtrian labourers were in a majority.

The economic decline had attracted many Marathi labourers to the Sena, as had the anti-communist stance of Thackeray.

Keeping these numbers in mind, why a Sena-like sons-of-the-soil movement did not arise earlier?

Lack of organisation is not a plausible enough answer to the question, considering the kind of political energies expended by Maharashtrians during the first six decades of the twentieth century. The timing of the Sena movement is therefore not explained by the presence of demographic factors. We have to take a look at other conditions.

It may have been something about the numbers of 'outsiders' that provoked the local people. It may have been a perception that they constituted social threats, or that they majorly affected the political and economic position of the native populace.

Either way, how did the native-migrant issue raised by Thackeray through *Marmik* contribute to anti-migrant mobilisation and organised protest?

A survey carried out in the early 1950s by D.K. Lakdawala et al., whose findings were published in a book entitled *Work, Wages and Well-Being in an Indian Metropolis* showed Maharashtrians lagged behind other communities staying in Mumbai in terms of occupational status and education. According to his study, the percentage of Maharashtrians earning a middle- to upper-middle-class salary (500–1000 rupees per month) was conspicuously lower (4.0 per cent) than people from the South Indian (7.9 per cent) and Gujarati (10.2 per cent) communities.

A study by Mary F. Katzenstein,[25] too, concluded that Maharashtrians were inadequately represented in higher status jobs (administrative, professional and clerical).

Katzenstein in her book *Ethnicity and Equality* writes:

> The extent of Maharashtrian underrepresentation is revealed by Mumbai-wide occupational figures; but the picture of economic competition confronting middle-class Maharashtrians is even more striking when a distinction is made between the newer and older industries of the city. A survey of employment rolls, conducted by the author in 1970, focused on selected industries, including relatively older ones, such as textiles, tobacco, and printing, and relatively new ones, such as chemicals, pharmaceuticals, insurance and other service industries. It is in the newer industries that Maharashtrians are most poorly represented. In several of the older companies whose records were inspected, Maharashtrians at all salary levels were present in large numbers – well above the Maharashtrian percentage in the population (although, interestingly, even in large textile companies, the percentage of Maharashtrians decreased with an increase in the salary level).

> In the new companies, with rare exceptions Maharashtrians are employed in proportion to their population percentage of 43 per cent only in the lower-income brackets designating manual labor.

Maharashtrians share in the better-paid jobs in the older industries but are excluded from those jobs in the newer industries.

The economic competition between Maharashtrians and "outsiders" in Mumbai is not a canard set afloat by Sena propaganda to delude Maharashtrian voters. Maharashtrians are economically behind several other communities in Mumbai. As evidenced by the recruitment patterns of newer industries in the city, this situation substantially intensified prior to the Sena's emergence.[26]

The economic dominance of non-Maharashtrians in Mumbai can be traced back to the mid-nineteenth century, when Marathi-speaking elites like the Pathare Prabhus were displaced by 'the more enterprising Bhatias and Banias'.[27] By and large, Maharashtrians in the metropolis were involved in occupations outside the industrial and commercial sector.

It is for this reason that Maharashtrians never played a pre-eminent role in Mumbai politics in the nineteenth century. During the British Raj, suffrage was confined to tax payers, and wealth, rather than numbers determined political power. Maharashtrians beat other communities in Mumbai as far as numbers were concerned, but their role in municipal politics was inferior. The representation of Maharashtrians in the municipal council of 1875 was 12 per cent, though they constituted 50 per cent of the city's population.

After universal suffrage was introduced in 1948, and especially after the creation of Maharashtra in 1960, the political status of the Marathi-speaking people underwent a major change. The gaining of political strength led to a widespread questioning, within the community, of their continued economic backwardness and the desire for an improvement in financial prospects.

But their expectations of economic betterment were not met, despite the booming of the Mumbai economy and the growth of new industries.

Striking early roots

Curiously, the Sena's formation was preceded by phases of economic development. According to an estimate, between 1962 and 1967, the number of office jobs went up by 28 per cent as against an 8 per cent increase in blue-collar employment.[28] In the organised sector, where most middle-class jobs lie, employment grew steadily in the first half of the 1960s.[29] But the bright employment scenario did not match Maharashtrian perceptions of job opportunities.

At the time, there was also an explosion of educated/qualified job seekers in the metropolis and other parts of the state. Enrollment in Bombay University spiralled from 24,000 in the early 1950s to almost 90,000 in the early 1970s, a rise of nearly 300 per cent.[30] The primary educational enlistment in western Maharashtra was 2 million in 1960; in 1966, it had doubled to 4 million students. Secondary enrollment went up from a little under 2 million to 6.5 million students.[31] Thus, competition was intensified. And compared to their percentage in the population, Maharashtrians held few top-ranking and white-collar slots in Mumbai.

The Sena's roots lay in this economic inequality between Maharashtrians and non-Maharashtrians. Thackeray's portrayals of Maharashtrian worries, fears and apprehensions, and his protests through the columns and cartoons of *Marmik* were not fictional constructs or political lies. They were economic truths.

Accentuating the concerns was an emotional string, a feeling that the economic situation was made more unfair and one-sided due to the 'attitudinal habits' of dominant non-Maharashtrians, not only in providing employment but in the social and cultural sphere. And Thackeray tugged at it and set off an alarm.

The journalist Kumar Ketkar, no supporter of Thackeray and the Sena, has this to say about the Marathi sentiment of the period:

> The carving out of Maharashtra state in 1960 was an emotional moment for the Marathi manus. Chauvinistic? No more so than Bengali, Punjabi, Tamil or Telugu chauvinism. Liberal, cosmopolitan and modern leaders or litterateurs may have lectured the Marathi people on the broader Indian vision, but they still defended linguistic cultural sub-nationalism in their respective states. This hypocrisy angered the Marathi Mumbaikar, who was by now passionately drawn towards the street-smart approach of Balasaheb Thackeray. Thus, ironically, Thackeray drew his strength from his critics.[32]

Chhagan Bhujbal, one of Sena's top-ranking leaders who defected to the Congress in 1991, ascribes Thackeray's apparent wizardry of the time to a combination of the mood created by the Samyukta Maharashtra movement and the feeling of deprivation among Maharashtrians in

Mumbai, who felt left out of the increasing opportunities in a fast-developing city.[33]

Iqbal Masud, former income tax commissioner-turned-columnist and commentator, confirms this. 'The Shiv Sena is the expression of the ground feeling, particularly among the lower-middle-class Maharashtrians, which has existed in the city. Thackeray realised the potency of the local, regional aspirations, and exploited it to the hilt.'[34]

As does V.S. Naipaul, in his book *India: A Million Mutinies Now*. Quoting a Sena leader, Diwakar Raote, a Sena leader who says *Marmik* had started working on his young mind during that era, Naipaul writes: 'Every week the magazine spoke about the injustices done in Mumbai and Maharashtra to the sons of the soil. And I found I was terribly attracted to the emotional personality of Bal Thackeray and his father, as expressed in the magazine. I even tried to meet Bal Thackeray.'[35]

By then, Thackeray had already begun a full-fledged campaign for jobs for Maharashtrians, and, in response to an announcement in *Marmik*, hundreds of youths stood in queues outside Thackeray's residence to submit job applications.

Prabodhankar then gave a decisive push to popular demand. 'For how long are you going to continue like this?' he asked his son. 'People come, go and come back again. Why not give this collective voice an organised form?'[36]

That settled the matter.

Bal, who had been seriously considering the idea of floating an outfit, decided to take the plunge.

'One day, when Dada (Prabodhankar) was resting, he asked me whether I had thought of a name for the organisation,' reminisces Thackeray. 'When I said I hadn't, he himself suggested the name: Shiv Sena. Shivaji's Army.'[37]

In May 1966, there appeared an announcement in *Marmik* about a youth organisation that was to be founded. It was to be called the Shiv Sena.

The auspicious and inaugural breaking of the coconut took place on 19 June 1966.

'There were very few of us present,' Thackeray recounts. 'We didn't consult any pundit, nor did we bother to see if the stars were favourably inclined or not. At around 9:30 in the morning, one of our family friends, Naik, brought a coconut from the grocery store and broke it. And intoning *Chhatrapati Shivaji Maharaj Ki Jai*, we started the Shiv Sena.'[38]

Sena leader Diwakar Raote recalls the ceremony.

'I was one of the 18 people there. Four of the 18 were from Bal Thackeray's own house: Balasaheb himself, his father and his two brothers. The first meeting lasted about half an hour. It was in the main room of their small house. Their father occupied that room.'[39] And the name Shiv Sena given by Prabodhankar, according to Raote, 'just seemed natural and right. And we pledged ourselves at that meeting to fight the injustices done to the sons of the soil'.

Who can be a member of the Shiv Sena?

Exactly a month after the Sena's inception, directive principles were laid down for those desirous of joining it. Anyone wanting to be a Sainik had to take an oath which constituted the following principles:[40]

1) The Marathi people should help each other, and see that the Marathi *manoos* takes the path to prosperity.
2) Maharashtrians shouldn't sell their property to outsiders, and if any local is found doing so, the nearest shakha should be immediately informed.
3) As far as possible, Marathi shopkeepers should buy their goods only from Marathi wholesale traders and treat customers with decorum.
4) Maharashtrians who have their own establishments should only employ sons of the soil.
5) Young Marathi-speaking boys should develop excellent communication skills in the English language, and learn English typing as well.
6) Casting away laziness, the Marathi people should form their own co-operative housing societies, and they should show willingness to go to any place for a job.
7) Celebrate Marathi festivals and functions with Marathi brothers and sisters by participating eagerly in huge numbers.
8) Locals should involve themselves in the activities of institutions, schools, ashrams, etc. belonging to Maharashtrians and donate generously for their cause.
9) Boycott all Udipi hotels and do not buy anything from shops of non-Maharashtrians.

10) Don't discourage the Marathi-speaking people involved in business and other professions, and keep them from losing heart; instead, extend as much help as you can.

11) Do not behave arrogantly and crudely with your own Marathi brethren, and in case any one of them faces any difficulty, others should collectively support him.

Hundreds of youngsters signed this statement of oath and enrolled themselves as Shiv Sainiks.

A function was held soon after at the Ravindra Natyamandir, an auditorium in Prabhadevi in north-central Mumbai, to make the formal announcement of the establishment of the Shiv Sena. Chief Minister V.P. Naik, a friend of Thackeray, was the chief guest.

Barrister Achyut Chafekar, later counsel for the Sena during the Madon Commission of Inquiry into the 1971 Bhiwandi riots, attended the function. He told me:

> Though there were tickets for the programme, the hall was packed to capacity. A performance of the play *Andhala Daltay* (The Blind One Grinds) was part of the function. The metaphor of a crab had been used in the play to depict the attitude of the Marathi *manoos*. A fisherman's basket carrying crabs has no cover, because whenever one of the crabs tries to clamber up and get out, the others pull him in. This had been portrayed in the play, as reflecting the attitude of Maharashtrians.[41]

A favourite with *Marmik* readers at that time were cartoons Thackeray drew under the columhead *Ravivarchi Jatra* (Sunday Fair). Spread over two pages, they presented national and international events from a political cartoonist's perspective. After the Sena's formation, the *Jatra* became more special: in a box at the bottom of one of the pages, announcements began to be made about the Sena's public meetings.

Four months after the establishment of the organisation, *Marmik* readers were informed about a public meeting to be held on the issue of 'injustice', at Shivaji Park on 30 October 1966, the Dussehra day.

The invitation extended to readers read thus: 'Paying obeisance to Maharashtra's deity, Chhatrapati Shivaji Maharaj, a meeting of Shiv Sena's Sainiks who are ready to bring about a Maharashtrian resurgence will be held on Sunday, 30 October 1966 at 5:30 pm at Shivaji Park, Dadar. You are justly proud sons of Maharashtra. I request you on behalf of Shiv Sainiks to be present for the meeting.' The editor of *Marmik* signed off the letter designating himself as 'Your humble Maharashtra Sevak, Bal Thackeray.'

For mobilising people for its first rally, the Sena effectively used the popular *mitra mandal* (neighbourhood clubs) and *vyayamshala* (gymnasium) culture of Mumbai-Maharashtra.

Vijay Gaonkar, Sena corporator between 1968 to 1978 who joined the Sena immediately after it was formed, describes how the network of *mandals* and gymnasiums was approached by the organisation and exposed to its influence:

> Padmakar Adhikari, Shyam Deshmukh, Pujari Master, Bhai Bhonsle, myself and a few others set ourselves to the task of mobilising people for the meeting. We went to all gymnasiums in central Mumbai and explained to them the importance of the Sena, urging them to participate in the Dussehra rally. At the same time, we formed a joint mandal for the Govinda celebrations that year, which brought different mandals together. Thus, the Sena early formed a strong bond with these cultural organisations of Mumbai, which are important places for societal interaction with long traditions of popular mobilisation. Most of Mumbai's gyms and mandals took part in the rally.[42]

Thackeray himself shared:

> A few days before the rally, I was busy drawing cartoons at home, when one of our well-wishers, Professor D.V. Deshpande, arrived. "Bal, I read today's *Marmik*. All your announcements appear here, don't they?" he asked. I told them there was no other place I could print them. "But why have you chosen Shivaji Park for the meeting?" he questioned. "It's such a huge ground [with a capacity of about 2 lakh]. What if people don't respond well?" I told him I had already gone ahead with the announcement. He came up with a suggestion: "Take the King George High School ground (about one-tenth the size of Shivaji Park). If the crowd increases, you can always have loudspeakers outside." I refused: "The arrow has left the bow. I can't backtrack. Let's see if I am proven a fool, or the people are." But neither emerged as fools. The turnout was so big, Shivaji Park was full to overflowing. There was tremendous excitement and enthusiasm.[43]

The *Nava Kaal* of 31 October 1966 described the rally as 'massive' and said that from 4 pm on Dussehra day, processions of Sainiks from various parts of the city had wound their way to Shivaji Park. In all, nearly 4 lakh people thronged the maidan, a figure well beyond the organisers' wildest expectations.

Prabodhankar was present on the occasion and gave a speech:

> Today, Marathi brothers are celebrating Dussehra in the true sense by crossing new frontiers. Let us, through the Shiv Sena, fight and overcome our problems and attempt to realise our goals. This will be the real crossing of boundaries on our part (Dussehra is the festival that marks the symbolic crossing of boundaries). You have today demonstrated that Maratha blood has not yet become impure, and Maharashtrians are ready to combat injustice. The Marathi people should now resolve not to fight among themselves but establish cordial relations with their brethren.

He stressed:

> Maharashtra is not a land of the weak and the timid. It's the land of tigers. History has shown time and again what happens when attempts are made to sting this tiger. If in the future too, anyone wants this fact to be tellingly demonstrated, his wish will be fulfilled.[44]

Barrister Ramrao Adik, Prof S.A. Ranade and Balwant Mantri also spoke at the rally. The last speaker was Bal Thackeray.

'Maharashtra has never achieved anything without strenuous efforts, great struggle and sacrifice,' he addressed the audience.[45] 'S.M. Joshi has, under the pretext of nationalism, called the Shiv Sena communal. I throw an open challenge to him – he should fight an election on the issue of whether Maharashtra is today in dire need of Maharashtrianism or nationalism.'

'The Shiv Sena isn't communal', the Sena pramukh said, 'Anybody who establishes a sincere friendship with one in one's troubled times is a Marathi *manoos*. Today, society needs social work more than *rajkaran* (politics). It has been decided to keep the Sena away from politics. Because *rajkaran* (politics) is like *gajkaran* (ringworm, a deadly skin disease).'

The cartoonist then detested politics and hated politicians attached to any party, and he made it clear in no uncertain terms. Of course, as the phonetic character of *rajkaran* matched that of *gajkaran*, it is obvious that the temptation for wordplay – one of Thackeray's favourite indulgences to this day – had prompted the use of the term.

Thackeray also demanded that 80 per cent of seats in the Maharashtra Housing Development Corporation be reserved for Maharashtrians, and government jobs given only to those who could read and write Marathi or those who could speak Marathi well. 'The Marathi *manoos* has awakened. He will never in the future tolerate injustice. The Maharashtra government should take note of this before it's too late,' he said.

The journalist Kumar Ketkar, who attended the Sena's first meeting along with 'hundreds and thousands of other young boys,' later wrote: 'To him (Bal Thackeray) all southerners were Madrasis and all northerners, Bhaiyyas... He thundered against Madrasis for snatching jobs that he thought belonged to the Marathi people. His philistinism was transparent as much as his political innocence.'[46]

This is surprising because Mumbai, at the time, was a highly politicised city with strong trade unions. Comrade S.A. Dange was the uncrowned king of the textile workers. S.M. Joshi was the nationally recognised socialist leader who was in the vanguard of the Samyukta Maharashtra movement. Together, Dange, Joshi and Acharya Atre, the fighter-editor of the daily *Maratha*, had led the vintage Left Front, known as Samyukta Maharashtra Samiti. Mumbai was the epicentre of that movement and the Marathi-speaking people earned a glorious victory when they succeeded in carving out the state of Maharashtra.

Yet, here was a man condemning all parties and politicians, with an aplomb that surprised the first-generation Thackeray-watchers and, of course, the Leftists who had concluded that Mumbai was the quintessential city of working class with Leninist consciousness. They had totally overlooked the rise of the generation that was born in the mid-1940s. This generation, then in its teens or early 20s, was not enamoured by either the socialist movement or the freedom struggle. They felt that their future had been stolen by someone.

Thackeray said he knew the thief. And abused the lungi-wearing Madrasi.

After Thackeray's first speech, the crowd that had shown up for the rally attacked Udipi restaurants as it dispersed, immediately marrying the new organisation's image with its mascot, a growling tiger.

Dilip Ghatpande, one of Thackeray's earliest associates, says: 'The boys' blood had started boiling after listening to Balasaheb's speech. On the way to Dadar station, there was an *adda* (den) of South Indians where illegal activities like *matka* (gambling) took place. The angry youth stormed the place.'[47]

The *Nava Kaal* of 31 October 1966, nevertheless reported that stones were pelted and soda-water bottles thrown at the crowd returning from Shivaji Park. The assault allegedly took place from a hotel on Ranade Road. 'As a result, the atmosphere became tense, and a little amount of ravaging and despoilment is also understood to have taken place. But the police soon appeared on the scene, calmed things down and arrested the owner of the hotel from which the stone-throwing had taken place,' the paper reported.

Thackeray was pleased with the Sena rally's success. He recollects: 'At around 10:30 in the night, Deshpande, who had asked me why I had chosen Shivaji Park as venue, came home again. "Bal, you have won," he said. "Haven't we?" I told him. "We are Thackerays. We never speak of defeat, only of triumph."'[48]

Four lakh people had gathered for the Sena's inaugural rally, and the response to Thackeray's appeal was such that the *Marmik* editor was himself left a little bewildered.

The rally overnight established the Shiv Sena as a force to reckon with in Mumbai. The city got a Tiger, and the state a new slogan: *Jai Maharashtra*.

The then chief minister of Maharashtra, V.P. Naik, was incensed by reports of Sainiks' violence following the rally. He condemned it, saying, 'This is not the way to fight for rights of Maharashtrians.'

The Left parties not only said they were opposed to the Sena, they declared on 2 November that a meeting of all Left parties would be convened to decide on steps to be taken to 'strike down' the Shiv Sena.

4

MOBILISING THE SENA CORPS

Buoyed by the instant ascent to 'Tigerdom', Thackeray began holding meetings in the narrow bylanes, winding alleys and spacious maidans of Mumbai. Wherever he went with his fiery talk, he drew crowds and embraced controversy.

The mobilisation of a corps of Shiv Sena workers began at the same time. The Sena chief then had a handful of people around him, such as Wamanrao Mahadik, Dattaji Salvi, Vijay Parvatkar, Shamrao Deshmukh and Madhav Deshpande, to manage the organisatonal machinery.

Salvi, Thackeray says, was the first of what came to be known later as his inner circle, to have met him:

> I was in the box during a mock court proceeding in the Amar Hind Mandal. George Fernandes [Socialist leader, later India's defence minister and Thackeray's good friend] was the prosecutor posing questions to me, and Dattaji Salvi was in the chair as judge. The next day, Dattaji came to my house and said, "I heard you yesterday. I want to work with you." He had quit his job in a mill, he said. I told him not to quit rightaway, as the organisation still had to take shape. "I've quit already," he said. After Salvi came Wamanrao Mahadik. He was a clerk in the BMC. And after that, I met Manohar Joshi [who became chief minister during Sena rule]. I had a rally at Shaniwarwada in Pune, and from there I went to my sister's house. Srikant, my brother, and Joshi arrived there. I did not know Joshi; Srikant introduced him as the man who ran the Kohinoor technical institute. Joshi told me he had come for my rally, and Srikant said they had all come from Mumbai in Joshi's car. We then returned to Mumbai in Joshi's car. After Manohar Joshi came his nephew, Sudhir Joshi [who went on to become Mumbai mayor and revenue and education minister during Sena rule].[49]

With these aides, Thackeray undertook the task of building the party structure and setting up Sena branches across Mumbai, called shakhas.

All the work did not have to be done by these few people, for many youngsters came forward saying they wanted to form Sena branches in their respective areas. Most of them did not ask for funds for the purpose; they established branches on their own with their own money and turned their own cloth into Sena banners.

Those days, Sena shakhas were not elaborately built fortress-like structures like the ones we see today. At some places, even the verandah of someone's house, a small vacant place next to the staircase of a chawl, a shop, a stall or the benches of some classes functioned as a Sena shakha.

Till the construction of the Parel shakha was over, Wamanrao Mahadik held meetings in the street right in front of his house, with a chair and table forming the 'shakha furniture'. Sudhir Joshi ran his shakha for some time on the terrace of his Dadar building.

Showing considerable drive, youngsters attracted to the Sena plastered the city's walls with Thackeray's slogans and cartoons and worked to garner public support. Through their community self-help projects too, Sainiks took the Sena to ordinary people.

What was the nature of these Sena activists who took such initiatives? What was it that set them apart from workers of other parties and organisations? Was there any distinguishing characteristic of the Sena worker *at all*, who had been attracted to the outfit by Thackeray's anti-migrant fulminations and the sons-of-the-soil slogan? Was he 'lumpen proletariat,' or was he merely a representative of the middle class?

The one attribute that most vividly distinguished the Sena worker from his counterparts in other party organisations was youth.

Thackeray was himself 40 when he launched the Sena, and the Maharashtrians who were quickly attracted to him were either his contemporaries or younger. Most Sainiks who manned the new shakhas, and a large percentage of those who attended Thackeray's early meetings were students or of student age. Even the 'senior' organisers accompanying Thackeray during those days were either his contemporaries or younger. Of the group of 37 shakha pramukhs (branch heads), upshakha pramukhs (deputy branch heads) and active Sainiks that Katzenstein interviewed during her research on the Sena in 1968, the average age was twenty-six.[50]

And most of these youngsters had education. Only 22 per cent of Sainiks she interviewed had not matriculated, though they had attended school; 35 per cent of them had completed matriculation; 16 per cent had matriculated and received an additional diploma; and 27 per cent had completed college and obtained an advanced degree.

Communist leader Roza Deshpande, daughter of S.A. Dange, told me that the image of the Shiv Sainik as a lumpen proletariat was incorrect and had been entertained by 'petty bourgeoise intellectuals':

> The Sena's support base wasn't lumpen. Even Communist leaders' children joined the Sena. They were, of course, members of the working classes, they were from the labour and the poor constituencies. Would the Communists call their own children lumpen? The Sena was a mass upsurge, and lumpens may have been one of the constituents of the Sena's support base, as a mass upsurge involves every section of society. But the Sena wasn't dominated by lumpens, as it is made out. The educated classes backed the Sena, many professors and intellectuals swore allegiance to it when it appeared on the scene. Plus, the party has won so many elections over the years. Does the lumpen dominate the whole of the electorate? Lumpens will wither away, they will associate themselves with elements like Haji Mastan, Yusuf Patel and Arun Gawli. But the Shiv Sena was a genuine movement, a movement of the people against the establishment. Lawyers, doctors, actors and actresses all joined the Sena and supported it. Their background was intellectual. The whole Kapoor family, a legendary family in the history of Indian cinema, had belonged to the Shiv Sena. They weren't just sympathisers or supporters from outside, they were Sainiks. Unfortunately, Communists haven't objectively analysed the Sena's growth.[51]

The references that attracted the youth to the Sena were multiple. What were they? And how did their curious concatenation come about?

Of the diverse strands that commingled in the mid-1960s to draw youngsters towards the Sena kind of protest movement, the first one – which we have dealt with earlier at length – was economic.

It was not as if a financial fire storm had raged through Mumbai, ravaging the Marathi population and abruptly snatching all opportunities for economic advancement. The process had been gradual: it was a slow but steady build-up of conditions that had caused the economic impasse to reach worrying proportions.

And the politics of the time was mingled with economics. The Samyukta Maharashtra movement had galvanised the Marathi people and breathed new life into Maharashtrian youth, but the Samyukta Maharashtra Samiti witnessed internecine conflicts following the formation of Maharashtra and got badly splintered.

Thus, the energies of popular leaders like Dange, S.M. Joshi, Prabodhankar Thackeray and Atre got diffused at a time when their collective strength could have mobilised the youth segment and pressured the establishment to redress their grievances.

The shrivelling of this front enabled the Congress to win 215 of the total 264 Assembly seats in the elections held in 1962. Holding total sway over the state, the new Congress regime did its utmost to strengthen its vested interests across the Maratha land and took no steps to better the lot of Mumbai's Marathi youth, who were getting increasingly restive.

Maharashtra, and, along with it, Mumbai, had been won after 105 people had laid down their lives for it.[52] This was deeply embedded in the Marathi mind, as were Congress leader Y.B. Chavan's proclamations opposing the cause of Samyukta Maharashtra. Chavan had caused consternation among young Maharashtrians by saying 'Nehru is greater than Maharashtra' and by terming Samyukta Maharashtra as 'home-grown colonialism'. After his advocacy of the Centre's stand, his act of getting the *mangalkalash* as a tribute to the 105 Hutatmas on becoming the first chief minister of Maharashtra did not go down well with the people. Nor did the reluctance of his government to address problems of Mumbai's Marathi youth.

The anger against Congress grew rapidly after 1960, but after the Samiti lost its force, a void was created and there was no one to articulate the anger and concerns of the discontented young lot.

Thackeray filled this void. The same youngsters who had given momentum to the Samyukta Maharashtra movement welcomed him.

Maharashtrians had hoped their economic dependence would end once Mumbai was made a part of a United Maharashtra, but the landscape grew bleaker. The Sena, with its avowed aim of 'Maharashtra for Maharashtrians' and its demand for preferential treatment for sons of the soil, lifted sagging spirits and rekindled aspirations. It emerged as a ray of hope for a distressed generation.

Second, the organisation was named after the iconic figure, Chhatrapati Shivaji.

'Who will not feel a surge of pride on hearing the name of Shivaji?' Communist leader Ahilya Rangnekar told me. 'After all, anything that touches the heart is attractive. So what if the behaviour of those taking Shivaji's name is at variance with his teachings? The Sena used Shivaji's name to capitalise on the sentiment attached to it'.[53]

Bharatiya Janata Party (BJP) leader L.K. Advani says: 'Like so many others, I have learnt the lessons of Hindutva in our RSS shakhas and the ideal before us always used to be Chhatrapati Shivaji. Shivaji has an appeal for the whole country and one of the best poems on him was written by the great Rabindranath Tagore. But in the state that gave birth to Chhatrapati Shivaji, Balasaheb put Shivaji on a pedestal, idolised him and even named his party after Shivaji.'[54]

Thus, the significance of the name Shiv Sena – Shivaji's Army – could not have been lost on a people proud of the Maratha warrior tradition and disappointed with their current status. In 1966, Maharashtrian youth saw that their hero's name seemed once again to radiate hope.

Blended with this was the personality of Bal Thackeray. Though we will later explore in detail the equation of Shiv Sena = Bal Thackeray, it is pertinent at this point to refer to the impact his aggressive posturing had on impressionable young minds in the 1960s.

How did Thackeray capture young hearts in the Sena's early days?

He expressed concern over the status of Maharashtrians and lambasted 'outsiders' who had 'snatched away the rights of the Marathi *manoos*'.

He spoke of the manifestoes of political parties with disdain.

He damned a democracy which 'placed obstacles in the path to progress'.

He condemned a law which 'couldn't provide justice to people' and said he did not have faith in *any* ideology.

What he solely and firmly believed in, he said, was 'Maharashtra Dharma', which abhorred the piece-meal division of Maharashtrians and instead unified them, secured for them their rights and led to the establishment of a just state.

Thackeray did not dish out any grand promises then, nor did he sell grandiloquent dreams. He only exhorted the vast number of urban unemployed youth to launch an assault on the establishment.

He came on the scene as an angry young man, assumed an anti-establishment stand and urged youth to hit out at injustice.

The young sons of the soil, who looked aghast at the economic revolution that was side-stepping them, were in search of a leader who thundered against the powers that be. In Thackeray, they found a tiger who roared, and they responded.

Soon, they began barging into offices, gheraoing top officers, delivering physical blows to 'lungiwallahs' and 'bhaiyyas' who had 'robbed' their jobs and attacking Udipi hotels.

By January 1967, 60 Sena shakhas had been formed all over Mumbai and Thane. Thackeray and the chief organisers around him had created these offices. After this was done, the Senapati (Sena chief) and his close aides cautiously selected seven vibhag pramukhs (division chiefs) conterminous with parliamentary constituencies and more than a hundred shakha pramukhs (branch chiefs) conterminous with municipal seats. The branch leaders were followed by upshakha pramukhs (assistant branch chiefs), and after them came the rank and file.

All these people, right from the netas to the upshakha pramukhs, were hand-picked by the leader. Many of them had zero political experience, though they were not without any organisational background. While selecting the divisional and branch chiefs, focus was placed on a person's capabilities, his *nishtha* (allegiance), his conversational abilities, contacts, ability to identify himself with youth and his interest in physical activity.

When experience proved that estimation of certain qualities had been wrong, quick corrective measures were taken. In one public meeting in 1967, Thackeray told Sena activists he had sent the Malad shakha pramukh packing, and others in the *Sanghatna* (organisation) who deviated from its principles would be similarly ousted.

The same year, Balwant Mantri, a senior leader who criticised the Sena's undemocratic way of functioning, was forced by Sainiks to prostrate before Thackeray and was freed only after he had apologised profusely. From the beginning, it was made clear to everyone in the Sena that there was no place for 'indiscipline'.

Three things were given prime importance in the Sena scheme of things: orderliness, party regulations and concentration of power. The way Sena meetings were held, and the way communication within the organisation took place demonstrated this well enough.

Care was taken to ensure that the Sena's public meetings were held at the scheduled hour, and party activists were made to sit in the midst of the crowd to keep people from leaving. Chatter and shouts among listeners were also never noticed during meetings, and the speakers were never disturbed by unruly noises. On the other hand, rallies of other parties were routinely ruined by disorderly behaviour, and constant chitchat, screams for those in the front to sit, heckling and even throwing of pebbles dominated the proceedings regularly.

Even the meetings of Thackeray and his confidants with vibhag pramukhs and shakha pramukhs were characterised by orderliness: office-bearers were asked to sit in a particular order, individuals were asked to report their division and branch activities and voting was not even the exception to the rule.

Having observed the mode of communication between various levels of the Sena heirarchy in the early days, Katzenstein gives an account of it in her book:

> In one of the very active shakhas of Girgaum, leaders were appointed from each street or major chawl in the neighbourhood and were instructed to report into the ward office each week to check the bulletin board for notices and announcements. The financial accounts and books noting the shakha activities and meetings were regularly inspected by the higher party organisers... Communication with the individual shakhas took place with amazing speed and messages and directives from Thackeray and his cohorts reached the ward office almost instantaneously. It is sometimes satirically observed that the only more efficient network of communications in Bombay is matka, the illegal numbers game.[55]

The RSS: A role model?

The Sena's mobilisation of activists through a systematic organisational structure is often compared to that of the Rashtriya Swayamsevak Sangh (RSS), the Hindu nationalist outfit which is the ideological anchor of the BJP.

This comparison is, in a way, unavoidable. Like the Sena, the leadership in the RSS is centrally controlled, finalisation of decisions rests with the Sarasanghachalak and the code of discipline is exacting.

The Sangh also lays stress on paramilitary preparedness and physical prowess, as does the Sena. And a large percentage of activists of both organisations come from the middle and the lower-middle classes.

In fact, it is also suggested that Bal Thackeray, who was an RSS member in his student days, copied the RSS's organisational structure to build his own Sena.

'I used to go to the Dadar shakha of the RSS for 3-4 years,' Thackeray admits.[56] 'Must be between 1941 to 1944. But the Sangh never really left any deep impression on my mind. One day, Dada (Prabodhankar) told me, "Don't just sit at home. Go there for some physical training." I thought of the Sangh shakha as a gymnasium.'

The Sena chief has all along maintained he does not have any opinion on the RSS. But some of his statements have given away his feelings. 'They behave like one-man soldiers,' he says. 'There are still some old men in the RSS who are haughtily stubborn. If something good takes place, they'll say, "Our men were there!" But if anything goes wrong, their escape route is: "It happened because we slightly overlooked it.".... When I'd gone to Nagpur to meet Balasaheb Deoras once, all the RSS people in the "Mahal" there were moving about in a glum-faced way. Now, the people may have changed, but the Sangh's cheerless, mournful appearance persists.'[57]

No matter how much the extent of similarity between Sena and the RSS, Thackeray strongly denies he borrowed the Sangh's structural set-up. 'After the Sena was formed, shakhas were established, office-bearers came, and so did Shiv Sainiks. But it was as if the edifice came up on its own. How the Sena took shape would be difficult to say. One doesn't know if it was the result of divine guidance. But the structure was formed. And it proved successful. Now even national parties are copying the organisational structure. All this has nothing to do with the RSS.'

Whether the resemblance between the Sena and RSS structure is accidental or carefully designed, the Sena's well-formulated set-up and its stringent internal discipline brought a high level of orderliness to its actions. This, too, attracted large numbers of youths.

Very early, the Sena got a firm handle on the cultural dimensions of Mumbai's Marathi society and through its synergist of 'action', infused a sense of involvement among youths drawn to it.

The sense of direction, and of being absorbed and engrossed, that its activities imparted succeeded in weaning away a large section of fence-sitting youngsters to its side, and many of those who were members of other, longer-established parties also slowly gravitated towards this organisation whose swelling ranks were seen to be filled with enthusiasm.

Energies of most Sena activists were directed towards organising two of Mumbai's most popular festivals, the Shivaji Jayanti and Ganesh Chaturthi. These festivals are the two biggest cultural events in Maharashtra, and anybody playing a stellar role in organising their celebration automatically stakes claim as the upholder of the Maharashtrian way of life.

In addition to taking up the vital centres of the Marathi cultural consciousness, the Sena, through its shakhas, held classes conducting physical training courses, and provided solutions to neighbourhoods facing problems such as water shortage, poor drainage and dilapidated buildings.

The Sena shakha functioned almost as an extension of the family for many Mumbaikars: it placed a premium on cultural activities, sports, educational establishments for the underprivileged, ambulance service, assistance to the disabled, improvement of living conditions, opening of employment channels to the unemployed and several other social tasks. The handling of such things was as valued in the Sena scheme of things as the 'fight against injustice,' and these responsibilities almost entirely occupied young Sena workers, giving them an otherwise hard-to-find sense of commitment.

There were many Sena shakhas, for instance, which kept employment registers in which job-seekers wrote down their names, qualifications and the posts desired. When the shakha was informed about availability of jobs, the roster was referred to and youngsters were made aware about the opportunities and existing vacancies. Many were offered suggestions on how to fill application forms and how to present themselves at interviews. Naturally, youth looking for jobs found the Sena shakhas linked to their short- and long-term interests.

Typing, stenography and English classes were also held by some shakhas, and poor students securing good percentage in matriculation and higher-level exams were felicitated and offered free notebooks and other stationery as incentive. Study rooms were sometimes arranged for students in local schools, so that they got sufficient study space, and shakhas also took the responsibility of paying school fees of some 'poor and deserving' students.

What was more, the Sena's Madhyavarti Karyalaya (central office) distributed money among the shakhas, which in turn gave these funds as capital to young Marathi boys eager to start small entrepreneurial ventures.

Bal Thackeray's early exhortation to Marathi youths to start *vada pav* stalls of their own has faced strong criticism from the anti-Sena school of thought, which feels he kept the vision of young Maharashtrians confined to small ventures and did not encourage them to think big. *Vada Pav*, they have maintained, was too restrictive a concept forwarded by Thackeray.

To take the *vada pav* slogan of those days literally is, however, to miss out on the shrewd nature of Thackeray's appeal. In the 1960s, the *vada pav* stall stood as the symbol of the self-dependence and self-reliance of the Marathi youngster, more than anything else. Maharashtrian youth then did not have any capital to invest in big business ventures and to take huge entrepreneurial leaps; they could, with the money they had with them – or the lack of it – at that time, only have started something on the scale of some such refreshment stall.

If Thackeray had then suggested that Maharashtrians open up factories and industries and launch companies, he would have been laughed off as crazy. He saw that the first step he could suggest for unemployed youth was a *vada pav* stall, and he went the whole hog advocating the setting up of such stalls and extending party funds for the purpose.

The social activities of Sena shakhas motivated Sainiks towards further involvement in organisational work and made youngsters outside the party join the fold of the combative and well-directed Sena.

The spirit of action and the enthusiasm of Sainiks has cast the Sena in a mould different from that of other organisations. It is often satirically observed that a Sainik can be over-enthusiastic and over-active, but he can never be found *lacking* in enthusiasm and action.

About the zeal of Sena activists, Katzeinstein recounts:

> An almost clublike, fraternal spirit was exhibited in the way Shiv Sena activists talked among and about each other and the party. The occasional boyishness and constant exuberance obtained at the highest level of the organisation as well as among the Shiv Sainiks working in the shakha office... In the shakha offices the

highly charged atmosphere and excitement were almost always in evidence. There was constant laughter. Talking, crowds of young boys, arms on each others' shoulders, and excited shouts interspersed the hushed conferences of several Shiv Sainiks huddled on benches or chairs.[58]

The fraternal spirit shown by the Shiv Sainiks, thus, contributed in sending inviting signals to youth. As did many other factors.

5

BAL THACKERAY:
THE PERSON AND THE PERSONA

T he personality of Bal Thackeray played a key role in attracting youth to the Shiv Sena and also in inviting stringent criticism from non-Marathi-speaking people about the methods he advocated for 'securing the rights of the Marathi population'. From the time of the Sena's inception, Thackeray positioned himself as someone outside the political establishment. We have seen in earlier chapters, how he equated politics with a disease and said the Sena would do '80 per cent social work and 20 per cent politics'. The manner in which he went about building his political persona reflected these political priorities and stratagems. For starters, Thackeray did not dress like the average Indian politician. He scrupulously avoided khadi clothes, till date the hallmark of the Indian neta. For the first Sena rally, he wore a simple full-length shirt and trousers, portraying the image of a middle-class Maharashtrian. He was suitably thin and wiry to carry off this image, and he wore thick-rimmed glasses. He gradually took to wearing a *bandh gala* safari suit, and sometime in the 1970s switched to a kurta and pyjama, with a shawl draped delicately around his neck. The kurta-pyjama and shawl would be either off-white or saffron in colour. At home, he would always be dressed in a saffron kurta and a lungi of the same colour. In the early 1990s, as champion of the cause of a militant Hindutva, Thackeray took to wearing a string of beads of *rudraksha* on his left hand, which he would often raise in impassioned gesticulation while making his fiery and often-provocative speeches. The *rudraksha*, given to him by spiritual guru Gagangiri Maharaj, was discarded after his wife Meena, called Meena-tai or Maa-saheb by Shiv

Sainiks, died in 1995; at that time, Thackeray also declared he had no reason to keep his faith in God who took away people so cruelly. Before his wife died, Balasaheb would routinely visit the Thackeray family's deity, Goddess Ekvira, at Karla near Lonavla, more than a 100 km from Mumbai; after her passing, his visits reduced and at one point stopped altogether, though his son Uddhav and nephew Raj continue to go there every once in a while along with their families. In the early years of the Sena, Thackeray prepared himself well for his political role. He read the history of India's freedom struggle in considerable detail a little before he launched his party, so that he would have a good grip on India's political past and would be in a strong position to provide a historical perspective to events and modern-day developments. He intensely disliked novels then, as he does even today, and avoided reading them. 'I don't like the fake romance in the novels, and other kinds of fakery you see there,' he once said. But he was a voracious reader of newspapers: by his own admission, he went through more than 10 newspapers in a day. The number went up to 16 in later years as the Indian media witnessed an expansion. He has had, for the past five decades, a habit of marking media reports he considers significant and forwarding the newspaper cuttings to Sena leaders, legislators, corporators and activists for follow-up action. For example, he says that if he sees a picture of garbage accumulated in an area, he sends a copy to the Sena corporator from the area, and if the party does not have a corporator there, to the vibhag pramukh (party head for the Assembly constituency concerned) or shakha pramukh (party head for the civic ward concerned). This practice, which he began in the 1960s, continues to this day, though in recent times his reading of newspapers has reduced as a result of age and illnesses.

The young Thackeray loved a glass of warm, lager beer, and his pipe and cigar equally. He would enjoy his pipe even while he drew cartoons or had lengthy meetings with party aides; in July 2000, when he left Matoshree to go to court over his arrest in the Mumbai riots case, he walked out of the house with his favourite cigar in hand. His evening beer sessions with filmstar-friends such as Dilip Kumar on the terrace of Matoshree (the friendship with Dilip Kumar ended when the actor accepted the Nishaan-e-Pakistan award, with Thackeray saying, in Hindi, 'Abhi chana bhi hain, beer bhi hain, lekin Dilip Kumar ke raaste badal gaye [The beer and chana are still there, but Dilip Kumar has gone elsewhere]'), or with cricketer-friends such as Bapu Nadkarni, Ramakant Desai and Madhav Mantri, with whom he would take the local train every day from Dadar to Churchgate during his *FPJ* days, are well known. Warm beer gave way to wine after his bypass surgery in 1996 because the doctors told him wine was good for the heart, and he took to playfully chiding his doctors for imposing restrictions on him and even for converting his body into 'a medical laboratory'. The strict discipline extended itself to eating habits. This meant that while Thackeray could have his beloved *varan bhaat* (dal–rice) and vegetables, he could not, as a member of the Chandraseniya Kayastha Prabhu community that loves fish and chicken, have non–vegetarian food the way he had always loved to as there were limits on eating seafood and meat.

Cricket was another favourite of the man. In his youth, he had often gone to Shivaji Park situated a stone's throw away from his Ranade Road residence, to watch the likes of Mantri, Nadkarni, Desai and Sandeep Patil's father Madhusudan Patil play. That love has continued to this day, and even as he has remained firm in his opposition to Indo–Pak cricket relations over the past two decades, he clapped deliriously as he watched, on his TV set at home, Virender Sehwag get his triple century against Pakistan in 2004. Once, in the 1970s, he surprised the famous cricket coach Anna Vaidya who had stood in a queue to meet him. As the queue moved slowly, the people who had lined up touched Thackeray's feet, one after the other; the moment Vaidya tried to bend, Thackeray held his hands and prevented him from playing the supplicant. 'You cannot touch my feet. As a youngster, I have seen you coaching youngsters at Shivaji Park,' he told the cricket guru. There is also a picture of a 40–something Thackeray, bat in hand, launching into a drive. The backlift is decently high, always a thing a good coach will appreciate. Another passion Thackeray has shared with a majority of Indians has been Bollywood. He has not only enjoyed Hindi film movies but has counted Amitabh Bachchan among his best friends. When Amitabh was injured on the sets of the film *Coolie* in 1982, it was a Sena ambulance that quickly arrived at the spot to take him to hospital; and when a collection of poems written by Thackeray's grandson Aditya was to be released, it was Amitabh who was invited by the Sena chief to do the honours. In the early years of the Sena, Thackeray invited numerous personalities from Bollywood on to the Sena platform and felicitated them. Among those who attended party functions in the 1960s and 70s were Mohammed Rafi (whom Thackeray's musician-brother Shrikant got to sing for Marathi films), Asha Bhosle, Dharmendra, Rajesh Khanna, Sanjeev Kumar, Kishore Kumar and R.D. Burman. While Dharmendra, Asha and Rajesh Khanna were all given small busts of Shivaji as mementoes, R.D. Burman was presented with a huge lamp by Thackeray. In the 1980s and 90s, Thackeray increasingly turned arbiter in disputes in the Bollywood and mediated not only in the professional matters of Bollywood personalities but even helped them sort out personal issues. When Sanjay Dutt was arrested under the TADA law for his role in the 1993 Mumbai serial blasts, Bal Thackeray was the sole political leader who supported him and demanded his release from jail. Thackeray even reprimanded his Sainiks who took out a morcha to protest against another morcha taken out in support of the actor by film-maker Subhash Ghai and others. Sanjay's father, actor and Congressman Sunil Dutt, was one of Thackeray's close buddies, and Thackeray said he was convinced of Sanjay's innocence after he had spoken to Dutt Senior. Thackeray has periodically sent out warnings to Mumbai's film-makers and even extra-legally 'cleared' films. When Mani Ratnam's film *Bombay*, set against the backdrop of the 1992–93 Mumbai riots, was set for release, it was reported that one of the characters shown in it – a Hindu leader – bore a serious resemblance to Thackeray. The Sena chief said: 'If the filmmaker showed anything mischievous, the screen will be torn by my boys.' In 2005, Ram Gopal Verma had to organise a special pre-release screening of *Sarkar* – a film based on the Sena chief's life and family – for Thackeray, and only after he had 'approved' of it was the film released. This public image of being a stern, insistent and even extra-legal judge on issues notwithstanding, Thackeray has had his softer side as well. He has adored his pets: a dog called Pampu was among his earliest pets, and then there was an Alsatian, Major, and a dog called Marshal. And he has loved the aquarium he's had in his home for decades now.

His love for gardening is well-known, and in a letter written by him to his children from Yerawada Jail in 1969, after he was arrested in the wake of riots in Mumbai over the Maharashtra-Karnataka border dispute, he implored his three sons to take care of the *baug* (garden) outside their home and to place the seeds of the sunflower plant, which he had sent to them, in an earthen pot so that they could grow. 'There are beautiful sunflowers here,' he added in the letter from prison. Also, for all his endorsement of violence, Thackeray has hated, from his early years, the idea of beating up children. He was, and remains, an indulgent father, and he even allowed his three sons – the eldest, Bindumadhav (a filmmaker, Bindumadhav died in a road accident in 1996), the second, Jaidev, who is estranged, and the third, Uddhav, who lives with him at Matoshree – to give him a special name: Pilga. Nobody has been able to figure out till date the etymological origins of this name, but Thackeray not only did not mind it earlier, he still does not. He also gave his children fond names when they were young: Binda, Dinga and Tibba. And Raj Thackeray, the nephew, has always been 'Raja' to him. One more aspect of his personality, largely unknown, has been his love for the number 13, considered inauspicious by many. Thackeray says it is his lucky number. He married Sarla Vaidya, who became Meena Thackeray after marriage on 13 June 1948 and he launched *Marmik* weekly on 13 August 1960. He also considers the number 27 lucky, as Uddhav was born on 27 July 1960. When I asked Thackeray to release the first edition of this book in June 1999, he chose the 27th of that month for the function, saying it was 'a good date'. Thackeray has also been known for his excellent relations with political rivals, despite the harsh language he has often used for them. Sharad Pawar is a thick friend, and so is Sushilkumar Shinde, whom he has criticised strongly for defending the resumption of cricketing ties between India and Pakistan as the Union home minister.

Thackeray extended unconditional support to Pawar's daughter Supriya Sule's candidature to the Rajya Sabha because she was his 'friend's daughter'. He wrote in the Sena mouthpiece how he had watched her grow. He said that once, when she was a toddler, her parents had come along with her to Matoshree for dinner. She had high fever then, and the Pawars had left the same night for Pune. Thackeray remembered how he had then called them up in Pune early next morning to find out how Supriya was doing. Similarly, George Fernandes and Thackeray may have been famous rivals, but they also got along famously, and he enjoyed a good rapport with Socialist leader S.M. Joshi and Communist leader S.A.

Dange, perhaps representatives of the only two parties with whom he has never had a truck. Thackeray has shown remarkable political flexibility otherwise. While he was alleged to have been propped up in the second half of the 1960s by the Congress, he tied up with Madhu Dandavate's Praja Socialist Party in 1968 and even joined hands with the Muslim League for a mayoral poll in the 1970s; he brought Pawar and Fernandes on the Sena podium in 1982 and supported Pawar's claim to chief ministership at the time; and his alliance with the BJP has of course lasted for more than 25 years, making it the longest alliance within the NDA. But he has never tied up with the Communists and with Joshi's Samyukta Socialist Party. At a personal level, Thackeray has been the one contemporary Maharashtra politician who has perhaps seen the maximum number of tragedies. His estrangement with his brother Ramesh – he has two brothers and five sisters[59] – took place sometime in the 1960s; his second son, Jaidev, was estranged in the early 1990s, with Thackeray saying of him, a touch of melancholy clear in his voice, 'That boy is a tragedy'; he lost his wife in September 1995 to a heart attack just months after his greatest political triumph, the capture of power in Maharashtra; and seven months later, in April 1996, his eldest son Binda died in a road accident. The circumstances of his wife's death were tragic. Thackeray had gone with her and a few aides to their farmhouse in Karjat, some 100 km from Mumbai. When she suffered a heart attack, there was no power in the house, so emergency calls could not be made to the doctors (there were no mobile phones then); by the time the doctors arrived, it was too late. Thackeray was devastated and, perhaps for the first time, could not hold back his tears in public. On other occasions, he has, quoting Swami Vivekananda, said he is like a fish in water: he has his moments of sadness and of grief, but nobody can see his tears. The estrangement with his nephew was also bitter, as Raj has been among the people closest to him, and though things have improved there, with both Raj and he having started the process of reconciliation and Raj visiting him frequently to check on his health, Uddhav's illness of late – Thackeray's son got eight stents placed in his body after undergoing angioplasty in July 2012, and then underwent a second angioplasty in November 2012 – has worried him a great deal and even affected his health. The day after Uddhav was released from Lilavati Hospital in Bandra in July 2012, Bal Thackeray was admitted to the same hospital for ailments of the lungs and pancreas; his close aides said his anxiety about Uddhav's health had a lot to do with this.

While Thackeray raged and ranted against migrants in the Sena's early days and urged Marathis to thrash anyone who blocked their progress, for his Sainiks, he played friend, philosopher and guide, and was gentle with them. He would win them over with the way he treated them. He would unfailingly walk any Sainik who visited his home to his door, that is, before security became a concern for him and his family; and his wife would treat them to delicacies and enquire about their families. Even while drawing his cartoons, Thackeray would often discuss the characters or his 'models', as he called them, with his party aides and regale them with stories about these personalities. He thus developed a bond with his loyalists. And while his booming voice was a big draw for the youth, so was his oratorical style. He never read out his speech, and he never referred to notes. His speeches were conversational in nature, and they did not follow any set pattern or even a fixed line of thought. He would flit from subject to subject, beginning with politics, going on to Bollywood, switching over from there to cricket and culture and then return, with gusto, to politics. That was part of his appeal, for it gave the listeners the impression that he was talking to them. He has certainly imbibed the lesson well, because his regular listeners have sworn, right from 1966, that he could make the Marathi language dance to his tune, and they have loved his penchant for word play. He has often called Sharad Pawar '*maidyacha pota*' (a bag of flour), labelled the Communists 'the red monkeys' and, during a visit to the US in the 1980s, told a local there, when asked where he had come from, 'I am an Indian, but not a Red Indian'. His listeners have appreciated the fact that he has not spared his allies and friends either: he light-heartedly uttered the line from the famous Hindi song '*O Sajna, Barkha bahaar aayi*' when BJP leader Gopinath Munde, whose dalliance with a *lavani* dancer by the name of Barkha had just become public knowledge, was sharing the dais with him. He once accused his ally, the BJP, of getting between Mayawati and Mulayam when the two of them had briefly 'come together'. There have been two responses to his ribald humour: one of denunciation, and the other, of wholehearted acceptance. This is just part of the reaction he evokes: no middle-of-the-road response, people either love him or love to dislike him. So why was his humour accepted by a wide constituency of Marathi-speaking people? Part of the reason is that bawdy talk has been part of classic Maharashtrian satire, and even the Marathi political tradition allows for such talk. Before Thackeray, 'Acharya' P.K. Atre used colourful language and even sexual innuendo to describe and ridicule his political opponents. Atre's persona helped Thackeray adopt a similar style and build a similar persona of a person who was not afraid of using his creative imagination as a cartoonist to target his opponents. Thackeray also systematically built his reputation as a person who spoke about what was on people's minds but which they would not dare say. So he made accusations against people and ethnic groups that an ordinary person would hesitate to make, even if he/she felt like doing so, for fear of sounding politically incorrect, called people names that one would not normally use, and cracked the kind of jokes in front of a crowd of lakhs that hardly anybody, out of concerns for respectability and public perception, would make in front of people other than those in their inner circle. His histrionic art has involved non-verbal communication as well. I was once witness to an incident where he sent across a firm message to the crowd without uttering a word. This was during the Lok Sabha poll campaign in 1998. Thackeray had just stood up to address a huge crowd at Girgaum Chowpatty when people seated closest to the dais got up because of some commotion behind. He urged them, twice or thrice, to sit, but the commotion increased, and people seated behind too got up. He then simply squatted on the floor of the dais. Members of the crowd, nonplussed, looked at him, then at each other, and sat down. He had, with that act, made it clear that if the crowd wanted to stand, he would sit, and it was only when they sat that he would get up to speak. But verbal or not, his communication has always been contentious. The non-Marathi-speaking people of Mumbai – and even a strong section of the Marathi-speaking population – acutely resented his accusations of discrimination, made against South Indians, of cornering jobs that he said 'Maharashtrians ought to have got', and they denounced the cult of violence that he wanted to encourage and spread. But Thackeray stuck to his stand, calling his violence 'constructive'. This theory of 'constructive violence' later helped him woo a section of other Hindus with his condemnation of 'pro-Pakistani Muslims' and his advocacy of an aggressive Hindutva, and neither the new converts who had denounced him earlier nor his loyal followers saw anything wrong with the shift in the target from South Indians to Muslims. Bal Thackeray had, with his personality, his booming voice, gift for oratory, political talk bereft of well-entrenched political theories and his militant methods succeeded in casting his spell over a wide constituency of Maharashtrian and, for a while, a section of non-Marathi-speaking youth. So much so, that for 46 consecutive years, he has attracted a crowd of at least a lakh for his Dussehra rally, every year, a record of sorts. To have attracted almost three generations in this manner has been his political achievement, and to have provoked extreme reactions of hate and unflinching loyalty, a measure of his controversial personality.

6

POLITICS, PROMISES AND VIOLENCE

Tremendous activity took place in the Shiv Sena within a year of its birth, and the way other political parties reacted to its emergence and growth was intriguing.

The Congress took an ambiguous stand. Thackeray had gone head-to-head against the Communists and pledged to fight the 'red monkeys' tooth and nail, so the Congress had reason not to go in for a straight confrontation. The enemy was common. At the same time, the ruling party could not be seen hobnobbing with the militant group.

So it devised a delicate strategy that combined a little bit of conflict and a little bit of tacit co-operation.

The Left-of-Centre forces resolved to 'nip the menace in the bud', and significant sections of society, including Maharashtrians and non-Maharashtrians alike, saw the Sena as a 'dangerous development'.

Equally significant sections of society, mainly comprising young Maharashtrians, welcomed the fledgling front and pledged support to it.

The Sena became a topic for hot debate. At the same time, its activities, some outside the ambit of the law, continued to grow.

One such action, which invited controversy, was an attack on a South Indian hotel in Kalachowki in central Mumbai in February 1967. Thirty-two persons were injured in the stone-throwing by Shiv Sainiks, and four Sena activists were arrested. Bal Thackeray, however, showered praise on Sainiks involved in the attack.

Right from the beginning, he made no bones about his advocacy of violence.

Such activities apart, the Sena – whose leader had likened politics to ringworm in his maiden speech – soon found itself borne upon the tides of politics.

When the Lok Sabha elections were announced to be held in the first half of 1967, the Sena chose to take a leap into mainstream politics, though it was firm on *not* putting up any candidates of its own. It was equally firm on another thing: its animosity towards Communists. That ostensibly impelled the foray into politics.

Former Defence Minister V.K. Krishna Menon, who had earned notoriety following the Chinese aggression in 1962, had sought a Lok Sabha seat from north-east Mumbai from the Congress. In fact, he had been Congress candidate from the constituency since 1957. But S.K. Patil, then the undisputed Congress leader from Mumbai, saw to it that Menon did not get the party ticket. Factional fights within Congress put paid to Menon's hopes, and he finally chose to contest as an Independent from the same constituency.

After the Samyukta Maharashtra Samiti was torn to shreds, the Communist and the Samyukta Samajwadi Party had combined in May 1966 to create the Sampoorna Maharashtra Samiti.

The purported aim of this Samiti, led by S.A. Dange, was to complete the unfinished task of the Samyukta Maharashta movement: to integrate Belgaum-Karwar-Nipani with Maharashtra. These areas, with a strong Marathi-speaking population, had not been included in Maharashtra at the time of its formation in 1960. This front decided to put its weight behind Menon. The Congress's official candidate against Menon was S.G. Barve, a revenue officer, and for S.K. Patil winning the seat became a matter of prestige.

At this time, the Sena surprisingly announced it would work to bring about the defeat of the 'rhinoceros-skinned' Krishna Menon because he was standing as a Communist.[60] This meant backing Congress candidate Barve; the Sena was willing to do it. Thackeray then concentrated not on whom to elect, but on whom to oppose. His slogan was 'Bury the Five Demons'. The demons, as he saw them, were Menon, Dange, Acharya Atre, George Fernandes and H.R. Gokhale, all having more than just Communist sympathies. He also supported candidates from the Jan Sangh, Swatantra and Socialist parties against the 'Reds' in other constituencies in the city. In central Mumbai, the Sena backed Harish Mahindra, director of Mahindra and Mahindra, against Dange, and in north-west Mumbai propped up Maharashtra Home Minister and Swatantra Party candidate Shantilal Shah against Krishna Menon's pal Gokhale.

But if Thackeray took up cudgels on behalf of Congress nominee Barve, Maharashtra's leading writer Acharya Atre launched a campaign in support of Krishna Menon.

Atre held several meetings in the north-east Mumbai constituency, which then extended up to Thane-Dombivli, warning people against the perils of the 'jingoistic' Sena.

He left no stone unturned in running down the Sena. And the Sena left no turn of his unstoned.

The campaigning prowess of both sides came to the fore as election day drew nearer, and north-east Mumbai's voters were asked more for a referendum on acrimonious exchanges than on matters ideological. Atre declared he would hold a 'rally' at Thane's Gamdevi Maidan. 'Disrupt my meeting if you can,' he challenged Shiv Sainiks.

Gamdevi Maidan saw a capacity crowd; the Communist flag, the *Lal Bavta*, looked omnipresent and Atre began his speech on a note of jubilation. Just then, a chappal was hurled at the dais. But Atre continued: 'You shameless ones, why do you hurl stones? You'll finally have to run away to save yourself!'

At this, all hell broke loose. Countless chappals found their way on to the stage, and a bonfire of all the *Lal Bavtas* was lit. Shiv Sainiks themselves had crowded the ground carrying Red flags.

Atre had to seek shelter in a hospital that stood next to the maidan. Enraged Sainiks followed him there, but Atre somehow escaped.

His car, however, bore the brunt of the Sainiks' wrath. It was smashed to pieces.

Many Sainiks saw this humiliation of Atre as retribution, for, before the Sena was born, Thackeray's *Marmik* office had been assaulted by followers of Atre, Dange and George Fernandes for an allegedly mischievous cartoon.

On the cover of the *Marmik* issue dated 29 August 1965, there had appeared a caricature showing *Bharatmata* shorn of all her sparkle and glory, in a state of helplessness, and Atre, Dange and Fernandes standing in front of her with a mischievous glee on their faces.

Atre, Dange and Fernandes were quick to take action. All three were powerful leaders in their own right and had plenty of followers.

In the night of 29 August, their faithfuls took a morcha to Thackeray's Ranade Road residence in Dadar, which also served as the *Marmik* office. Bal and his brother Shrikant were not at home then, only Prabodhankar and his younger son Ramesh.

The crowd chanted: 'Bal Thackeray is the stooge of the Congress!' 'Bal Thackeray polishes [Congress leader] Balasaheb Desai's boots!'

The board of *Marmik* was removed and thrown on to the road, slogans of 'Atre-Dange-Fernandes Zindabad' were raised, stones and chappals hurled, and copies of *Marmik* burnt. According to Atre's *Maratha* daily, which carried a report on the protest: 'Seeing the crowd's anger, Prabodhankar Thackeray was at his wits' end. He came out on to the gallery of his house and, hands folded, told the demonstrators, "My son doesn't have brains. You should forgive him. I will make efforts to prevent him from insulting political leaders again."'

Atre also held a public meeting at Shivaji Park to protest against Thackeray's brush-strokes, and displaying the issue of *Marmik* to the gathering, said: 'Look at this filthy cartoon on the cover of *Marmik*. Thackeray has been hired by the Congress for its campaign. He cleans Balasaheb Desai's footwear. I condemn this vulgar cartoon.'[61]

Bal Thackeray replied to Atre by penning a piece in *Marmik* entitled 'Uncontrollably violent mob provoked by *Lalbhai* Atre brings a morcha to *Marmik* office'.

Extolling the virtues of democracy, Thackeray wrote:

> Atre, Dange and Fernandes evidently have zero belief in the people. All they believe in is browbeating, intimidation and violence. What display of muscle were the anarchists sent by Atre and Fernandes going to make before an 80-year-old social worker (Prabodhankar)? Were they going to tear his clothes and assault him physically to prove how strong they were? And why do this to Prabodhankar? Because his son only writes that which appeals to reason and is in the interest of people? Or because he fearlessly presents before the masses truths that Atre, Dange and Fernandes dislike and find difficult to digest? ... Fernandes is an old friend of ours. Not just because he's our friend, but also because he's our compatriot, we will never physically attack him. But we'll surely assault him ideologically, with our ideas.

To come back to the third general elections in 1967. Applying the same anti-Left principle as it did in the case of Menon, the Sena declared its support for Congress candidate S.K. Patil, who was pitched against George Fernandes in south Mumbai.

Thackeray had consistently heaped abuse on Patil through his writings, cartoons and speeches. The Lok Sabha poll changed the equation. The Congress, for its part, welcomed the Sena's help in its effort to defeat Menon and Fernandes.

This invited the argument that the Sena was the brainchild of the Congress, and that the 'relationship' between the two was about securing common benefits. Atre then called the Sena the *SadaShiv* (S.K. Patil's first name) Sena, and the nomenclature stuck for a while.

Although Fernandes defeated S.K. Patil, the Sena played a role in bringing about the downfall of Krishna Menon. Attacking him as an 'outsider', it put the might of its cadres behind Congress nominee Barve and saw to it that the latter won the numbers game against Nehru's trusted ally by a comfortable margin.

This was a heady victory for the Sena, and it boosted its confidence.

The Shiv Sena in the region/regional politics

The Thane municipal corporation elections were scheduled later in the same year. Thackeray, encouraged by the role played by his outfit in the Lok Sabha polls, decided the Sena would contest these elections by putting up its own candidates.

The organisational strength had increased in one year, and there had come into being a team of activists which was expanding. In Thane itself, the Sena had begun its activities on 1 January 1967, with one Dr Dhawle as pramukh of its first shakha in the township.

But why did Thackeray, who had maintained the Sena did not have political intent, choose politics and get his own candidates into the fray?

Dilip Ghatpande, one of Thackeray's close companions since the Sena's birth, points to a lack of fruition of its activities and ideas, due to a lack of political power, as the reason for the Sena entering politics.

Political power bestows clout and public representatives like Mumbai's municipal corporators enjoy powers of patronage and job appointments. The Sena's full-fledged entry into politics was thus inevitable, considering the widening sphere of its influence, the taste of success from 'outside participation' in the Lok Sabha elections and heightened expectations of sections of the Marathi populace from it.

The first test of the Sena's electoral strength threw up unexpected results. On its political debut, that too in suburban Thane, the Sena bagged 17 out of 40 seats and emerged the largest single party in the municipal corporation.

The Sena also reaped a whirlwind of criticism. The English media skewered it, and non-Maharashtrians looked upon it with increasing dread and distrust. To counter this diatribe and explain the party's political philosophy to the English-speaking classes, the Sena published an official statement in English, in the form of a book entitled *Shiv Sena Speaks*.

Shiv Sena Speaks soon led to the publication of another book on the Sena in English, but not by the Sena.

Barrister Achyut Chafekar, who appeared as counsel for the Sena during the Madon Commission of Inquiry set up to probe the Bhiwandi riots in 1970, used to work as a junior to Barrister H.R. Pardiwala, one of the leading Mumbai-based lawyers of the time.

He recounts:

> In Pardiwala's chamber, most of the lawyers were non-Maharashtrian, and they used to criticise the Shiv Sena severely. I asked Pardiwala and his friends why they were so critical of the Sena. I told him the Sena had some good points, and suggested he read the book *Shiv Sena Speaks*, which, it was believed, was the brainchild of Manohar Joshi.
>
> Pardiwala then asked me: "Can you get me 25 copies of the book?" I said I'd try. I went to Bal Thackeray's Ranade Road residence, and one of the men there, Sule, agreed to give me 25 copies. The book cost ₹ 1.50 paise.
>
> I handed over the copies to Pardiwala. He distributed them among his friends, most of whom were IAS and IPS officers, and held long discussions with them on the subject.
>
> (Thereafter), he wrote a book *The Shiv Sena – Why and Why Not* (Popular Prakashan, 1967), in which he upheld the Sena's sons-of-the-soil proposition. Where he disagreed with the Sena, however, was on the use of violence. It's significant that one of the prominent lawyers of the time, a Parsi at that, appreciated some of the Shiv Sena's points.[62]

The Sena and '*yandugundus*' (South Indians)

Thackeray's campaign against *yandugundus*, as he referred to South Indians, received a fillip early in 1968, when cinema houses in Madras took a decision not to screen Hindi films.

The Shiv Sena chief, in Mumbai, set out to squash the outburst of nativist sentiment in southern India. He appealed to owners of Mumbai's theatres to stop screening films made in the South.

When the appeal did not work, coercive action was taken. In February 1968, Sena activists attacked Ganesh Talkies in Lalbaug and stopped the screening of the film *Aadmi*. Thackeray's argument was that South Indian film-makers earned money in Mumbai and took it down South.

When Madras-based producer A.V. Mayappan met the Sena chief on 2 March 1968, asking him to allow release of his film *Do Kaliya* in Mumbai, Thackeray said only if three conditions were fulfilled could the screening be permitted. The conditions were: 1) Hindi films would have to be shown in Madras cinema houses, and Mayappan would have to meet the chief minister to get this done; 2) If the chief minister did not agree, Mayappan had to shift his studio to Mumbai; 3) When he set up his studio here, he ought to employ technicians and workers from Mumbai and not get them from the South.

Mayappam went back and met the chief minister and sent a message to Thackeray that the chief minister had assured the ban on Hindi films would be lifted. Following this, *Aadmi* was allowed to be released at Dadar's Kohinoor cinema, and a big banner beneath the film's poster at the theatre said: 'This film has been released with the blessings of the Shiv Sena.'

But the reported assurance from the South proved untrue, and Madras theatres refused to go back on their earlier stand. So the Sena, on 11 March 1968, conducted a simultaneous attack on 17 theatres in Mumbai and stopped screening of Hindi films made in the South.

Around the same time, South Indian actor Sivaji Ganesan arrived in Mumbai for a film shoot. 'The Shiv Sainiks made up their minds to stop the shoot at Goregaon, but they cancelled their agitation after Shiv Sena pramukh ordered them not to protest,' said *Marmik*.[63]

Thackeray's exhortation to Sainiks vis-a-vis Sivaji Ganesan was also published by *Marmik*. It went like this: 'Sivaji Ganesan contributed some measure of funds for the construction of Chhatrapati Shivaji Maharaj's statue at Shivaji Park. At the same time, when Bal Gandharva (one of Marathi theatre's towering figures) was felicitated

at Shivaji Park, Ganesan offered tw
publicly acknowledged his gratitud
of theatre and also had the sincerit
guru. What are you going to gain b
a man?'[64]

But the campaign against films m;
and the 'total ban' became operati
Sena stand, a section of the Mumbai
the same month. Several producer
were present for the function held at Ranjit Stu...,
was presided over by producer-director Adarsh. On the dais were
producer Bakshi Jangbahadur, Mandaloi, Govind Ghanekar, Gajanan
Jahagirdar, Anwar Husain, Tiwari and Pandit M.

'To see that the ban was properly implemented', *Marmik* reported,
'Sainiks visited quite a few cinema houses, but the theatre owners said
they had themselves stopped showing films from South India.'

When Madras theatres revoked their stand, Thackeray's campaign
ended, and the screening of Madras films resumed in Mumbai's theatres.

This was the beginning of Thackeray's longstanding influence in
the Mumbai film industry.

In an article entitled 'The Moving Hand Writes', published in
Eastern Economist, it was noted:

> The economics of the celluloid has triumphed over the politics
> of the DMK. The screening of Hindi films has been resumed in
> Madras state simply because, if this is not done, the Shiv Sena
> will not allow the exhibition in Maharashtra of Hindi films made
> in Madras studios. The answer to the Annadurais of this world,
> evidently is the Bal Thackerays. This may not be the most desirable
> way of ordering our affairs, but I fail to see what else there is to
> be done.[65]

This drive against Madras films came during the run-up to the
Brihanmumbai Municipal Corporation (BMC) or the Mumbai civic
elections, scheduled to be held on 26 March 1968. Having notched
up success in Thane the previous year, the Sena was eager to get a grip
on the BMC. Its stamp over Mumbai was already evident, and in the
1967 Lok Sabha polls, it had performed a key role in dealing a blow
to Krishna Menon.

e: The first official alliance

me for Sena to test its strength as a political player on
in Mumbai. And also as one which was willing to give
team to the Praja Socialist Party (PSP).

Sena sprang a surpise by striking an alliance with the Praja
list Party for the BMC polls. This was the first official alliance
e party had entered into. The PSP had not joined the Sampoorna
Maharashtra Samiti, and it was looking for a political bedfellow who
could help it gain a toehold in the metropolis. Its leader Madhu
Dandavate took the initiative in approaching Thackeray, and the PSP-
Sena alliance materialised. The PSP agreed to contest as many seats as
the Sena was willing to give it.

The Sena was the senior partner in the alliance. Though PSP was
a national party, its presence in Mumbai was negligible, and a tie-up
with Thackeray's party – even if it meant playing second fiddle –
could only help it acquire political space in India's financial capital.

The Sena, on the other hand, could not have got any tangible
benefits in the city by allying with the PSP. Then why did it join
hands with Dandavate's party?

There is a section of Sena leaders which believes that since the
Sena then had no representative of its own in Parliament, it needed
someone who could take up cudgels on its behalf in Delhi. In case
of criticism of the Sena in Parliament, Thackeray wanted someone
who would stand by his party and defend it in the House. With this
objective in mind, he agreed to a tie-up.

The PSP too recognised its role and performed it well in Delhi. In
February 1968, Communist leaders like A.P. Chatterjee, Bhupesh Gupta
and Chitta Basu raised the issue of an attack by Shiv Sainiks on Dalvi
building, the headquarters of the Communist Party in central Mumbai.
At that time, PSP's Banke Behari Das defended the Sena in the House.
Surprisingly, performing a tightrope walk, the then Union Home
Minister Y.B. Chavan had told MPs that though it was unfortunate that
an attack had taken place on the office of a political party, it needed to be
pointed out that members of a political outfit had launched an assault on
a procession of Shiv Sainiks prior to the Dalvi building incident. When
the Sena's opponents argued that the Sena was backed by businessmen
and industrialists, Chavan noted that this class extended its support to all
political parties, and added that it was its duty to do so.

The Sena's avowed Maharashtrianism had brought about a change in the political behaviour of all parties in Mumbai, and during the countdown to the polls, most of them had started attempting to pick up its language. During the seventh anniversary function of *Marmik* in 1967, Chief Minister Vasantrao Naik stated: 'It's a great weakness of the Marathi *manoos* that he allows the progress of non-Maharashtrians but poses obstacles in the path of his own people. Unless this is rectified, Marathi-speaking people cannot progress.'

The Sena had charged the Congress, and especially S.K. Patil, with selling Mumbai to non-Maharashtrians in general and Gujaratis in particular, and had elicited ready approval from the Marathi people. When the Congress made public its first list of candidates for the BMC elections, it had an unprecedented number of Marathi candidates – thirty-four.

After the BMC polls were announced, the Peasants and Workers Party's Bapusaheb Lad declared a 'programme for the youth', which was mainly a reiteration of the demands made by the Sena for Maharashtrians.

Everybody was trying to get the Marathi vote.

The Sena started its poll campaign in earnest. The Sena-PSP alliance's first public rally was held on 28 January 1968 at Kamgar Maidan, Parel, in central Mumbai.

A huge crowd had turned up, and Dandavate himself must have been astounded by the response, considering the impassioned speech he made that day.

'Regional sentiments and aspirations have risen all over India, and these sentiments have to be understood and not condemned', he said in defence of Thackeray's outfit, adding, 'The Shiv Sena is a party fully committed to nationalism. Only because the PSP has faith in the nationalism of the Sena has it joined hands with it. The Marathi-speaking people were displaced after the creation of Samyukta Maharashtra, and because of the unworthy Congress, their dreams and hopes were crushed.'

As the meeting was held in the Communist bastion of Parel, Sena leaders too were aggression personified. 'Now that the funeral of Communists is being held at Kamgar maidan, they should organise a condolence meeting at Nare Park (which is also in Parel),' Manohar Joshi said. Pramod Navalkar remarked: 'Dange should now go to the terrace of his building. He will see the sun has set on the Communist empire.'

The Marathi cause taken up by the Sena attracted crowds to its meetings across the city, and its anti-Communist stance also grabbed attention.

Just how well-organised was the electioneering can be seen by the rules laid down by Thackeray during the campaign for party activists. The list of rules, under which was stamped the Sena chief's signature, was as follows:

1) Shakha pramukhs of different areas should arrange to bring the speakers to the scheduled meetings in their respective areas and also arrange for their return home.

2) There must not be too many speakers for one meeting.

3) Prominence should be given to the main speaker.

4) Since the speakers have to address many rallies in a day, take care to see that all meetings begin at the fixed hour.

5) Since it is not possible, owing to time constraints, to hold a meeting in every municipal ward, some wards should organise joint rallies.

6) It is not necessary to have a chairperson for every meeting.

7) The thanks-giving ceremony should take place before the main speaker begins his speech.

8) After the end of the main speaker's speech, only the national anthem should be sung.

9) Names of speakers should not be announced without their prior permission.

The results demonstrated the efficacy of the Sena-PSP's well-orchestrated campaign. The Sena won 42 seats on its electoral debut in Mumbai, and the PSP got 11 seats. The Congress was the single largest party with 65 seats, the Sena the second largest.

Interestingly, the Congress had gained 59 seats in the 1961 BMC elections, with 45 per cent of the total vote share, and the Samyukta Maharashtra Samiti, which emerged the second largest group, had got 34 seats with 26 per cent of the vote share. In 1968, with 65 seats in its favour, the total polling percentage for the Congress had gone up by just 1 per cent, i.e., 46 per cent; and the Shiv Sena with 42 seats had replaced the polling percentage gained by the Samiti in 1961, with a vote share of 30 per cent.

The Sena had won from nearly all the principally Maharashtrian middle-class constituencies in Mumbai, and between the Marathi middle-class societies of Girgaum and Dadar, it had polled between 54 and 67 per cent of the popular vote.

Evidently, the Sena had, along with working-class support, also conquered the middle classes.

A crack had been made in Communist bastions, and it looked like it would be a matter of time before all of them would be wrested.

For those opposed to the well-entrenched Communist unions in Mumbai's industries, their intimidatory tactics and their penchant for organising strikes at the drop of a hat, the Sena's extremism was 'an answer to the Reds in the same coin'. Thackeray had made no secret of his stand that the Sena would fight Communists on 'their own terms', meaning, it would use methods as violent as those of the Communists to break their dominance. And since *Marmik* was launched, he had been unrelenting in his criticism of Communists.

After the Sena was formed, the verbal opposition to Communists was translated into action.

On 10 September 1967, it was declared through *Marmik* that 'one of the main objects of the Shiv Sena' was 'emasculation of the Communists'. Sainiks set out to accomplish this task for the first time on 27 December 1967. They attacked the Communist Party's office in Dalvi building, Parel, burnt all the files therein and set afire the furniture on the road. 'The boys were so furious, they flung the typewriter on to the road from the window of the office and wrecked whatever came within their sight. In fact, we wanted to burn the entire Dalvi building,' Thackeray says, 'but some of our voters were also staying in the building. So we only targeted the office'.[66] It was this attack that a PSP MP had defended in Parliament.

When a couple of days later, Shiv Sainiks hurled stones at a CPI rally at Kamgar Maidan, Parel, Thackeray proclaimed: 'I am proud of the Shiv Sainiks who fought the Reds on Wednesday and Friday.'

The *Indian Express* on 22 January 1968, reported that Sainiks had attacked two CPI members, who had to be rushed to a Lalbaug hospital, and on 24 March 1968, with the BMC polls two days away, the CPI's Gulabrao Ganacharya told the *Express* that Sainiks had indulged in violence during the election campaign and attacked a prominent Leftist worker, Dr Taraskar, with knives.

Factors responsible for drawing a significant percentage of the labour class from the Communists to the Sena in such a short period was the services and the supply of essential goods, tackling drainage and water problems and constructing buildings and repairing roads, as provided by Sena shakhas.

In the *New York Review of Books*, V.S. Naipaul has described his visit to a slum where – he was proudly shown the dustbins the Sena had placed along the lanes and where its infrastructure was strong:

> The most important discovery was the extent and nature of Shiv Sena's control. A squatters' settlement, a low huddle of mud and tin and tile and old boards, might suggest a random drift of human debris in a vacant city space; but the chances now were that it would be tightly organised. The settlement... was full of Sena "committees"; and these committees were dedicated as much to municipal self-regulation as to the Sena's politics: industrial workers beginning to apply something of the discipline of the factory floor to the areas where they had lived...
>
> There were eight Shiv Sena committee rooms in the settlement. The one we went to was on the main lane. It was a stuffy little shed with a corrugated-iron roof; but the floor, which the engineer remembered as being of earth, was now of concrete; and the walls, formerly of plain brick, had been plastered and whitewashed. There was one portrait. And interestingly, it was not of the leader of the Shiv Sena or of Shivaji, the Sena's warrior-god, but of the long dead Dr Ambedkar...

According to Naipaul, 'Lower down, in the chawls and the squatters' settlements of the city, among the dispossessed, needs are more elemental: food, shelter, water, a latrine.'[67] In the working-class areas of Mumbai, the Shiv Sena had addressed some of these needs.

Dipankar Gupta has cited in his book the example of a Christian lady factory worker in Goregaon who was helped by the Sena.[68]

Mary Katzenstein too, recorded that a large number of people in the Cumballa Hill slum area, where the Sena had got 50 per cent of the vote, told her the Sena men had 'put out a fire when some of the huts had been accidentally set ablaze, and that the Sena had been responsible for arranging the *zopadpatti* (slum) connection to the city's water main.'[69]

Her visit to a large slum in the suburbs, she writes, gave her the same impression:

One of the leaders of the Shiv Sena organisation in the colony, not a Maharashtrian but a Muslim from Andhra Pradesh, guided his visitors through Shiv Sena-paved lanes of one of the colony's sections — a stark contrast to the muddy paths and refuse-strewn alleys of the farther section of the slum. Elsewhere in the city, Shiv Sena shakhas, or committees, have organised other "civic improvements": an electric connection, permits to set up additional dwellings, etc.[70]

A Christian lady of Goregaon came to the Goregaon shakha because she had been dismissed from the factory where she worked, and her payment had also been held up. This factory was in Worli. So the shakha of Goregaon together with the shakhas of Worli and Dadar worked on her case and managed to persuade the factory management to pay her salary.

Such assistance, the results of the 1968 BMC elections revealed, had created goodwill for the Sena in Mumbai's working-class pockets.

But Janata Dal leader Mrinal Gore felt that Thackeray duped working-class youths. She told me:

His appeal was to youngsters whose reasoning faculty wasn't fully developed. He told them outsiders were taking away their jobs and suggested a quick-fix solution: Hit them, drive them away and get your rightful position. The youngsters who still hadn't matured liked his theories because he offered simple solutions. Little did they know the methods he was advocating were not only full of danger but also abhorrent.

Another reason he caught the fancy of youngsters was that he told them not to read and increase their corpus of knowledge. He pooh-poohed all social, political and economic theories, and told the youth they were useless and not worthy of study. Thus, he kept the vision of the youngsters confined to the Marathi issue. One who wants to know about societal problems must read a lot, but he deliberately discouraged the reading habit among youths to hide the hollowness of his own philosophy. He stunted the intellectual and cultural growth of Marathi youth and made headway.

We, the Socialists, and the Communists, however, should have paid more attention to the needs of the youngsters. We didn't.[71]

7

THE BATTLE WITH THE COMMUNISTS

H aving emerged a challenger to what was essentially the proclaimed role of communists, there was also a growing demand within the Shiv Sena to set up a workers' front. On 9 August 1968, Thackeray established the Bharatiya Kamgar Sena (BKS), the party's labour wing. A rally was held that day at Nare Park, Parel, in central Mumbai – the ground for many a Communist agitation – to announce its founding, and thousands of factory workers attended it, braving rain.

Thackeray appointed Dattaji Salvi as president of the BKS, and Arun Mehta as general secretary. Both had been involved with trade union activities. Salvi, himself a factory worker, had been part of the Congress-affiliated Rashtriya Mill Mazdoor Sangh (RMMS), and Mehta had been with the Indian National Trade Union Congress (INTUC) before he joined the Sena.

The BKS's agenda was to stamp out Communism from factories and from the minds of factory workers because although many workers functioned as Sainiks outside their factories, they took up the Red flag on the premises and were activists of entrenched Communist unions. Thackeray said at the launch: 'Till date, we didn't have a union, yet we punctured all strikes detrimental to workers' interests. Now we have our union. If the owner is good, we'll salute him. If he treats workers respectfully, we'll shake hands; else, we'll strike!'

Calling trade unionism 'our dharma' (set of ethical principles), he attacked other unions. 'Their leaders fill their pockets with the membership fees of poor workers and ignore workers' problems. We'll never exploit workers. We don't subscribe to the notion that the owner is an enemy. Large-hearted owners certainly aren't. We will never organise strikes in factories where the owners identify

themselves with the interests of workers and of Maharashtra.'
The guidelines set for the BKS were:[72]

1) It will not exploit workers the way the Communist Party has.
2) Workers will be taught to produce more and only then ask for more. The hue and cry raised about the class struggle has fooled the worker; he has remained mired in poverty because he has held up production by striking work.
3) The BKS will relentlessly attack CPI and CPI(M) strongholds.
4) The Sena will never use its participation in trade unions for gaining political capital.
5) Unlike Communist unions, the BKS will use donations to help workers facing difficulties.

Immediately, allegations were made that the BKS was a front set up by the Congress, its then Chief Minister V.P. Naik and industrialists to end Communist dominance in Mumbai's industrial sector.

Communist leader Roza Deshpande says:

The Congress found the Sena useful in destroying the labour movement. Industrialists too wanted to eliminate the Left, and the Sena helped them. Congress leaders treated Thackeray sympathetically, and he became a Frankenstein's monster.

The Sena acquired its base by raising the *bhoomiputra* (sons of the soil) issue. Communists in Kerala too spoke of 80 per cent reservations for locals, and Jyoti Basu in Bengal said preference should be given to Bengalis in Bengal. Thackeray did reflect the aspirations of the Marathi-speaking people, and the Communists knew he was right in many respects, but the clash between them and the Sena was because the Sena targeted South Indians. Thackeray said no Madrasis should get jobs here. We said the question was of providing jobs to Maharashtrians, not taking away others' jobs.

Unfortunately, the Communists opposed Thackeray as a fascist without understanding where the appeal of his party lay and were isolated. The masses weren't inimical to us, but they went to the Sena. The question, finally, is who delivers the goods. The Sena did.[73]

CPI(M) leader Ahilya Rangnekar told me:

The Sena slogan was *Jala Do, Jala Do, Lal Bavta Jala Do*. It sought to attack the Left and progressives because it knew that if these powers rose and the worker obtained a voice, it wouldn't be able to impose its will on society and mill workers. Hand-in-glove with mill-owners and industrialists, it struck deals with managements and worked to break unions. It spread terror and punctured union activities. Only industrialists and other market capitalists benefited by its actions.[74]

The BKS initially had one president, a general secretary, a secretary, eight field workers, legal workers and office staff. Two small rooms in Dadar's Purandare Wadi constituted its office.

Soon, clashes between the BKS and Left unions were reported from various mills, factories and industries, with each side accusing the other of crimes ranging from intimidation to murder.

B.S. Dhume, then leader of the Leftist All India Trade Union Congress (AITUC), a powerful union in many Mumbai establishments, narrated to me some of his experiences during the time the BKS was attempting to obtain a foothold:

> The Sena tried to create discord among workers and to break strikes, and our centre, the Communist Party's Andheri centre, has fought some of the fiercest fights with it at T. Manecklal, Larsen & Tubro (L&T), Parle Bottling Company and Gold Spot, where I led the AITUC unions.
>
> Manecklal was one of the big engineering companies in Mumbai, and its 500 workers – 60 per cent of them Marathi – were united under the Communist flag. When the owner didn't grant the workers' legitimate demands, we called for a strike, which continued for 90 days. The owner then went to Bal Thackeray and asked him for help. A puja was organised on the factory premises, and the Sena chief attended it. There was a huge tamarind tree on the premises. A chair was laid out for Thackeray under this tree, and as Marathi labourers gathered to see the man who had awakened curiosity among local youths, Thackeray began his speech. He told the workers: "The ones with the Red flag are misleading you. We are all Marathis, and you should act as Marathis and resume work immediately."
>
> This caused a split among workers. More than half of them still weren't willing to restart work, but others were willing to back down. Some immediately went back to work, some fought it out for some more time, but ultimately everyone went with the tide. The strike was broken.

In L&T, where again our union was dominant, they used intimidatory tactics. That factory has no railway station near it [both Andheri and Vikhroli are distant], so if you have to hold a rally, you can mobilise workers from the factory but it is not easy to call in workers from elsewhere. We had demanded certain things from the management, but the Sena started playing the Marathi vs non-Marathi game. They started holding meetings of workers inside the premises in the evenings, unleashed their anti-Left propaganda, and also brought in workers from other factories in trucks, so the crowd looked huge.

We then decided that we, too, would bring in workers from outside. But when we decided on a rally, the police commissioner called me and asked me how we were going to mobilise people. I said, the same way the others did. I asked him if it was a crime for us to bring people in trucks, while the Sena freely did that. Why one rule for us and another for them? At the meeting, a clash took place between workers sympathetic to the Sena and those affiliated to our union.

Soon, the clashes became frequent, both within the factory premises and outside. The Sena also caused friction in various factory departments in order to divide workers, and stones were hurled by Sainiks at the car of L&T's general manager Purothe. Finally, Thackeray's boys resorted to murder. When a supervisor in the switch gear department named Joshi, who wasn't even a member of our union but merely a sympathiser, was on his way home in the night, he was accosted by Sena men near Kurla railway station and stabbed to death.

The Sena just wanted to spread terror. Despite all this, we fought it out but could not win because the Sena was backed by the Congress government.

V.P. Naik, the then chief minister, was a sweet talker but thick-skinned. When we met him after Joshi's killing, he said he sympathised with us. I said, we don't want your sympathies. What are you doing to rein in the Sena? We told him it was getting difficult for us to function because of the Sena's terror tactics.

But we got no help. At Gold Spot in Andheri, workers led by us went on strike after an officer called Surve refused to concede their demands. The stir was so successful, it looked like the management would be forced to retreat. So Surve gathered the Sena's boys from neighbouring Parsiwada. He promised them jobs, saying he'd drive out the striking workers if the Sainiks helped him crush the agitation. Work on the highway was going on then, and heaps of stones lay on the road. Our workers would throw stones from outside the company's gates, and Sainiks would hurl bottles at them from inside. Pitched battles were fought for some time, but the hired fighters won.

At the New Standard Engineering Company in Goregaon [also in Mumbai's western suburbs], where again our union was influential, the Sena beat up one of our union leaders when he was emerging from Goregaon railway station. He was shocked and felt helpless. The other workers got the message and withdrew from our movement.

In 1972, a strike by government employees went on for many days, so the chief minister got in Thackeray as mediator as most employees were Marathi. Thackeray asked them to resume duty, saying, "Climb the stairs of the Mantralaya proudly, as Maharashtrians and as victors." Nobody responded to his appeal, but it was evidence of how the government used the Sena and how the police too protected it.

And yet, there was a shift among the masses too. Among our workers, there were Marathis, Malayalis, Tamilians, and Gujaratis. They used to fight unitedly. But after the Sena raised the Marathi vs non-Marathi slogan, their unity was shattered.

We at least knew the direction in which we were going, but the Sena had no such direction. Its rise was in the nature of a response to challenges, without any sense of perspective.[75]

The BKS Chief Salve not only refuted charges of anti-labour activities but maintained that workers and the management were the two wings of production. The Sena, he said, did not believe in class struggle but in cooperation between these wings. Responding to the Left's allegations about the Sena's violent ways, he said: 'When have the Communists believed in democracy and fair play? They are here to sabotage India and help Russia. We are acting in the country's interest'.[76]

How did the BKS enter a factory or a textile mill?

First, all Sainiks employed there established a BKS unit and launched a drive to win workers to their side. One of the Sena leaders was then asked to address the unit, and Sainiks from adjoining shakhas were called in for the meeting to demonstrate strength.

Second, whenever a strike continued for long and no settlement appeared in sight, Sena men worked to persuade workers that a prolonged stir would get them nothing. A Sena leader would then hold negotiations with the management and arrive at an arrangement acceptable to both workers and the owners.

After the management thus conceded demands made by the Sena, the BKS would walk away with the credit, and rival unions would appear ineffectual.

Third, whenever owners of small establishments approached the Sena for assistance in obtaining licences, power connections and the like, the Sena extended its helping hand by laying down a condition: that Marathi youngsters be employed in the establishment. Once the owner accepted this, the formation of a Sena unit in the establishment would be guaranteed.

In the first year itself, according to Salvi, 55 BKS unions were set up in different establishments, and workers joined them in large numbers.

The Sena condemned industrial strike and unrest, and increasingly, the Marathi *manoos* seemed to agree with Thackeray when he said: 'Anyone who gives bread and employment to Maharashtrians is ours, be he Tata, Birla or any other.'

The BKS was also going to be helpful to the Sena in acquiring news about the employment scenario in the industrial world and about vacancies. For unemployed youth who approached shakhas, the Sena would thus be in a better position to provide information.

To underscore the employment issue, Thackeray at the same time set up an Employment Bureau, and three Sainiks – Arun Joshi, Ram Dandekar and S. Palekar – were given charge of it. Both Joshi and Dandekar were employed with the Bank of America and were feeling badgered by the management. They approached Sena leader Pramod Navalkar, who took them to Thackeray. The Sena chief said he would support them, so they joined the party.

But the bureau did not have its own office. All its work was done through Sena shakhas. Joshi and Dandekar were sent in to negotiate only in situations where the management was reticent, or when discussions were necessary on the general principles of employment.

About the Sena's demand with regard to employment, and the work done by shakhas for the Employment Wing, Dipankar Gupta notes:

> The Shiv Sena stand is that apart from highly skilled jobs in factories, other jobs, that do not require any special skill, should be given to

Maharashtrians. Similarly they feel that in white-collar occupations, Maharashtrians can easily be employed as clerks, in offices and as lobby managers, bell hops, waiters, etc. in hotels. Every shakha office has printed forms for those looking for jobs. These forms have columns eliciting information regarding the applicant's education, experience and economic background. Highly educated people with degrees in Science, and Arts and even engineers figure in these forms. When the Shiv Sena officials get any information regarding vacancies they submit these applications depending on the type of job.[77]

Bani Deshpande, son-in-law of S.A. Dange, talks of how the emotional appeal blended in with such organisation:

> Thackeray once said, satirically, that he wanted even the prostitutes on Foras Road to be Marathi. He said all smugglers are non-Marathi and flush with money, then why can't Marathi youth earn money? Even when it came to gangland, he said if Dawood killed 10 people, the Marathi youth in the underworld should kill 50. He wouldn't mind if his boys broke a few heads for the Marathi cause. He didn't denounce his violent Sainiks or Maharashtrians in the underworld. He still supports the Marathi element in the underworld.[78]

Stirrings of Hindutva

An incident in the second half of 1967 marked, for the first time, Hindu nationalism as an undercurrent to the Sena philosophy.

In Kalyan, a township close to Thane, a communally sensitive problem had arisen following claims made over the Durgadi fort shrine by both Hindus and Muslims. While local Hindus believed the shrine atop the fort was that of Goddess Durga, the Muslims believed it to be a mosque and started performing namaaz there. To add to the tense atmosphere was neighbouring Bhiwandi, a Muslim-dominated town which regularly witnessed communal disturbances.

When Thackeray got wind of the matter, he declared he would unfurl the saffron flag atop Durgadi fort on 8 September 1967.

'We made it clear to the Muslims that we didn't want to rake up communal issues. But there was incontrovertible evidence that the shrine was Hindu. There were distinctive Hindu symbols: the Om, Swastik and Ganpati. We addressed meetings on the issue. Then the Navratri festival came, and Chief Minister V.P. Naik declared a ban on the puja at the shrine. I was furious. I first issued a statement that no such ban could be enforced. Then I said I'd go with my wife and perform puja there; if anybody had the guts, they should arrest me,' says Thackeray.[79]

Tension grew as word spread that Thackeray, along with Manohar Joshi and Dattaji Salvi, would break the coconut in front of the Durgadevi temple amid splashing of *gulal* and display of religious fervour. Police declared a ban on assembly in the area.

Thackeray said he would defy the ban. When he arrived in Kalyan on 8 September with his two lieutenants, he was greeted by Sainiks and local Hindus at the base of the fort. The crowd performed all its sacramental ceremonies on the fort.

The ban on assembly had remained on paper, and for the rally held at Kalyan's Subhash Maidan after the religious observances, the turnout was big. Joshi told the crowd the Sena had decided to 'throw pro-Pakistan Muslims out of India', and Thackeray, referring to local legislator Krishnarao Dhulap to whom local Muslims had made a representation, said, 'To get the votes of 6,000 Muslims, this Dhulap won't even hesitate to sell his mother.'

Later in the same month, the Sena chief addressed another 8,000-strong rally at the fort, and on 12 October 1968, the ban on assembly went unheeded a third time as Thackeray held yet another meeting and denounced 'those disloyal to India and opposed to a Common Civil Code'.

8

GREATER MAHARASHTRA AND
THE FIRST ARREST

After its first experiment with Hindutva, the Shiv Sena returned to its sons-of-the-soil plank. Resentments from 1960, when Belgaum, Nipani, Karwar and other border areas with a strong Marathi population were included in Mysore (as Karnataka was then called) were fresh in Marathi minds. They were reignited when incidents of discrimination against Maharashtrians were reported from these areas.

The dispute had been alive since 1960, but after the Samyukta Maharashtra Samiti was torn to shreds, Maharashtra's voice on the issue came to be mired in sense of comparative unimportance, and the perception within the state was that the Congress government would not do much to make Marathi voices heard.

The Sampoorna Maharashtra Samiti, comprising Socialists and Communists, was formed in 1966 to get Belgaum, Nipani and Karwar back into Maharashtra, but it was disbanded in 1968.

Though the Sena made noises on the issue intermittently from the time of its inception, with Thackeray highlighting the 'swallowing of Belgaum-Karwar-Nipani by Mysore' in his two-page cartoon spread *Ravivarchi Jatra* (Sunday Fair) in *Marmik*, it did not speak of organising a mass agitation on the issue before 1968. But when it did lead to a stir, it acquired such momentum that it dragged Mumbai into a whirlpool of violence.

On 25 February 1968, Thackeray gave salience to the dispute in an editorial in *Marmik*. Headlined *Rajkaran Mhanje Dombaryacha Khel* (Politics is the game of acrobats), it said:

> There is a serious shortage of statesmen in India. That is why questions like the border dispute, instead of being solved, have

come to acquire a cancerous nature... When a suggestion was made to divide Uttar Pradesh into three states, the then home minister, Govind Vallabh Pant, said: "Who has the power to divide the land of Ram and Krishna? That soil will eternally remain Akhand (one)." But when Maharashtra was being torn into pieces, he didn't have the same feeling. The Maharashtra which was created after killing 105 people was divided!

When lakhs of unilingual people were being forced into the prisons of states having a different linguistic composition, Jawaharlal and other politicians didn't feel the twinge of humanitarianism... After all, aren't they mere politicians, full of the arrogance of power? When taking up a pencil to draw borders, they had to consider the selfish whims of their friends in states other than Maharashtra. So they at once tore our Belgaum-Karwar-Nipani away and gave it to the Demon!

In the last 10-12 years, Marathi brothers in Mysore have won the local elections comfortably and demonstrated many a time that they want to be part of Maharashtra. What national consensus, then, are politicians talking about?

Prime Minister Indira Gandhi has said the opinions of both chief ministers would be taken into account before arriving at a final decision, because they have to face the situation, after all. Quite right.

But what to speak of Central leaders? Rome is burning, and they're playing the fiddle! If things get too bad, they throw at us some vague ideas like national consensus.

The Congress chief of Mysore, Nijalingappa, is like a live wire. Press the button anywhere, anyhow, this spark goes off instantly. He said this solution isn't acceptable to us, and Hegde, backing him, said the Mahajan report[80] is the judge's final decision and should be implemented as it is.

Under such circumstances, how are the leaders in Delhi going to consider opinions of both chief ministers?

Terms like "national level," "popular consensus" and "opinion" are just part of the acrobatics indulged in to fool people.

The Maharashtra government's position is pathetic. Within the state, there are MLAs who, showing opposition for the sake of opposition, spare no opportunity to defame the government and rubbish every step it takes. The group of MPs from Maharashtra also can't be looked at with hope, because only a handful can strongly defend Maharashtra's stand in the Lok Sabha. Every MP is caught in the swamp of party politics, and his talk of loyalty to the people is confined to elections.

We have read Chief Minsiter Vasantrao Naik called a meeting of state MPs a few days ago and told them about Maharashtra's suffering. But what can one expect from those who've done nothing beyond taking advantage of the MP's quota of funds? The truth is, Marathi people don't have a saviour!

But this is Shivaji Raje's Maharashtra. It has faced many Asmanis and Sultanis (momentous difficulties) in the past, and is today carefully watching the exploits of democracy and that of the Congress. It has shrewdly examined the verbal slough of so-called nationalism. The Maratha's study of the enemy camp is now complete. And he's aware of the strength of the ballot box... Shivaji's Maratha is dignified. WE WILL SEE.

In November 1968, he visited Belgaum and was warmly welcomed. The day after his return, he addressed a meeting at Shivaji Park and warned that if the border dispute was not resolved within a specific time-frame, the prime minister, central ministers, the Mysore chief minister and the Congress president would not be allowed to enter Mumbai.

At another rally at Kamgar Maidan, Parel, in central Mumbai on 29 December 1968, Thackeray said the 'ban' would be effective beginning 26 January 1969. 'We will carry out our threat, no matter what the consequences.'

In the first week of January 1969, Thackeray went to Nagpur for a seminar and, during his stay there, met RSS *Sarasanghachalak* Guru Golwalkar at the Sangh's headquarters.

When he arrived at Nagpur airport on the midnight of 5 January to catch a flight to Mumbai, he and his associates were accosted by 10 goons.

As Thackeray sat reading a book in the airport lounge, these men began hovering around him. Noticing their movements, the Sena chief's aides went to a police jeep stationed outside the airport for Thackeray's security and apprised the cops of the matter. But Sainiks maintain the policemen did nothing even as the goons grew abusive and let loose a string of unmentionables on the Sena chief. The Sainiks then besieged the goons and handed over three of them to the police. The rest fled. Two of those who ran away, Sainiks claimed, were Communists, their names Chowbey and Shukla.

Back in Mumbai, the Sainiks began preparing their strategy for 27 January 1969, the day Union Home Minister Y.B. Chavan was scheduled to visit the city. Thackeray reiterated that unless a time-bound programme was announced for solving the border tangle, the Sena would not allow the prime minister, the deputy prime minister, the home minister, President of Congress S. Nijalingappa and chief minister of Mysore Veerendra Patil to enter Mumbai. If they did come, he said, Sainiks would fling themselves in front of their cars and block their path.

'Agreed that no harm should be caused to national property, but if there's an upsurge of popular sentiment, people can't be blamed', he pointed out, adding, 'Sainiks will assemble in groups at places like Mahim, the road near Siddhivinayak temple, and Worli Naka, and will lie down in the middle of the road to stop Chavan's car. This is the first step of the struggle. Its intensity will depend on the government's behaviour'.[81]

Police were keen to ensure that Chavan's visit passed off peacefully, and the Sena was just as determined to see it did not.

Some 500 Sainiks set up camp at 9 am on 27 January near Mahim Church, and a posse of about 100 policemen stood guard to avert any incident. When Chavan's car, led by an escort vehicle, arrived at 10:05 am, police formed a chain on both sides of the road to prevent Sainiks from surging forward. But nearly 150 Sainiks broke the cordon and stood in the middle of the road.

Vasant Marathe, the Sena's Thane unit chief, along with some partymen, jumped into the sparse space between the escort vehicle and Chavan's car, and lay on the road. Around 100 Sainiks surrounded the car and, raising black flags, began shouting slogans against the government and the home minister: '105 Hutatmas for Mumbai! How many do you need for Belgaum?' The scuffle between the cops and Sainiks continued for 5 minutes, and when Sainiks resorted to stone-throwing, the police lathi-charged them.

Chavan's car moved, at last, and in anticipation of further trouble at Shivaji Park and Worli, a change of route was decided upon. The atmosphere at Shivaji Park, Prabhadevi and Worli was much the same as that at Mahim. Sainiks had gathered in large numbers. But the official entourage took the Senapati Bapat Marg to Prabhadevi and later went along Tulsi Pipe Road. Still, near

Kismet Cinema, a little distance away from Siddhivinayak temple, demonstrators again stopped Chavan's car awhile, and protests were staged at Worli Naka.

The altering of routes helped, and Chavan went his way.

Later, around 11:30 am, when the various groups of Sainiks who had assembled at different locations marched with celebratory fervour to the Sena's main office at Ranade Road, Dadar, Thackeray addressed them.

'Chavan had to change his route. We've won a moral victory,' he said.[82]

The first spark had gone off.

And the Sena had chosen to intensify its agitation. So Chief Minister Naik marshalled the Special Reserve Police (SRP) to assist Mumbai's cops.

On 2 February, Thackeray addressed a rally at Shivaji Park to outline the Sena's plan of action and obtained an oath from party workers to face lathis, teargas shells and bullets. He told them:

> Police have been given instructions to finish off the Sena. But we're prepared. We care neither about lathis nor bullets. We've also made up our minds to carry out our agitation in such a way that the lathis will crack...We don't wish to take the law into our hands, but if just demands are killed unjustly, we'll retaliate. Sena leaders may be put into prison in the next few days. But if that happens, Sainiks will be furious, and the police force will prove inadequate if they protest. The Army will have to be called.

> Chavan should have got off his car and asked the Satyagrahis what he could do for them. This would have placated them. For 12 years, the Marathi population in the border areas has been fighting for justice, and our Marathi brothers recently won the Belgaum Council elections. But without telling them when they would get justice, Chavan fled like a coward... Naik is a good person, our relations with him are good, but they are going to come unstuck on this issue. I don't care if that happens.

> Today, I've brought a Kannada newspaper with me. See the pictures in it. Boards in Marathi and shops bearing Marathi nameplates have been smashed. Baban Prabhu wasn't allowed to perform his Marathi play in Hubli yesterday. And while all this was happening, there wasn't a single cop on the road! When we, without doing any such abominable things, ask for justice, we are

besieged by police. Despite the mess in the South, the government there does nothing.

Next, it was Deputy Prime Minister Morarji Desai's turn to visit Mumbai. On the morning of 7 February, the date of his visit, Thackeray met Mumbai Police Commissioner Emmanuel Modak and assured him that Sena's *aandolan* would be peaceful. According to an agreement reached between the police commissioner, Deputy Commissioner of Police Dafle and Thackeray, the Sena would hand over a written representation to Morarji at Mahim.

'We wanted to stop his car, but we were told there was no need for it,' Thackeray recounts. 'We were assured Morarji would accept our representation.'[83]

But the arrival of Morarji, a hate figure in Maharashtra because of the attack on SMM activists in 1960, could only be a climate-deranging phenomenon for the Sena.

By 8 pm, Thackeray and Manohar Joshi reached the venue where the Sena was to hand over its statement to the deputy prime minister. On both sides of the road, thousands of youths had occupied a nearly 100-ft-long stretch, holding saffron flags, cheering the Sena and chanting 'Morarji Shame Shame' and 'Why are there so many policemen around? For Morarji's funeral, of course.'

At 9:30 pm, Morarji's car was seen coming from a distance. As it approached the promised rendezvous, it did not slow down but whizzed past the Sena crowd and delegation. A Sainik leapt forward and tried to stop it, but slammed against the right wheel and collapsed, hurt. Three other Sainiks were also injured.

Emotions flared with much the same speed that Morarji's car had taken, and the crowd hurled stones on the vehicle, which was making a desperate attempt to speed away.

'What a lowly man!' Thackeray says.[84] 'He made all the vehicles proceed with breakneck speed. Despite the promise, he didn't stop. Our cameraman (Karambelkar) too was hit by his car, as were our vehicles. The boys were so furious, they pelted his car with stones.'

The windshield of Morarji's car was smashed, but he somehow got past the hostile crowd and went his way.

Police had by then begun lathi-charging the Sainiks. As the blows fell, some Sainiks rushed to the nearby Navjivan Society for shelter, but the cops chased them down and used the lathi.

Those demonstrators who were still near Mahim Church and the Mahim bus depot, and who had started hurling stones, also faced batons and teargas shells. But inflamed passions flared further due to the police offensive, and the Mahim railway station too witnessed incidents of stone-throwing.

Shivaji Park was tense, too. Sainiks had turned up on the streets in hundreds, and ringed by police officers, were waiting for Morarji's car. Soon Manohar Joshi came to Shivaji Park and told party workers that the deputy prime minister had 'committed a breach of trust' and left from Cadell Road. The Sainiks stirred in response, but before they could launch their protest, Joshi announced over the loudspeaker that Thackeray had gone to his Ranade Road office and that everyone should move there. This message was reported at various places, and 10,000 Sainiks soon thronged Ranade Road.

Thackeray, who never made any secret of his belief in the certainties of violent protests over the ambiguities of quiet demonstrations, told them: 'A Shiv Sainik's blood has been spilled. We will take revenge.'

From now on, it was to be straight fight between the police and the Sena activists.

The whole of Dadar turned into a battlefield. Stone-throwing intensified, and the clock, refreshment stalls and showcases at Dadar railway station were smashed. Three police chowkies – at Cadell Road, Lady Jamshetji Road and Ranade Road – and two BEST buses were torched. Police used lathis and teargas to try and quieten things down, but not only was there no let-up in violence, the disturbances spread to Byculla in the night.

Mahim, Prabhadevi (here too Morarji's car was stoned) and Worli were badly affected, but Dadar disintegrated into complete chaos.

After midnight, police said that 185 persons had been arrested, and two police officers and 15 constables injured. The figures given by KEM Hospital in the night were: 6 seriously injured, 3 of whom were in a critical state and 50 other injured persons discharged after they being given treatment.

Thackeray's statement to the media, released late night, read: 'Police have betrayed us. The haughtiness with which Morarji went away is infuriating. Now we'll put up a struggle like the one which had to be waged for Mumbai. The responsibility for the consequences doesn't lie with us. People can't be faulted for today's happenings.'[85]

Unrest swelled on Saturday, 8 February, with masses of Mumbai's Marathi youths, transformed by the Sena into a political army, registering increasingly violent protests.

The stretch between Lalbaug and Mahim saw a continued onslaught on BEST buses and incidents of stone-throwing all day, causing total disruption of normal life.

The Sena had said that Thackeray would address a rally at Bhoiwada Maidan, Parel, in central Mumbai in the evening in defiance of the police ban on meetings. So tension in the area increased.

Thackeray himself did not turn up for the rally. He despatched Dattaji Salvi, but Dattaji was arrested along with other Sainiks as he was about to enter the maidan for flouting the police ban.

This led to escalation of violence. Stone-throwing intensified, buses were torched, all tubelights on Ambedkar Road and in Dadar were smashed, a police chowky was burnt near Swan Mills, BEST services from Byculla to Dadar and from Haji Ali to Mahim had to be suspended in view of the disturbances, and all shops and commercial establishments were shut.

At around 9:30 pm, a 1,000-strong morcha was taken out from Naigaum's BDD Chawls, and when the protestors refused to heed orders given by police to disperse, lathis and teargas were used.

A little after 10 pm, a mob tried to set fire to a petrol pump near Chitra Talkies, Dadar. Police rushed to the spot and averted a disaster, but they were bombarded with stones not only by the Sainiks but also by residents of chawls adjacent to the theatre. As the cops tried to fend off the attack, buses were torched on the other side of the road.

Finally, after having exhausted measures like lathi-charge and use of teargas shells, police fired 11 rounds at Ambedkar Nagar to quell the rioting mob.

9 February 1969.

Just when hopes of the cessation of violence, or even a brief hold-off, were fast being extinguished, the state government decided to clamp down on Sena leaders. Early morning, Bal Thackeray and Manohar Joshi were arrested under the Preventive Detention Act (Thackeray was released from jail after three months).

Jail and violence

Unprecedented violence rocked Mumbai after Thackeray's arrest. News of the arrest spread throughout Dadar well before 8 am, thanks largely to Sainiks who not only put up blackboards announcing the development at street corners, but also wrote down the piece of news with chalk on every road in Dadar.

For the first two days, the targets had been BEST buses, milk-booths and police chowkies. Now, shops, commercial establishments and hotels became sitting ducks.

Hotel Visaava on N.C. Kelkar Marg was reduced to ashes, and so bad was the fire that five shops adjacent to it were badly burned.

Amid choking smoke and massive ravaging, Sainiks entered into an open duel with the police, and the police operation to contain the conflagration began to look small.

Hotels between Naigaum and Matunga were torched, property at Century Bazaar was destroyed, and two petrol pumps were burnt at Lamington Road in south Mumbai. An assault was made on Mahim railway station, forcing cops to open fire. Two died as a result, and two were seriously injured.

Deputy Police Commissioner R.S. Kulkarni was besieged by a crowd at Sewri Chowky, and police had to fire six rounds in the air to scatter the protesters.

An armoured police vehicle approaching Mahim station was attacked by a mob. The firing that ensued claimed one. On Central Railway, a first-class compartment was destroyed at Byculla, and obstacles were placed on the CR route, with the result that services were paralysed for a while.

At 5 pm, Sena leaders Sudhir Joshi, the Kamgar Sena's General Secretary Arun Mehta, Bhai Shingre and Satam Guruji were arrested. And the police had decided to impose a curfew from Worli Naka to Mahim from 8 pm to 5 am for three days.

By 8 pm, seven persons had been killed in police firing and 35 injured. At 10 pm, disturbances grew in Girgaum in south Mumbai, and one more person died in police firing.

Late in the night, Chief Minister Naik issued an appeal to citizens to cooperate with the authorities to restore peace and severely chastised the Sena.

Monday, 10 February 1969.

Naik's request for peace was rebuffed, and the state machinery continued to creak.

Curfew stood clamped between Girgaum and Mahim from 1 pm to 6 pm and 8 pm to 5 am, but Dadar's Kirtikar Market was burnt early in the morning, and 30 buses damaged in stone-throwing at the Marol bus depot in Andheri in the western suburbs.

In the afternoon, three vehicles belonging to the Atomic Energy establishment were stopped and torched near Dadar's Plaza cinema. The figure of those dead in police firing went up to thirty.

The Army was asked to be on alert, and the State Reserve Police platoons were brought in from other states to assist the city police.

Along with this, the Maharashtra government took another decision: it asked Thackeray, who had been lodged in the Yerawada Jail in Pune, to issue a written appeal exhorting people to establish peace in Mumbai.

Perhaps for the first time in the history of independent India, an appeal issued by a man detained under the Preventive Detention Act was distributed by police to bring the law and order under control.

Disseminated across the city by police vans, Thackeray's appeal to Shiv Sainiks read:

> It has caused me immeasurable agony to know through newspapers that the Army has been called in to restore law and order. In view of the broader national interest, all nationalist Indians should ensure the Army isn't required to establish internal peace. Its job is to guard the nation's borders. I appeal to all Shiv Sainiks to see to it that law and order is immediately established in Mumbai. At the same time, Sainiks should also see that under no circumstances are the Communists able to take advantage of our struggle.

Dexterous draftsmanship, this, to explain the reasons for withdrawing the 'agitation'? 'No,' said Sena leader Pramod Navalkar. According to him, Thackeray had isssued the appeal in the name of 'national interest'.[86]

By Tuesday afternoon, only a few stray incidents of rioting had taken place.

Sainiks were now in the forefront of the clean-up operations, removing obstacles they themselves had placed on the roads to slown down police movement.

On 12 February normalcy was restored and curfew lifted during the day, though it was still in place in the evening.

On 13 February curfew was totally lifted, and the following day, the chief minister met Prime Minister Indira Gandhi in New Delhi and apprised her of the improving law and order situation. Home Minister Chavan had already handed over a report to Mrs Gandhi on the Mumbai riots: in all, 59 persons had died, 56 of them due to police firing, and property worth crores had been destroyed.

Shiv Sena, only in its third year, had realised what it could do. It had completely disrupted normal life in Mumbai for close to five days and paralysed state machinery.

The budget session of Parliament was to start in the third week of February, so it was natural that Mumbai's violence should dominate proceedings. Violence had also broken out at the same time in Telangana too detailed commonly known knowledge makes the narrative text bookish. But though the situation in Telengana too came up for discussion, the Mumbai violence stirred maximum debate.

A chorus of condemnation echoed from across the political spectrum against the Sena's actions.

Maharasthra's Congress government was lambasted for its inability to deal firmly with the rioters.

The Communist Party of India was the most strident. It demanded Chavan and Naik's resignation and asked for the setting up of an inquiry commission to probe the riots and accused ministers in the state of having sympathy for the Sena's objectives, if not for its actions. 'When Chief Minister Naik addressed people over the radio and appealed for peace, he didn't even make a mention of the Shiv Sena. Why?' he asked.[87]

In his statement to the House, Chavan had said the use of violence, even if it was to draw attention to key issues, called for condemnation.

Referring to this, the Communist Party's Bhupesh Gupta said: 'The home minister's statement has shocked us. He has not realised the gravity of the situation. Many Congressmen have built the Shiv Sena, and, I say with regret, Chavan and Naik too initially contributed to its growth.'

Gupta also came up with a conspiracy theory: 'I have information that the American embassy provides funds to the Shiv Sena. There should be a parliamentary inquiry into this. Thackeray and his goons have to be controlled and brought to book. If the home minister and the state chief minister cannot do this, they should resign.'

Chavan replied: 'I have been the first to denounce the Shiv Sena as a fascist organisation. The allegation that I have relations with the Sena is unjust and made with a malicious intent. The Shiv Sena is a blot on Mumbai's social life. Everything possible should be done to foil its designs.'[88]

The next day, Left parties moved a no-confidence motion in the Lok Sabha against the Congress government for its failure to curb the riots.

During the debate on the no-confidence vote, which was defeated by 213 votes as against 83, Chavan reiterated his position and sought to dissociate his party from the Sena. 'I find that the Shiv Sena by its very character, by its very nature and ideology, is an Indian fascist movement... and as every fascist movement takes advantage of the gullibility of other political parties, they have exploited the gullibility of other political parties in Bombay, including the Congress,' he said.[89] 'At the time of certain polls and by-polls, the Sena's members infiltrated into the Congress and campaigned for our party. That does not mean the Congress is linked to the Sena. Some businessmen and industrialists openly supported the Sena, because they knew it would fight Communists... Now, all parties have learnt a lesson about the Shiv Sena!'

Indira Gandhi said during the debate: 'The Shiv Sena is a threat to the unity, progress and development of the country. It is regrettable that the name of Veer Purush Shivaji should be given to such a movement. Shivaji Maharaj was the hero of the entire nation. From various parts of India, people have brought intellectual wealth, money and trading and business activities into Mumbai. A movement which seeks to bring Mumbai to a standstill will pull down the great city. There's a need for all of us to do some deep introspection on why movements like the Shiv Sena flourish.'[90]

Kerala Chief Minister EMS Namboodiripad, Tamil Nadu Chief Minister M. Karunanidhi and Mysore Chief Minister Veerendra Patil added their bit. Namboodiripad said he had met the prime minister and home minister and demanded assurance of safety of Keralites in Mumbai; Karunanidhi said he had sent letters to Chavan and Naik, asking them to halt the Sena menace; and Patil proclaimed in the

Mysore Assembly that he had, in a letter to the prime minister, demanded the Sena be banned.

The session of the Maharashtra legislature began a month after the riots, and the opposition parties in the state too moved a no-confidence motion against the Naik government.

But before a debate could begin, Minister of State for Home Kalyanrao Patil made in the House a statement on the riots which read like the government's admission of failure.

'As incidents of violence grew, those of police firing too went up. True, police bandobast was crippled at places. But responsible for it was the rioters' policy of placing obstacles on roads and escaping after an attack. At certain points, obstacles cleared by the police were replaced by rioters. As stones were hurled from rooftops and from the middle of crowds, the lathi-charge and teargas shells proved rather ineffective. And as children constituted a significant percentage of the rioters, it was difficult for police to open fire everywhere.'[91]

He attributed the gradual cessation of violence to the appeal issued by the chief minister and at the same time trotted up a weak excuse for the dissemination of Thackeray's plea.

'After police took strong peace-enforcing measures and after the chief minister appealed to people over the radio, the situation gradually improved. Anyone's appeal for peace under such circumstances would have had to be considered necessary. That is why the government did not hesitate to issue the appeal made by Thackeray from Yerawada,' he said.

The no-confidence motion was defeated by 169 votes as against 52, but the Opposition held the government responsible for the mess.

Around the same time, Home Minister Chavan visited Mumbai and, addressing an audience, said every Indian should be ashamed of the pernicious ideology of the Sena and added that everyone had the right to seek employment in any part of India. He pronounced himself 'sick and sad' over the Sena's acts.[92]

During the same visit, Chavan met Bal Thackeray at the railway headquarters. Vijay Gaonkar, then Sena corporator from Parel who was present at the meeting, told me: 'Balasaheb was furious, and he severely criticised Chavan for the deaths of 59 Shiv Sainiks. I'd never seen him assail anybody like this. Chavan kept mum, and ended the meeting saying: "Now it has all happened. What can we do?"'[93]

The Muslims

Before embarking on his first Konkan tour in February 1970, Thackeray sensed a 'winning number' in yet another religious issue. It held out the promise of implanting the Sena in the coastal Konkan region of Maharashtra and taking it further afield as the professed guardian of the Hindus.

The Mahikawati shrine in Mahad was claimed by both Hindus and Muslims. The Sena's Panvel shakha pramukh, Madhav Bhide, who inaugurated the party's Mahad shakha prior to Thackeray's visit, set the ball rolling: 'Till now, no party has given thought to the Hindu religion. The Mahikawati temple was demolished and idols in it taken away, but nobody thought of reconstructing the mandir. In fact, Muslims have begun a campaign saying this isn't a temple, but a masjid. We should build a temple here, and re-install the Goddess's idol. Sena pramukh Balasaheb Thackeray is coming to Mahad to do just that. We should give him all our support.'

Addressing a rally at Girgaum Chowpatty on 2 November 1969, Thackeray said: 'Just as I gave the Durgadi Devi shrine back to Hindus, I'm going to hand over the Mahikawati mandir to them. I will myself break the coconut there, and if someone tries to block my way, I will break the coconut on his head.'

Tension gripped the Panvel–Mahad belt, and everyone waited with bated breath to see what transpired during Thackeray's trip.

On 17 January 1970, the Sena leader entered Mahad, accompanied by a fleet of vehicles.

'Along with my wife, Manohar Joshi and other associates, I went up the hillock on which the shrine stands, broke the coconut in the temple and unfurled the saffron flag,' says Thackeray.[94]

This done, in the blazing heat of afternoon, all the vehicles, along with the assembled Shiv Sainiks, moved to the nearby Azad Maidan in a procession for a rally. Nearly 7,000 people had gathered to hear Thackeray speak.

When Thackeray set off for his Konkan tour on 15 February, Shiv Sainiks in Mahad stood on the outskirts of the village to greet his vehicle and on its arrival, requested their boss to wait awhile in Mahad for tea and biscuits.

But just as Thackeray's car reached the village's entry point, a posse of policemen blocked its way and handed over the written order of the taluka executive magistrate. It said: 'As the visit of Sena leaders could create discord among Hindus and Muslims in Mahad, Bal Thackeray, Manohar Joshi, Datta Salvi, Pramod Navalkar, Madhav Bhide and others are banned entry under Section 144 of the Criminal Procedure Code.'

Thackeray's response was: 'A public rally will be held in Mahad on 22 February, on my way back from the Konkan. And if necessary, the Sena will flout the ban order.'

The very idea of challenging the ban enthused Sena activists. Truckloads set out for Mahad on 22 February from Mumbai and Thane. At around 2 pm, two trucks carrying Sainiks from Mumbra joined the other vehicles. There were three trucks in all, and some private vehicles. Sena leaders like Manohar Joshi, Sudhir Joshi and Dattaji Salvi were also accompanying the party workers.

Half-a-mile away from Mumbra is Koushe village. When the fleet was passing through it, shouting slogans of '*Shiv Sena Zindabad*', stones were hurled at an Ambassador, the last in the line of Sena vehicles. Sainiks who had gone ahead rushed back to defend their aides, but they were greeted with soda-water bottles from surrounding hotels.

Violence broke out, and many hotels and houses were set afire. Traffic on the road was disrupted for an hour, and the SRP finally had to fire rounds in the air to stop rioting.

The Sena had declared a bandh in Mahad that day, and the only activity that appeared to be in full swing was that of Sainiks. The rally was huge, but the Sena chief was conspicuous by his absence.

Nonetheless, Sena leader Wamanrao Mahadik sent out the party's warning: 'Whoever helps us belongs to us, is the Sena's stand. But if, instead of supporting us, the minorities stab us in the back, we'll have to crack the whip to prove the Hindu community is still alive.'

The town of Bhiwandi was to go up in flames in May the same year, in a demonstration of the role the Sena could play in a communal conflict.

9

BHIWANDI BURNS

Bhiwandi, nearly 12 miles away from Thane, has been known as much for its communally surcharged atmosphere as for its handloom and powerloom industry. Economic upturn in the town has been matched by the rising graph of communal tension since 1896, when Hindu–Muslim riots first erupted and the absence of access roads and bridges made it difficult even for police squads from Mumbai and Thane to reach in time.

On the occasion of Shivaji Jayanti in May 1970, the steady simmer reached full boil.

The Shiv Jayanti procession began on 7 May at around 7 pm from the Bhiwandi police station, with the sprinkling of *gulal*, raising of slogans, and all its attendant dazzle. When the nearly 10,000-strong crowd was passing through Bhusari Ali near the fish market, stones and bulbs were hurled at it from a street nearby.

The news spread quickly, and stones and bulbs began to be flung freely all over Bhiwandi. Shops and houses were burnt and looted, and many incidents of stabbing were reported. Power supply had been cut off at the same time, so there was darkness all around. Police fired teargas and rounds of bullets to control the violence, but far from showing signs of dying down, the fires burnt all the more fiercely.

Police squads from Mumbai and Thane were despatched to Bhiwandi, and at 10 pm, indefinite curfew was clamped. When Additional IGP E.S. Modak arrived at 11 pm to take stock of the situation, official figures put the death toll at two; the unofficial count was fifteen. More than 300 persons had been injured; 30 had been admitted to Thane Civil Hospital either with stab wounds, burns or injuries in police firing; and 105 had been arrested.

Notwithstanding the curfew, rioting continued the next day, and even country-made bombs were put into use by mobs. No shoot–at–sight orders had been issued, hampering effective police action. At least 100 houses were torched, 11 sizing units and 5,000 powerlooms damaged, and slums in Somanagar, Madhavnagar, Vetalpada and Darga Road were destroyed. At least 5,000 people were rendered homeless.

The same day, the violence spread to Jalgaon and Mahad. In Jalgaon, 20 persons were killed in an attack on a marriage procession. By 11 May 1970, when hostilities had stopped and Bhiwandi, Jalgaon and Mahad had begun limping back to normalcy, the death toll in Bhiwandi had reached 43, and it was 39 in Jalgaon.

The Assembly was in session at the time, and the Opposition took the government to task and pointed an accusing finger at the Shiv Sena and Jan Sangh. The Congress government set up a commission of inquiry headed by Justice D.P. Madon of the Bombay High Court.

During the commission's proceedings, Achyut Chafekar appeared as counsel for the Sena. He told me:

> Four days before Shiv Jayanti, Muslims in Bhiwandi had threatened they wouldn't allow the Shiv Jayanti procession to take place. Marathi writer and Hindutva protagonist Pu Bha Bhave also gave a speech in Bhiwandi a day before Shiv Jayanti, in which he allegedly said Shivaji had demolished a mosque in Bhiwandi and asked people to emulate his example against the nation's enemies. Thackeray was similarly accused of saying in a speech that the coconut he was breaking was intended to fall on the heads of Muslims.
>
> All this had already created tension in the township, and a peace committee had been set up to ensure there was no communal flare-up.
>
> But the attack on the Shiv Jayanti procession was planned in advance, because it was launched simultaneously from all sides. Till 4 am the next day, Hindus in Bhiwandi were assaulted and bore the brunt of the attack. But from 4 am, the retaliation began. For the next two days, all hell broke loose in Bhiwandi, and A.B. Vajpayee said in Parliament: "Hindus will no longer quietly allow themselves to be assaulted".[95]

Justice Madon summoned both Bhave and Thackeray, accused of making inflammatory speeches.

In his report, Justice Madon observed how Bhave had described in detail, in front of an assembly of nearly 800 people, Shivaji's act of demolition of mosques and *dargahs* in Bhiwandi after Aurangzeb razed Hindu temples:

> P.B. Bhave's said speech was a highly inflammatory and provocative communal speech. It greatly annoyed the Muslims in the audience including those Muslim leaders who had been striving for communal harmony and were endeavouring to see that the Shiv Jayanti procession passed off peacefully...

Bhave was booked for promoting enmity among different groups. Justice Madon also noted how the Shiv Jayanti processionists had raised provocative slogans which it clear that a large number of participants were workers or followers or sympathisers of the Sena, the Jan Sangh and the Rashtriya Utsav Mandal. Referring to Thackeray, he observed:

> Bhiwandi came in for a special attack by the Shiv Sena chief Bal Thackeray at a public speech made by him on 13 May 1969 in Thana in which he referred to Bhiwandi as a second Pakistan and alleged that such shameful things were being done by the Muslims in Bhiwandi that he was ashamed to mention those incidents in the presence of ladies...

The Bhiwandi episode was the first one in which the Sena openly resorted to violence in the name of Hindutva. Many such episodes, replete with drama and destruction were to follow in the future.

10

MURDER AND MANDATE

The Shiv Sena had by now made significant inroads in the Lalbaug-Parel area in central Mumbai, the heartland of the city's working-class population, and as cracks in the Communist bastion grew bigger, the Left sensed the edifice it had guarded for decades was in danger of collapsing.

Worried they might end up in the ash heap of history if the Sena's rise continued, the Communists powered up their cultural front, the Lok Seva Dal. The Sena's answer to the Lok Seva Dal – which it associated with the militant Red Guards of China – was the *Bhagwa* Guard (Saffron Guard).

Bal Thackeray quoted the 'growing goondaism' in Mumbai and 'the need to fight anti-social forces' to make his case for the Guard, which was to be not just a cultural force but the common man's shield against increasing insecurity. 'The police force is finished,' he told a gathering one evening in February 1970. 'Only those willing to give haftas get justice. In the Delisle Road area, goondas move around sword in hand, terrorising people, and police nurture them. But if a Shiv Sainik is found with a blade, he's arrested. It's futile to rely on cops any more. I've decided to form a special squad of 500 youngsters to fight this goondaism. 200 youths are ready, and 300 more will be moblised. This Saffron Guard will destroy all matka and hooch corners'.[96]

After Thackeray's statement, *Link* magazine carried a report quoting Communist leader B.S. Dhume as saying he too would form a squad of 500 youths to counter the Bhagwa Guard. Referring to Dhume's reported proclamation – which Dhume told me he had never made – Thackeray said: 'I throw a challenge to Dhume. Why 500, he should establish a squad of 1,000 youngsters. Ten of my Shiv Sainiks against his thousand. Let's *have it*, anywhere he wants. We'll see who stands firm and who falls flat.'[97]

The Bhagwa Guard became operative soon, and its rugged members started roaming Mumbai's roads on bikes fitted with saffron flags. Whenever Thackeray set out for a rally, these youngsters would position themselves in front of and behind his vehicle and escort him to the venue in the manner of a security cordon.

In response, Communists in Parel and Lalbaug, led by sitting MLA Krishna Desai, stepped up the activities of their Red Guard. And the conflict took a serious turn.

In the night of 5 June 1970, Krishna Desai was stabbed to death.

He and one of his party workers, named Patkar, had set out for Rice Mills, which was in the vicinity of his house in Tavripada, Lalbaug, to make a phone call. Darkness had engulfed the area then, as power supply was off, and it was raining. When the two entered a narrow gully en route to Rice Mills, some unidentified men, carrying weapons, besieged them. Patkar tried to cover Desai but was attacked. After this, two swords were thrust into Desai's rib-cage. He collapsed.

Parel and Lalbaug woke up to a funereal morning on 6 June, and word spread that the CPI legislator had been bumped off by the Shiv Sena. The Communist Party's blackboards put up in every street corner blamed Thackeray's outfit for the murder.

When Desai's funeral procession turned into a meeting at Dadar's Chaityabhoomi, Left leaders censured 'the political goondaism on the rise' and condemned the Congress government for supporting it. The Sena was painted as a spawn of awful coupling between fascism and communalism.

The same day, Thackeray issued a statement calling Desai's death 'unfortunate'.

On 7 June, an all-party rally was organised at Nare Park, Parel, to condemn the killing. At this rally, the Peasants & Workers Party's (PWP) N.D. Patil expressed concern over the rise of reactionary forces in Mumbai and underlined the need to wipe out such 'dangers to society'.[98] Referring to the statement issued by Thackeray following Desai's death, CPI's Prabhakar Vaidya said: 'Thackeray has expressed sorrow. But people will no longer be fooled. Thackeray is a pretender, and people haven't forgotten his statements in the past. When stones were hurled at Comrade Dange at a rally in Pune, Thackeray said,

"You hurled four stones, I felt bad. You should pelt him with more. Don't allow his rallies to take place, burn the *Lal Bavta* (the red flag)." What else can you expect from such a person?'

A meeting of the Samyukta Samajwadi Party's state committee was organised within two weeks of the killing and a resolution passed against the Sena's 'terror tactics'.

The attack from across the political spectrum was to be expected. But what irked Thackeray most was the criticism by PSP leader Dandavate. The Sena and PSP were allies in the corporation, and Thackeray was miffed that the latter should join other parties in condemning the Sena.

Lambasting Dandavate for attending Desai's funeral and making anti-Sena remarks, Thackeray wrote in *Marmik*: 'What was most surprising was that even a crow like Dandavate, who has so frequently had the prasad of Communist shoes and chappals, felt the need to come to the crematorium to feast on the oblation to the dead. Has he forgotten that when he was greeted with chappals after one of Dange's rallies, it was the Sena that saved him? Our alliance with the PSP has now virtually come unstuck. We will have a straight fight with them.'

Against this backdrop, a Lalbaug-based Sena activist Sadakant Dhavan was killed, and Thackeray put the blame for the death on the PSP, stating in *Marmik* that Dhavan's killer was a PSP worker.

Later, 19 youths, believed to be Shiv Sena volunteers, were arrested for Desai's murder. Three of them were acquitted, and the rest convicted. But even after the arrests, the PWP kept up the pressure: 'There isn't just Bal Thackeray's brain behind the killing; there are other "brains" and "sources of funds" behind such organised political terror.'

The Congress too did not lag behind. Early in July 1970, the Maharashtra Congress working committee passed a resolution condemning political violence, but it made mention only of Desai's murder, not of the killing of Sainik Sadakant Dhavan. When mediapersons asked why Dhavan's name had been left out, Congress spokesperson V.N. Gadgil said 'the Congress condemns all political killings'.[99]

When Deputy Home Minister Kalyanrao Patil admitted in the Assembly that most of the 19 youths held for Desai's murder were Sainiks, Opposition leaders asked why the government was not doing anything to nab the *sutradhar* (mastermind).

The police charge sheet in the case read:

> Desai's murder was the result of enmity between the Shiv Sena's anti-goonda front, the Bhagwa Samrakshak Guard, and the Communist Party's Lok Seva Dal. All the arrested accused, and some absconding accused, are either Shiv Sainiks or followers of the Sena. One of the Sena men, accused no 1 Dilip Hate, is the brain behind the killing. He took the lead in forming the anti-goon front, also called the Bhagwa Samrakshak Dal. Desai led the Lok Seva Dal, so the plot to kill him was hatched to wipe out the Lok Seva Dal.

Bal Thackeray denies his partymen had anything to do with Desai's murder but CPI leader Ahilya Rangnekar, however, had no doubt that Bal Thackeray's boys sought to finish off Leftists. She told me:

> This, they knew, was the best way to muzzle the voice of workers. Once, when we had organised a public meeting at Kamgar Maidan, it was disrupted by Sainiks. Krishna Desai and I were there, and stones were hurled at us, but we were protected by our workers. However, Desai couldn't save himself a second time. Not only he, one more worker of ours, named Naidu, was murdered by the Sena.[100]

The Parel Assembly by-election was declared to be held on 18 October 1970, and as the murder charge seemed to stick, right-wing parties like the Jan Sangh, Swatantra Party, Hindu Mahasabha and Congress (O) were faced with a dilemma – to be or not to be with the Sena.

The Communists had put up Desai's widow as their candidate and obtained the support of Socialist parties and the Congress (R).

Seeing the level of Left mobilisation – 13 parties had aligned to guard their bastion – the rightist parties determined not to allow the broad right-wing agreement to be torpedoed. Although hesitant, they entered into an accord with the Sena.

But the weight of the Left was much stronger in the mill-worker-dominated constituency, and the Jan Sangh, Hindu Mahasabha, Swatantra Party and Congress (O) did not count for much.

What the Sena could thus discover here was the extent of its own influence, which it had been trying hard to gain. The election results promised to show just how much Thackeray's organisation had, in its four years of existence, been welcomed by the ordinary Marathi voter of Mumbai, in the face of a series of accusations hurled against its controversial methods.

The Sena candidate was Wamanrao Mahadik, already a sitting corporator from Parel, chairman of the civic improvements committee and one of Thackeray's trusted lieutenants.

Originally a clerk in BMC, Mahadik earned his spurs in the RSS. He joined the Sena after meeting Thackeray at a rally in Parel. Thackeray too looked upon him with respect, and he was the natural choice for the by-election.

The Sena launched its campaign with a massive rally at Kamgar Maidan on 20 September, where Thackeray acidly attacked the party's opponents. He said:

> Those who have till date sucked the blood of the Marathi *manoos* should not teach us lessons in peace. If the anti-national Communists begin their Naxalite dance in Mumbai and Maharashtra, our answer will be tit for tat... We're fighting this election on the basis of principle, and we don't care if we lose it for that principle. But we will teach anti-nationalists a lesson. For the last four years, all kinds of charges have been made against the Sena in the Assembly. These charges can be answered only by a Sena MLA. Police use their whip against the Sena. The Sena is treated unjustly and abuses are hurled at it. If this has to end, we have to have a Shiv Sena legislator. But we're confident of victory. Even if Prime Minister Indira Gandhi comes here to campaign, we will win.

The 13-party combination against the Sena also braced itself for a showdown. At a huge rally held at Nare Park on 29 September, leaders like S.A. Dange (Communist Party), Baburao Samant (Samyukta Socialist Party), Sadanand Varde (PSP), T.S. Karkhanis (PWP) and Datta Deshmukh (Lal Nishan) hailed the 'unification of pro-democracy forces against fascism'.

The Indicate Congress also held a meeting in Parel in support of Desai's widow, and its leader Mohan Dharia said it was okay if *any other* party won, but the victory of a Sena candidate was unacceptable.

Dandavate and Communist leader A.B. Bardhan too campaigned vigorously.

According to Thackeray, the Sena held 28 meetings in all in Parel, and he himself addressed 15 of them.

Mary F. Katzenstein, who was in Mumbai then working on her thesis on the Sena, watched the poll campaign closely.

Though it was predicted that the tussle between the Sena and Communsits would be hard, as the election was crucial to the future of both parties, her visit to the party offices two days before the poll seemed to indicate the outcome was a foregone conclusion. Pointing to the contrast between the two offices, she wrote: 'The Sena offices were jubilant, crowded and noisy. The CPI office was half-empty, the workers muted.' Most volunteers in the Sena offices were 'young boys in their teens and early twenties,' while at the CPI office, almost all workers were 'in their forties and fifties.'[101]

She heard a Sainik telling journalists how his party was assured of a win 'in the quick-fire manner of a preassembled speech' and noted how a few workers denounced the Communists 'in the manner reminiscent of the ebullience of an athletic competition'. In the Communists' office, 'those gathered around were uninterested in making predictions or even in engaging in the usual campaign denunciations of the other party; instead, a tense discussion was struck up about the historical role of the party in the Bombay trade union movement.'

The contest eventually turned out to be a close one, but the Sena emerged the victor, polling 1,679 votes more than the Communists. Mahadik obtained 31,592 votes, while Desai's widow got 29,913.

The next day, the Sena held a mammoth victory rally at Shivaji Park. And the slogan of *Jala Do, Jala Do, Lal Bavta Jala Do* (Burn it, burn it, burn the red flag), was replaced by *Jal Gaya, Jal Gaya, Lal Bavta Jal Gaya* (Burnt, burnt, the red flag has been burnt). A beaming Thackeray told Sainiks: 'This is our *dharma yuddha* (holy war). It is the Sena's aim to destroy all those disloyal to the nation. We will use the language of *Thokshahi* against Communists, because they don't understand the language of *Lokshahi* (democracy). I am thankful to the Jan Sangh, RSS and the Swatantra Party for their support. I'm not ashamed to call myself a Hindu. Our victory is the victory of Hindutva.'

A stronghold of the Communists had fallen, and Wamanrao Mahadik had become the first Sena man to enter the Maharashtra Legislative Assembly.

11

THE TENETS OF *THOKSHAHI*
AND THE SUCCESS IN PAREL

Bal Thackeray aggressively put forward his theory of *Thokshahi* and called it 'constructive violence', which would deliver prompt justice and remove bureaucratic bottlenecks that blocked growth. In fact, the Shiv Sena's slow replacement of an inefficient system of delivery of services and amenities by its coercive acts, which were seen to be effective, was one of the reasons voters in Parel backed it.

A case in point was the action taken by then Sena corporator from the area, Vijay Gaonkar, who, according to Thackeray, 'demonstrated to everyone *our* idea of democracy'.

There had been a shortage of water in Parel early in 1970, and despite the people's demands, the BMC's hydraulic engineer, one Vhise, caused inordinate delay in providing a cross-connection to local residents over the main pipeline. Unrest among locals grew, but Vhise continued to put things off.

It was then that Gaonkar approached him, impatiently urging him to solve the problem. 'Don't make too much noise', Vhise shot back, only to get the reply that 'This work isn't mine but that of the people. If you don't address the matter immediately, it's not my mouth but my hands that will do the talking.'

The hydraulic engineer sat over the matter for some more days, and Gaonkar acted on his warning: he went and thrashed Vhise. The cross-connection was provided instantly.

Around the same time, when prices of essential commodities went through the roof, the Sena carried out a massive anti-price rise agitation. A morcha was taken to Mahatma Phule Market in south

Mumbai, and Thackeray warned traders that if they created artificial scarcity, the Sena would use its own methods to fight them.

The Mahila Aghadi, the Sena's women's wing, barged into several shops all over Mumbai, whose owners had claimed to have a scarcity of Dalda ghee (the Union government had then hiked rates of vanaspati) and brought out thousands of Dalda containers hidden in godowns.

The containers were sold by the Sena at the rates printed thereon, and housewives queued up in thousands to buy them. The Sena said it handed over all the money earned from the sale to the owners of shops who had surreptitiously stocked the ghee.

The families that thus obtained their essentials supported the party in the by-election.

The Sena stood out in one more respect, and that too was influential in swaying the lower-middle class and poor voters of Parel and Lalbaug.

It brought the longstanding barriers away Dadar, Girgaum and Lalbaug-Parel tumbling down.

All these areas were Maharashtrian in character, but the psychological divide between Dadar-Girgaum and Lalbaug-Parel was substantial in the 1960s, and no party had attempted to bridge it. As Vijay Gaonkar pointed out:

> A Marathi-speaking person from Parel would hesitate to go to Dadar, because it was supposedly an upper-class Marathi locality and Parel belonged to the lower-middle classes and working classes. But Balasaheb worked a miracle. He bridged the divide between the Marathi youth of Dadar and Parel. Lalbaug and Parel were known for their physical strength, and Girgaum and Dadar for intellect. It was believed they'd never meet. But Thackeray brought them together.[102]

In the 1960s, there were sharp divisions among Maharashtrians on the basis of sub-castes such as Maratha, Kunbi, Brahmin, 96 *Kuli* and 92 *Kuli*. The politics of different parties revolved around these sub-castes.

The Congress, for instance, was, and remains, an effective exponent of Maratha politics. People belonging to the Maratha sub-caste have traditionally dominated politics in Maharashtra, and nearly 42 per cent of the total Marathi population in the state is Maratha. The Congress thus regarded Maratha politics as a winning coin and pitted one sub-caste against the other. Y.B. Chavan, the supreme Maharashtrian

Congress leader of the time, was a Maratha, and though chief minister V.P. Naik, belonged to the Banjara–Laman community, his loyalty to Chavan was complete, and he kept the Congress policy intact.

The Jan Sangh and the RSS were choc-a-bloc with Brahmins and had brazenly allowed not only Brahminical leadership but Brahminism to flourish.

The Dalit population was split among various factions of the Republican Party of India (RPI), founded by Dr B.R. Ambedkar. And the Communists played the lower-middle classes and poorer classes against the middle and upper-middle classes.

The ordinary man from Lalbaug and Parel, belonging to the so-called lower classes and castes, originally hailed from Konkan and was a labourer. He was getting disillusioned with the Communists and Socialists, who he thought were exploiting his plight for political benefit, but he could not go to the Congress, the Jan Sangh, the RSS and RPI due to their caste labels.

The Sena offered him an opening. Its thrust on the economic upliftment of Maharashtrians and demand for preferential treatment of sons of the soil in employment drew the working class towards it. They wanted someone to focus on the issue that mattered to them most: jobs.

Besides, people of various castes worked together in the Sena. Though, from among the party's leaders, Thackeray, Manohar Joshi, Sudhir Joshi, Balwant Mantri, Dr Hemchandra Gupte, Shyam Deshmukh, Madhav Deshpande, Datta Pradhan, Vijay Parvatkar, Madhukar Sarpotdar and Pramod Navalkar came from the so-called higher castes (they were either Brahmins, Pathare Prabhus or Chandraseniya Kayastha Prabhus) and middle-class localities like Dadar and Girgaum, rubbing shoulders with them were leaders from the working-class areas of Lalbaug-Parel such Dattaji Salvi, Dattaji Nalavade and Wamanrao Mahadik, and those from the so-called lower castes such as Chhagan Bhujbal, Leeladhar Dake, Bhai Shingre and Vijay Gaonkar.

In fact, when the Sena had to select candidates for the 1968 BMC polls, it had mainly chosen youths from the lower castes – Other Backward Classes and Scheduled Castes – as its representatives.

As part of its cadre, the Sena had youths from all sub-castes, including Brahmins, Marathas, Chandraseniya Kayastha Prabhus, Bhandaris, Vaishyas, Kunbis, Malis and others.

Plus, Thackeray had the advantage of having a father known for his participation in the anti-caste movement. Prabodhankar's fund of goodwill among Other Backward Classes (OBCs) and the so-called backward castes enhanced the Sena's credibility in the estimation of these communities.

And the Sena clasped itself both to the affluent and the poor Maharashtrian, the Brahmin and the OBC, through religion and tradition.

Over the years, other than the Sena chief, there have been 12 senior leaders in the party, called the netas. Apart from Thackeray, Satish Pradhan has been the only Kayastha Prabhu. So two CKPs in all. Subhash Desai has also been from among the Prabhu castes, and Pramod Navalkar was a Pathare Prabhu. There have been four Brahmins: Manohar Joshi, Sudhir Joshi, Madhukar Sarpotdar and Sharad Acharya. That makes eight leaders 'upper caste'.

Of the remaining five, Wamanrao Mahadik was a Shimpi, Leeladhar Dake an Agri and Dattaji Salvi a Maratha. Before Chhagan Bhujbal left the Sena, he was among the top 13 leaders. He belongs to the Mali community, one of many OBC groups.

In fact, 70 per cent of Sainiks have belonged to the OBC category, and even after the party opposed the Mandal Commission recommendations, the percentage of OBCs in the Sena did not go down. And it has had not an insignificant percentage of Dalits.

Another reason the charge of upper-caste bias, levelled by Bhujbal when he quit the party, could not stick against the Sena was that the leadership of other parties – notably Socialists and Communists – was also dominated by upper castes.

Most of the Janata Dal's top leaders in Maharashtra were Brahmins. And among the Communists, all the top leaders were upper caste.

The umbrella under which the Sena united the Brahmin youth from Dadar and the Mali from Parel was the composite Marathi umbrella, and the Marathi youth from working-class Parel joined it with as much willingness as those from middle-class Dadar.

12

HUMBLED AT THE HUSTINGS

After the friction between Indira Gandhi's New Congress and the Old Guard caused the Congress split in 1969, the Union government, represented by Mrs Gandhi's New Congress, had been reduced to a minority. Sixty MPs now sat in the Opposition, though Mrs Gandhi could muster a working majority with the backing of regional parties and independents.

But with reduced numbers and dependence on other parties, Indira was insecure, and faced an aggressive Opposition. She had relied on extra-parliamentary devices to bring about the apparently socialistic transformation she desired in India, but her path had been far from smooth.

The Supreme Court had struck down nationalisation of banks in February 1970. In April, the bill to end special privileges of the Indian Civil Service (ICS) had not obtained a two-thirds majority in Parliament.

On 15 December, a special Supreme Court bench ruled the presidential order on abolition of princely privileges as ultra vires of the Constitution, and Mrs Gandhi thought she had had enough.

She needed a two-thirds majority to introduce certain amendments to the Constitution, which she deemed necessary to 'carry on the socialist processes to the climax of a social revolution'.

So a decision was made to go to the polls and seek a fresh mandate.

On the prime minister's advice, President V.V. Giri dissolved the Lok Sabha on 27 December 1970 and ordered mid-term elections to be held in two phases in February and March 1971.

Mumbai's political arena attracted nationwide attention due to the play of heavyweights such as S.A. Dange, George Fernandes, S.K. Patil and others, and as negotiations began between parties over sharing of seats, leaders of the Shiv Sena and Jan Sangh attempted to lay the groundwork for a tie-up.

Just a few days after the Sena's win in the Parel by-poll, Thackeray and Jan Sangh leader Balraj Madhok had jointly addressed a meeting at Shivaji Park, in which the Sena chief had mooted the idea of an alliance of Hindutva parties.

Now that mid-term polls were declared, negotiations appeared to be going smoothly and both parties came close to forging an alliance, but the deal was dashed when the Jan Sangh refused to yield the north-west Mumbai seat to the Sena.

As the deadlock continued, Thackeray said: 'We wish to have an electoral understanding with the Sangh in the national interest, but we don't accept the fact that while we consider national interest, others play political games keeping an eye on seats.'

Amid this uncertainty, the Sena announced the candidature of its nominees Manohar Joshi from central Mumbai, Datta Pradhan from north-central Mumbai, Nandu Ghate from Pune city and Dr Anil Birje from Ratnagiri North, and said it would support the nomination of retired army personnel like General K.M. Cariappa and Lt. Gen. S.P.P. Thorat – who were toying with the idea of contesting from Mumbai – if they stood as Independents.

When Cariappa decided to contest as an Independent from north-west Mumbai, Thackeray declared the Sena's support to him. And the Jan Sangh cried foul.

Cariappa, who had worked with the likes of General Ayub Khan in the Indian Army, was a candidate acceptable to all opposition parties who had come together against Indira's Congress. But suspicions of a Sena conspiracy rose in the minds of Jan Sangh ideologues, and they announced they would welcome Cariappa's candidature but not if it was a ploy by the Sena to checkmate Jan Sangh.

The Sena chief clarified there was no conspiracy, but the Jan Sangh's stand was firm, and negotiations between the saffron parties ended.

The Sena came in for flak from its opponents because of its support to a non-Marathi nominee, that too a South Indian, despite its avowed Marathi cause and anti-lungi slogans.

'They speak of the Marathi *manoos* and work to get a Cariappa elected', read poll posters put up by rivals.

By Thackeray's own admission, a Sainik from Chembur asked him why he had chosen to back Cariappa, though he was an 'outsider'. The Sena chief replied: 'Cariappa has been part of the Indian Army. He has been involved in protecting the nation from outsiders. Placing trust in him entails no danger. And he himself says he is an Indian first.'

But the loose alliance formed to oppose Indira, the 'grand alliance' as the media called it, could not unite under any common programme. The men in it were not comfortable in each other's company, and agreed only in their resolve to remove Mrs Gandhi. Their slogan *Indira Hatao* (Remove Indira) contrasted miserably with hers, *Garibi Hatao* (Remove Poverty), and an Indira wave swept across the country.

Most voters wanted a stable government, and in the absence of any alternative, felt the New Congress with adequate majority would not be at the mercy of extremists, even those in its own party.

It was believed there had been pressures on Mrs Gandhi during her friction with her own party and her year of reliance on other parties, and once relieved of these, she would display good judgement.

Still, her success was unexpected: the New Congress won 350 out of the 518 seats to the Lok Sabha, a two-thirds majority.

All of Mumbai's five seats were included in this number. The Sena's Manohar Joshi, Datta Pradhan and Cariappa were submerged in the Indira wave, despite polling 1,46,000, 75,000 and 90,110 votes respectively.

There was another reason for the Sena defeat: the split in Congress had not left Thackeray's party unhurt.

Just prior to the polls, a Sena worker along with 1,000 Sainiks had crossed over to the then energetic New Congress and was given a red-carpet welcome. Thackeray protested and accused Congress of encouraging defections, but even in the civic body, some Sena corporators who felt the tide was turning in favour of Congress quit the Sena.

After the Congress split, the Sena had supported the Congress (O) against the Congress (R), suspecting the latter to be full of Communists, but the floor-crossing on the part of Sena corporators placed the Congress (R) in a stronger position.

Despite the electoral setback, however, the Sena succeeded in getting its candidate, Dr Hemchandra Gupte, elected as Mumbai's mayor in April 1971. Taking advantage of the split in the Congress,

Sena secured the support of the Old Congress in these elections and derived satisfaction from humbling the PSP, its erstwhile political partner, whose candidate contested against the Sena nominee.

Cong-Sena dalliance: On again, off again

The Shiv Sena's relations with the Congress have always aroused curiosity among political observers, and some have even gone to the extent of labelling Thackeray's party the handmaiden of the Congress in its early years.

A great deal of tacit and open cooperation took place between the parties, though the relationship was never uniform.

Let us see the intriguing approach of the parties towards one another.

In its first two years, 1966 and 1967, the Sena was unstinting in its praise for some Congress leaders sympathetic to the Marathi cause.

In his first rally on 30 October 1966, Thackeray had lauded Balasaheb Desai, then state home minister, saying he was the only person from whom the Marathi people could have expectations. Congress leader Vasantdada Patil attended *Marmik*'s annual celebration in August 1967, and S.K. Patil was the chief guest on the same occasion the next year.

But after having obtained Sena's support for its candidates in the 1967 Lok Sabha polls, the Congress, to keep its pan-India image intact, began a volley of accusations against Thackeray's party, and the Sena replied by criticising the Congress.

Yet, some members of the Maharashtra Pradesh Congress Committee (MPCC) continually demonstrated their sympathy towards the Sena, and right from the outset, Thackeray assisted the MPCC against the Mumbai Pradesh Congress Committee (BPCC). The BPCC was dominated by non-Maharashtrians like Rajni Patel and was accused by the Sena of working against Marathi interests.

Thackeray at the same time maintained an antagonistic stance towards Congress leaders like S. Nijalingappa, K. Kamaraj and C. Subramaniam because he perceived them as backers of Mysore in the border dispute and called them incompetent and corrupt. He also regularly hit out at other individual members of the Congress who were 'dishonest' and 'in the pay of profiteers and a few businessmen'.

The Sena argued that the plight of Marathi people was worsened by such Congress mandarins.

Of course, condemnation gave way to cooperation in situations where the Communists were seen as beneficiaries of a Congress-Sena clash.

The Sena shrewdly frowned upon any move that would have a negative effect on the status of Maharashtrians in Mumbai, and the Congress carefully maintained its image as a national party by conveniently condemning the Sena for some of its violent, 'anti-outsider' actions.

The Congress at times vociferously opposed the Sena but took no step towards checking it or blotting it out because it knew the Sena could protect it from the onslaught of Left parties.

Whenever it was believed the Communists were likely to gain an upper hand, the Sena propped up the Congress and was in turn propped up by the latter, but at least till 1973, both took care to see that the lines between the distinctive ideologies and identities of the two parties did not get smudged.

After the defeat – both electorally and in terms of defections – to the Congress in 1971, the Sena got a chance to wean away certain Congressmen to its side and put up a stiff opposition to the ruling party at the time of the BMC polls in 1973. But before that, there was more defeat to swallow.

Indira Gandhi's leadership during the 1971 Indo-Pak War stood the Congress in good stead in the Assembly elections held early in 1972.

The Congress had an impressive success all over India. In Maharashtra, it got 222 of the total 270 seats. The second highest tally was that of Independents: twenty-three. The PWP had won seven seats, and the Jan Sangh five.

The Sena had put up a few candidates for the Assembly polls, but barring Pramod Navalkar, who won from Girgaum by a margin of more than 25,000, others were washed away by the second successive Congress wave. However, that year Manohar Joshi was nominated as a Member of the Legislative Council (MLC).

13

THE TIGER'S WHITE COLLAR

The reverses in the electoral arena notwithstanding, the Shiv Sena's activities were not affected.

Attacks on South Indian establishments continued, as did the vocabulary of the Marathi *manoos*, but the Sena took a real leap towards employment generation for the local populace in 1972 by establishing, in place of its earlier Bureau, the Sthaniya Lokadhikar Samiti (literally, committee to protect rights of locals) in several government and business organisations.

The Samiti was formed to press the Sena's chief demand that 80 per cent of all jobs in government and semi-government undertakings, and in banks, insurance companies and corporate offices in Mumbai and Maharashtra, be reserved for sons of the soil.

The striking feature of this wing was that it was set up to mobilise white-collar workers and salary-earners and to rally the employed to fight for the employment rights of the jobless.

The Samiti gave flesh to the Sena's central canon by spreading its units in institutions such as the Reserve Bank of India, Bank of America, State Bank of India, Life Insurance Corporation and the General Assurance Company within months of its formation. It also began to be recognised as the core unit of the Shiv Sena.

To push its demand for 80 per cent quota for locals, the Samiti did not demand any retrenchment, but declared that all future recruitments should abide by this principle. Other demands were 1) Maharashtrian workers should not be harassed, and their promotions and transfers should be just; 2) Ads announcing recruitment plans and filling up of vacancies should be placed in Marathi newspapers, even those at the district level; and 3) There should be at least one Maharashtrian on the panel of interviewers.

Thackeray realised the Samiti, to be led by his lieutenant Sudhir Joshi, would be a powerful weapon in his hands because 65 per cent of the nation's economy was concentrated in Mumbai, and 85 per cent of all bank headquarters were in the city. If the Sena got a hold in such institutions, the party argued, not only would the employment rights of Maharashtrians be guaranteed, but any move to try and separate Mumbai from Maharashtra could be foiled.

The first white-collar institution targeted by the Sena was Air India, where Marathi youths seeking a job apparently encountered a stumbling block in the Chief Personnel Officer S.K. Nanda.

In November 1972, the Sena took a morcha to Air India's Nariman Point office, and when Nanda came forward to speak to the Sena delegation led by Thackeray, he was greeted with kicks and clenched fists. Thackeray warned that if anyone was arrested, Sainiks gathered outside the AI office would not take it lying down, and possibly fearing violence, police stood mute witnesses to the incident. No action was taken against the Sainiks.

The Sena chief later said he did not regret the assault on Nanda. In fact, he said Nanda had asked for it.

Around the same time, the Sena took up the case of a Marathi peon, one Rane, in Bank of Baroda. Rane, despite being a commerce graduate, was being denied promotion by his branch manager, while people belonging to other communities, less qualified, had been promoted.

Thackeray led a delegation to the bank, but the branch manager justified the stalling of Rane's promotion. 'I'll do what I want,' he told Thackeray, who flung papers lying on the table on the manager's face. Sainiks got the message, and the manager was beaten black and blue.

After numerous such violent morchas to the Oberoi Sheraton, Reserve Bank of India, Fertiliser Corporation of India, Indian Oil and other institutions, the recruitment of Maharashtrians actually picked up speed.

Communist leader Roza Deshpande gave me an example of how the Sena operated:

> The Rashtriya Chemicals and Fertilisers (RCF) unit at Chembur had invited applications for certain posts. If the officials scrutinising the applications, most of whom hailed from Uttar Pradesh, saw the applicant was a Maharashtrian, they would tear the form and throw

it into the dustbin. The Sena got to know of this. Sainiks got hold of all the torn forms thrown into the dustbins, took them to the officials concerned and demanded an explanation. When the officials groped for a reply, they were beaten up. The next day onwards, the tearing-up business stopped, and Marathi youths started getting jobs at RCF.[103]

Triumph in BMC polls

Just when the Shiv Sena's agitations were thus gathering momentum, elections to the BMC were declared early in 1973.

The Sena once again sprang a surprise on Mumbaikars by joining hands with the Republican Party of India (RPI) and proclaiming the alliance would go a long way in improving the fate of neo-Buddhists.

The method of selecting Sena nominees this time marked a change from the past, when the party had relied solely on a person's personality and conviction. This time, shakha pramukhs and vibhag pramukhs were asked to draw a list of probables from various wards. Apart from party office-bearers and activists, professionals such as doctors, lawyers and other reputable persons in a constituency were also included. There was a condition, though, for their inclusion: sympathy and support for the Sena. Then, along with information about the background and qualifications of all the probables, the lists were submitted to the Sena chief. There was no limit to the number of probables shakha pramukhs and vibhag pramukhs could suggest from each ward, and in most cases, the count exceeded ten.

Interviews of candidates were jointly held by Thackeray and members of his *karyakarini* (executive), and on a few occasions, B.K. Desai, a friend of the Sena chief, was also invited to be on the interviewers' panel.

The Sena fielded 85 candidates and allowed RPI to contest 20, and in what was seen as revenge for the Congress' 1971 poll-eve actions, succeeded in wooing Congress (R) members to its side.

A controversy over the singing of Vande Mataram on the floor of the BMC proved to be the dominant issue in the elections. Congress corporator Amin Khandwani had opposed the singing of Vande Mataram and received the support of the Muslim League. The Sena made its advocacy of the national song its main poll plank. Success was swift. It won 40 seats, but was still five short to have its own candidate elected as mayor and defeat the Muslim League.

If the Opposition came together, it could keep the mayoral seat away from the Congress (R), so the Sena set itself to the task of mobilising the Opposition and held parleys with leaders of other parties.

Along with RPI's one seat, the Sena strength was 41, and it was possible that 4 Congress (O) nominees would extend support to it.

Ultimately, the Sena's mayoral candidate Sudhir Joshi secured 76 votes, while the Congress got 45 and the Jan Sangh 15. Congress (O) corporators had helped the Sena win.

Some Muslim League corporators alleged the Sena had used *dadagiri* against them, but could not prove the charge.

The Sena did a volte face after emerging the winner in the BMC: it made a concession whereby Muslims could abstain from singing Vande Mataram.

Anti-price rise agitation

Although Vande Mataram was conveniently abandoned after acquiring the seat of power in the corporation, the Shiv Sena kept up the momentum on its anti-price rise agitation, launched in February 1973, even after the poll triumph.

The February stir had centred around rising milk prices, and Sainiks had seized milk vans, taken charge of milk booths and distributed milk at reduced rates to people.

In July, it was the high prices of mutton and fish that prompted an *aandolan*. Shops of mutton sellers were picketed, and a demand made that mutton be sold at ₹ 7 per kilo. After the *Times of India* reported on 28 July that mutton prices had indeed fallen due to the Sena stir, veteran Shiv Sena leader Pramod Navalkar threatened Sena would now picket shops selling essential commodities.

The party put up price lists in the markets and at street corners and appealed to consumers to inform Sena shakhas if discrepanies came to their notice. According to Sena leaders, shopkeepers conceded their demands, and police said everything was fine. No disturbance, nothing.

The scope of the agitation slowly extended to vegetable vendors and other commodity stores, and on 30 July, Sena activists attacked the Grant Road and Kurla markets and looted a few trucks carrying *maida* (refined wheat flour) and vegetable oil.

Shopkeepers condemned these strong-arm tactics and downed shutters in protest, but the popular response was good. Seeing the success of the Mumbai experiment, the party took its agitation to Pune, where shops were attacked.

When the Ganesh festival came, the Sena 'fixed' the rate of *pedha* at ₹ 10 per kilo, and in the second week of September, Sainiks 'raided' some fish sellers and landed in jail.

By mid-September, Thane and Kolaba (now Raigad) districts were also caught in the thick of the agitation, and encouraged by the success achieved, Sainiks in Mumbai swooped down on wholesale dealers of potatoes and onions as well.

Rival parties slammed these 'goonda' tactics, and hoteliers said they could not run their establishments at prices suggested by Sainiks. But Thackeray's party refused to accept decisions taken by the price panel because the sole Opposition member on the panel, Navalkar, had been absent when the decisions were made. The agitation continued into October, but on 2 November, the government lifted price control, and the problem of rising prices stayed on.

14

SENA STAMP ON CONGRESS'S EMPLOYMENT DIRECTIVES: LOCALS FIRST

I f it could not allow prices to go through the roof, the Shiv Sena said it also could not allow Mumbai's population to 'reach unmanageable proportions due to the influx of outsiders'.

As the ruling party in BMC, it made an attempt on 29 June 1973 to pass a resolution to check the inflow of migrants to Mumbai from other states. But the bid failed, and the Sena also lost all its allies in the civic body, who voted against it on the issue, calling the move 'unconstitutional'.

The resolution flopped owing to opposition from all parties, but the Congress government in Maharashtra issued an order in September 1973 which underlined how effective the Shiv Sena propaganda had been. The move was a desperate political imperative to keep the Sena from hijacking the Marathi cause.

In 1968, the state had issued an order to government offices and big business organisations in Mumbai, asking them to employ local labour. It had maintained that local workers had greater stability and would thus bring about an increase in profits. The order also reminded employers of their duty to act in compliance with the notification about the Vacancies Act, but its tone and the fact that the Vacancies Act did not make the hiring of locals mandatory suggested the state's espousal of the nativist cause was tentative.

Moreover, as the preferences were defined in terms of a person's duration of stay in the city, many public and private establishments could argue their employment rosters fulfilled conditions.

Right up to 1973, the Congress regime had stuck to guidelines suggesting that preference be given to locals, defined as those staying in Maharashtra for 15 years, in Class III and IV government jobs, and semi-skilled and unskilled positions.

In 1973, a sharp deviation was made

On 25 September, the Maharashtra government's director of industries issued a directive to government and business establishments asking them to employ local persons in *all* categories of jobs. It urged that 60 per cent of managerial jobs should be given to locals, and 90 per cent of staff in lower positions should be selected from among local applicants.

The directive also made the definition of a 'local' more specific: it included 'native Marathi-speaking people'. Referring to the Factory Act of 1948 that required labour officers to talk to workers in the language of the majority, it stated that employers should hire personnel or recruitment officers whose mother tongue was Marathi.

This directive was attacked by the Opposition in Parliament, and the Centre made the Maharashtra government redefine the term 'local'. The redefinition excluded all reference to mother tongue and retained only the residential criterion. Later too, there was little or no application of official pressure to see that firms followed the directive, and no restrictions were placed on unresponsive establishments.

But the very fact that the Congress regime in the state had to go well beyond the Centre's policy, if only temporarily, pointed to the political urgency of the move.

When the Sena burst upon the Mumbai scene in 1966, its official policy statement, *Shiv Sena Speaks*, had listed the following as its top demand:

> In order to rescue Maharashtrians from the rut of poverty and consequent frustration on all fronts of life, 80 per cent jobs, skilled or otherwise, must be reserved in governmental, semi-governmental, private and public undertakings. Existing concerns should be persuaded to meet this demand, and licences to new undertakings should be issued only on this condition.[104]

This was followed by a campaign to push organisations to employ Maharashtrians. Morchas were taken to State Bank of India, Fertiliser Corporation of India, Glaxo, Indian Oil, Sarabhai Chemicals, Jayanti Shipping Corporation, Burmah Shell, New India Assurance and numerous other firms. Top-ranking officials were hauled up, often beaten, and strong-arm tactics were used and unabashedly justified.

In one case, often discussed among Sena workers, a Sena leader met an executive of Indian Oil and told him that he better hire more Maharashtrians. 'You may be sitting inside, but your oil tanks are outside,' the executive was warned.

After receiving such ultimatums, managers of many firms, under duress, requested the Sena's help in employing Maharashtrians, and more Marathi speakers were hired.

During a morcha to Glaxo, which had a substantial number of Mumbai-born Christians on its rolls, Thackeray and a group of Sainiks barged into the manager's office and asked him why very few employees were Maharashtrian. The manager said most employees were Maharashtrian and produced before the Sena delegation the company's records to show where most employees had been born.

The Sainiks replied: 'We want to know how many are really Maharashtrian – Marathi by mother tongue.'

Frequently, employed Sainiks approached their own managements in groups and made the party's pressure felt; Sena corporators rang up and met personnel officers of companies in their wards; and shakhas maintained employment catalogues. Marathi youth were urged to register themselves in the catalogues, and when any firm or Sena activist alerted the shakha of a vacancy, youngsters on the lists were informed and instructed on the manner of submitting applications.

Along with the Sena's pressure, perception grew among Mumbai's Marathi-speaking people that they were getting more opportunities. By 1973, feeling was widespread that their status was improving. This sentiment was, of course, most expansive in Sena offices, but it also existed among Mumbai's voters regardless of whether they were Sena backers or not.

In a survey held by Mary F. Katzenstein and Kartikeya Sarabhai after the 1971 parliamentary polls, 51.5 per cent of those interviewed said they felt more Maharashtrians were getting jobs than before, 19 per cent felt more Maharashtrians were not getting jobs, 25 per cent answered they were not sure, and 4.5 per cent refused to respond.

Did these perceptions match reality? Had the economic condition of the Marathi-speaking people really changed for the better after the Sena's emergence?

As census surveys do not record the demarcation of occupational divisions community-wise, one can only give illustrative findings about changes in the employment scenario.

Let us consider three studies of public and private employment in Mumbai.

The first was done by Mumbai-based management students who interviewed 125 managers from 25 companies based in Mumbai. The percentage of Maharashtrian managers employed by these firms before 1950 was zero; between 1950 and 1960, 10 per cent of the managerial positions went to Maharashtrians; after 1960, Marathi-speaking persons held 21 per cent of the managerial jobs. The corresponding percentage of Gujaratis employed as managers during the three decades was 56, 34 and 44 respectively, while that of South Indians was 25, 29 and 12 respectively.

The percentage of Marathi managers was still low, seen against the total percentage of the Marathi-speaking population in Mumbai (42). But the rise in the number of Marathi speakers recruited by companies went beyond that of any other community.

The second study is an analysis of the Mumbai telephone directory, done by two researchers, Neelam Kanodia and T.C. Daswani. In the listing of government offices and private companies, the directory had names, positions and telephone numbers of an establishment or firm's officers. It was possible to find out from the names the ethnic background of individuals and thus to estimate the number of Marathi-speaking and non-Marathi-speaking people employed. There were some names whose linguistic category was difficult to identify: the surname Desai, for instance, could be either Marathi or Gujarati. But in case of identification done by native speakers familiar with Maharashtrian names, there was more than 85 per cent accuracy.

Eleven Central government establishments were included in the analysis, and it was found the percentage of Marathi-speaking people in these, 19 in 1962, had risen to 25 in 1967 and to 29 in 1973. The establishments sampled were Air India, Indian Airlines, Reserve Bank of India, Atomic Energy Department, Indian Oil, New India Assurance, Directorate General of Shipping, Western Railway, Posts and Telegraphs, Bombay Telephones and Life Insurance Corporation.

In the seven state and municipal government establishments studied, the percentage of Marathi-speaking people had gone up from 64 in 1962 to 75 per cent in 1967 and 82 in 1973. The state and municipal offices included Industries, Labour and Employment offices, Western Railway Police, Directorate of Employment, Finance Department and the Brihanmumbai Electricity and Transport Supply (BEST) undertaking.

Fifteen private-sector establishments were analysed, and here too, the percentage of Marathi speakers recruited had risen from 7 in 1962 to 12 in 1967 and 16 in 1973. The firms studied were L&T, Mafatlal, Philips, Bajaj, Burmah Shell, Glaxo, Caltex, CIBA, Forbes, Forbes and Campbell, Indian Express, Crompton and Greaves, Podar Mills, Shree Ram Mills, Shree Nivas Cotton and India United Mills.

So the percentage of Marathi-speaking people in high-level and middle-level positions in both government and private undertakings had risen continuously.

The third study was a survey of 126 clerical workers in 12 public and private organisations, done by a marketing research group in Mumbai, and commissioned by the Migration and Development Study Group at the Massachusetts Institute of Technology in 1976. The study revealed that of clerical workers recruited during or before 1971, Marathi-speaking people formed 45.6 per cent. But of those recruited after 1971, they accounted for 61.7 per cent.

Even newspaper reports made observations about the bettered occupational status of Maharashtrians. In a piece headlined 'Flourishing Businesses of Udipi Hotels' that appeared in the *Hindustan Times (Sunday Standard,* Delhi*)* of 6 January 1974, it was noted that though it was undeniable that South Indian restaurants in Mumbai employed few Maharashtrians, 'importing their near and distant relations from their home districts, now considerable numbers of Maharashtrians work in them. Indeed, the Satkar group of restaurants, the biggest name in the vegetarian catering business, boasts that nearly 70 per cent of its staff is Maharashtrian.'

The Sena's official statement of 1967, *Shiv Sena Speaks*, had said:

> Ours (Shiv Sena's) is an economic demand. It is not directed against a particular community, but surely against their communal mentality. We claim an adequate representation in the services as our rightful due. We do not want any charity from anybody. This is our legitimate right... Shiv Sena, therefore, demands that 80

per cent of the jobs available in private or public sectors must be reserved for Maharashtrians.

The directive issued by the Maharashtra government in 1973 still exists. As noted earlier, successive Congress governments in the state did little or nothing to see that this directive was followed by employers.

The Shiv Sena, after coming to power in 1995, also did nothing to implement this order.

15

SUPPORT FOR CONGRESS,
THE EMERGENCY AND ZERO TOLERANCE FOR
ARTISTIC DISSENT

Towards the end of 1973, the Shiv Sena sprang into action on the Maharashtra-Karnataka border issue again.

There was considerable tension in Belgaum and Karwar, with Marathi speakers there alleging they were being discriminated against and attacked by police.

The Sena chief called for a Mumbai bandh on 18 December to protest the 'brutalities' in Karnataka. The bandh was total, and even local train services were paralysed after six suburban coaches were torched by Sainiks, who also resorted to stone-throwing and did not allow commuters to board trains. In all, police rounded up 1,074 Sainiks that day, 402 of them for arson and stone-throwing.

The so-called agitation continued for two more days after the bandh. Many Udipi hotels and restaurants were attacked, 'outsiders' assaulted, and factories, mills, commercial offices, docks, schools and colleges were forced shut.

The bandh declared by the Sena on the border issue was supported by the Congress, purportedly for securing the Sena's backing in by-elections to the central Mumbai parliamentary constituency due in January 1974.

Thackeray had in November 1973 ruled out an alliance with the Congress (R). He had also said he would not support Jan Sangh as it had announced it would oppose any Sena candidate.

But as the elections drew close, the Sena changed its stand and chose to join forces with Indira's Congress.

According to a section of Sainiks, the turnaround was because of the Jan Sangh's opposition in the mayoral polls and the Congress's support for the stir on the border issue.

The fact that the Congress candidate was Ramrao Adik, Thackeray's old friend who had addressed the first Sena rally in October 1966, also mattered.

The Sena chief justified his decision saying the Congress–Sena tie-up was intended to keep Communists at bay. But even when he said the alliance would be on his terms, not all Sainiks were convinced.

Disappointed, many Sainiks did not put in their all into the campaign, while a hard-core Sainik Bandu Shingre – known as a *terror* in Lalbaug – revolted and aligned with the Hindu Mahasabha. There was also a scathing attack on Thackeray and the Sena by the editor of the Marathi weekly *Sobat*, G.V. Behere, a Hindutva propagandist. Behere wrote a front-page editorial in *Sobat*'s 20 January issue, entitled 'Senapati or *Shen*apati?' *Shen* means cowdung in Marathi.

Thackeray had been on good terms with Behere ever since the two were introduced to each other by Bal's aide D.V. Deshpande, a scholar. Their friendship, which had blossomed because they had common deities – Shivaji and Savarkar – ended with Behere's editorial.

Soon after this indictment was published, Behere, on his way to attending a meeting of his magazine's readers was accosted by Sainiks near Sena Bhavan and thrashed. Not only that, the editor, who had appealed to Sainiks to strip the Senapati of his robes, was stripped. Undaunted, Behere put on a lungi offered to him by someone and walked to the venue in that garb.

Even before the Behere incident, the Sena had demonstrated its intolerance of dissent and criticism. It had sharply criticised, in its early years, Acharya Atre, who had labelled Thackeray's party the Vasant Sena owing to then Chief Minister Vasantrao Naik's support for it, and even physically assaulted him. In 1972, the year in which Vijay Tendulkar wrote his play *Ghashiram Kotwal*, which many believed was in response to the emergence of the Shiv Sena, the party targeted the playwright. The underlying theme of *Ghashiram*, based on the life of Nana Phadnavis, the prime minister in the Peshwas' court, is the deliberate encouragement of certain ideologies by the powers-that-be, and their destruction of such ideologies once their selfish ends have been met. The Shiv Sena and the RSS staged protests against the play, saying it portrayed Brahmins as well as Phadnavis in poor light, and forced cancellations of performances. The Sena even pasted blackboards, with abuses written all over them, outside the housing society in Vile Parle in suburban Mumbai where Tendulkar lived, forcing the playwright to find shelter in a friend's house for some time and causing distress to his family.

A little after the assault on Behere, in 1975, the Sena blocked the publication of a Marathi novel *Raada*, written by Bhau Padhye. The novel not only made direct references to the Shiv Sena but had a shakha pramukh from Goregaon, a fictional character called Nanasaheb Kharkar, as one of its principal characters. In the book, the protagonist, Mandar Annegiri, the rebel son of a Maharashtrian factory-owner, cocks a snook at the Sena shakha's activities, debunks the party's hypocrisy and its moral code inflicted on all of Mumbai and comments on the Sena labour wing's attempts to oust the Communist union from his father's factory. Some copies, nevertheless, were published, a second edition was out in 1997 and a third edition was published recently, in 2011.

In 1977-78, the Sena, along with the RSS and the Hindu Mahasabha, extra-legally banned *Bedtime Story*, a play written by Kiran Nagarkar. Thackeray's party could not have counted Nagarkar among its supporters in any case, as the writer had, in his novel *Saat Sakkam Trechalis* (later translated into English as *Seven Sixes are Forty-Three*) – considered one of the seminal works of modern Marathi literature – published in 1974 written about Shiv Sena violence. After the state censor board had cleared the play with 28 cuts (having first demanded 78 cuts), the Sena objected to it, and even rehearsals were not allowed. The play was finally staged after 17 years.

Despite the trouble caused by Shingre's rebellion and the Behere episode, Sena leaders put up a united front and approved of Thackeray's stance in favour of Congress.

But Ramrao Adik's way was not going to be smooth. In the earlier elections, the Congress candidate had won a landslide victory because of the support of the RPI's neo-Buddhists, who formed a significant percentage of the constituency's voters.

This time round, a new militant organisation of neo-Buddhists, Dalit Panthers, had come up in the heart of central Mumbai to take on the RPI and its factions. Its leaders Namdeo Dhasal, Raja Dhale and Ramdas Athawale refused to align with the Congress, which, they felt, had offered unjust treatment to neo-Buddhists. They put their strength behind the Communists.

Tension was exacerbated on 5 January 1974, when the Panthers held a public meeting at a BDD (Bombay Development Directorate) Chawl to justify their boycott call of by-polls to protest the 'continued ill-treatment of Dalits by upper-caste Hindus with the government's connivance'.

There, the Panthers leaders allegedly made derogatory remarks against Hindu gods, and stone-throwing began, followed by a lathi-charge from police. There was, soon, full-scale violence between the Sena and the Panthers.

Sena boards later sprang up in the area, saying the party would not forgive anyone who insulted Hindu gods. When the Panthers leaders were arrested, the Yuva Kranti Dal, an organisation of socialist youths, took out a morcha to demand their release. The morcha was attacked, and one Dalit youth lost his life.

Partly in response to the Panthers' boycott call, and partly due to violence, most neo-Buddhist voters did not step out of their homes to exercise their franchise.

The Congress thus straightaway lost more than 75,000 votes, and the Communist Party's Roza Deshpande emerged the winner by a slender margin of 11,000.

A Sena morcha taken out the same month to the Bank of India (BOI) invited flak because of Sainik violence and alleged police inaction. The crowd returning from the morcha targeted shops, hawkers' stalls and other establishments. Quite a lot of property was destroyed, and when the police finally resorted to a lathi-charge, officegoers and lawyers on their way home allegedly had to bear the brunt of the attack. Railway commuters were cornered by Sainiks, asked if they were South Indians, and beaten up.

Two days later, when hawkers took out a morcha to the police commissioner's office demanding protection, they were lathi-charged, and many of them were injured.

The defeat in the central Mumbai by-poll had come as a blow to the Sena, but it continued its association with the Congress and indeed strengthened it with the passage of time.

As the collaboration increased, Bal Thackeray, who had earlier been scathing in his criticism of Indira Gandhi, discovered qualities in her and said he had faith in her leadership.

At the same time, the Sena worked on strengthening its unions, allegedly with Congress patronage. But as it came closer to the Congress, it became increasingly unable to set itself apart from other political parties in the eyes of voters.

When Indira Gandhi imposed the Emergency on 25 June 1975, Bal Thackeray declared his support for it.

This may have been the result of self-interest, or it may have been the result of his belief that authoritarian rule would bring 'discipline' and give the country a sense of direction. Or, the two factors may have combined to determine Sena policy.

Advocates for both theories are many.

Some suggest Thackeray dreaded the prospect of a ban on the Sena, the unleashing of repressive tactics against his party men, and imprisonment for himself. Mrs Gandhi had reduced the scene to a warlike confrontation between the Congress and other opinion, leaving no room for compromise or maneouvre.

But regardless of whether he simply wanted to play safe, the truth is that opposition to the Emergency would have meant for Thackeray a negation of his publicly proclaimed convictions.

Here was a political technique employed by Indira Gandhi which Thackeray himself had advocated as being desirable.

Policy and decision were seen as being handed down during the Emergency by a single person, and that is what the Sena pramukh believed in. 'I don't have faith in *Lokshahi*, I believe in *Thokshahi*', he had said time and again, and in his own outfit, he tolerated no dissent.

'This country needs a dictator', was his refrain, and Indira Gandhi had just become one. Just as Thackeray wanted a ruler to do, she had taken steps to dismantle democratic processes, gained absolute control of the state apparatus and established an all-powerful command.

Support to such authoritarianism did not do the Sena any good. *Marmik*'s publication was anyway banned, as part of curbs on press freedom, and the Sena injured its image in the eyes of the people because its interests came to be closely identified with those of Indira's Congress.

The Emergency's excesses angered the people, and support increased in favour of Jayaprakash Narayan and other Opposition leaders who dared to speak out against the Congress regime.

But Thackeray overreached himself by consistently showering praise on the leadership of Mrs Gandhi during the Emergency years – 1975 to 1977 – and overlooked the fact that her growing unpopularity could invite political retribution for the Sena.

Later, justifying his stand, the Sena chief told his followers:

> I did not support Indira Congress during the Emergency because I was afraid of being put behind bars. It's true the Sena faced a serious crisis during that period, because Shankarrao Chavan [then chief minister] was sitting on our head, so to say. I had a bad toothache at the time, and lay in Jaslok Hospital in a sickly state. Blood was trickling out of the mouth, cotton had been put inside; I couldn't even speak.
>
> Under such circumstances, Rajni Patel [then Congress strongman in Mumbai] sent a typed statement to me through Dr Shantilal Mehta, and asked me to sign it. Rajni Patel had himself inserted two lines in the statement! I told Dr Mehta I wouldn't sign it. Who the hell is Rajni Patel, I asked. Dr Mehta warned me that if I refused to sign, all Shiv Sena leaders would be put in prison. I replied: tell Rajni Patel, if that happens, his funeral is sure to take place. How dare they tell me that if I didn't sign, they would ban the Sena?
> We had not mortgaged our self-respect during the Emergency. We were studying the Indira regime.[105]

The 'study' continued even after the Emergency was lifted, when Bal Thackeray backed down on his earlier stand and supported Congress candidate Murli Deora for the Mumbai mayoral polls in March 1977.

When Indira Gandhi called a general election in March 1977, thinking that an Opposition, which for 19 months had remained out of public gaze with no chance to make its views heard, would be no match for her, Thackeray again stood behind her.

Mrs Gandhi believed the election would renew her mandate, but the Sena leader took no chances and campaigned all over the state for the Congress. He defended Indira's experiment in dictatorship and eulogised what he called the dynamism and tough political armour of Sanjay Gandhi.

The Congress suffered a shattering defeat. Roughly 60 per cent of the total Indian electorate of 320 million voted the Janata Party to power, reducing the Congress to a minority for the first time since Independence.

In Maharashtra, the Congress won 20 of the 47 seats contested, while the Janata Party bagged 19 out of 31 seats fought.

The Sena had not contested any seat but had intimately connected itself with the Congress. Now, with Congress hopes dwindling, its own future was a crossroads.

Realising what lay ahead, a section of the Sena leadership began efforts to strike an arrangement with the Janata Party – then riding the crest of a success wave – for the Assembly polls scheduled early in 1978.

Thackeray expressed his willingness to tie-up with the Janata Party, but talks did not yield any results. The Sena finally aligned with the Congress-I, which had come into being on 2 January 1978 following disagreements in the party about its course of action, as against the Congress (ARS).

It put up a few candidates for the elections. None was elected. Dr Gupte, who had joined the Janata Party after quitting the Sena, defeated Manohar Joshi from the Dadar constituency, a Sena stronghold.

The Janata Party obtained 99 seats, but the Congress-I and Congress-URS, with 62 and 69 seats respectively, got together and formed the government.

16

THE SURPRISE ANNOUNCEMENT

Faced with a serious crisis as a result of increasing identification with the Congress, the Sena had to fight the BMC election scheduled for November 1978. Bal Thackeray knew it would not be smooth sailing in the wake of electoral reverses and the erosion of the party's mass base. The Congress and Janata Party were at loggerheads, and the fight between the two centred mainly at all levels – national, regional and local. The Janata had brought with it a whiff of fresh air, and after its Lok Sabha triumph, renewed hope in the idea of total social, economic and political revolution. Two erstwhile Sena leaders, Dr Hemchandra Gupte and Datta Pradhan, had also joined the Janata Party.

Seeing the journey to the seat of municipal power strewn with obstacles, Thackeray decided to put all he had at stake, his leadership included. 'If I can't unfurl the saffron flag atop the BMC, I will resign as Shiv Sena chief,' he said during the poll campaign.

The people of Mumbai paid scant attention to the warning. They returned 21 Sena corporators, a nearly 50 per cent decline from the 40-member bloc the party had after the 1973 polls. When the Sena first fought BMC elections in 1968, 42 of its candidates had been elected. The November 1978 polls cut that strength by half.

The Janata Party won 83 out of 140 seats and Congress was relegated to the third position with 17 seats, fewer than those of the Sena.

The results showed the Sena's power in Mumbai had waned. Already, it had no member either in Parliament or the Assembly. Now, even the civic body was no longer in its grasp.

At this moment, Thackeray's baffled and disconcerted Sainiks were caught unawares. At a rally at Shivaji Park after the poll debacle, he pulled out a piece of paper from his pocket in the middle of his speech and started reading: 'I have failed to unfurl the saffron flag on top of the corporation. If the people have no faith in me, why should I waste my time reflecting their grievances? I am a man who lives by his word. As the people don't want me, I'm quitting the Shiv Sena.'

For the assembled Sainiks, the pronouncement was a shocker. They chanted in unison: 'You can't leave. You're our leader.'

He wouldn't listen. The intonations grew louder, the persuasion more frantic. Finally, after they had all repeatedly reaffirmed their loyalty to him, Thackeray reneged on his stand. 'It is only your extraordinary love and affection that is forcing me to withdraw my decision,' he said, tearing the resignation note.

The act was in keeping with Thackeray's style of functioning, and it helped him accomplish his goal. He had shrewdly made his party cadres, demoralised after the electoral defeat, renew their commitment to him and the Sena.

The Sena minus Thackeray was unthinkable for the ordinary Shiv Sainik, and Thackeray had renewed his bond with the Sainik by making a dramatic gesture of tendering his resignation.

Under Antulay's cover

The Congress regime formed in Maharashtra after the 1978 Vidhan Sabha elections did not last long. Sharad Pawar defected from the coalition of the Congress-I (led by Nasikrao Tirpude) and Congress-U (led by Vasantdada Patil), formed the Samajwadi Congress, struck a deal with the Janata Party and established a government of the Purogami Lokshahi Aghadi (Progressive Democratic Front).

The Sena remained a silent spectator to these developments, taking no sides and lauding or rubbishing no tie-ups.

The squabbling in the Janata government at the Centre had begun from day one, and by the end of 1979, all hopes it had generated were dashed, and people saw the Centre as weak and incompetent. As the government came apart, President Sanjiva Reddy called an election in January 1980, and the Indian people returned Indira Gandhi to power.

Soon after recapturing the prime minister's *gaddi*, Mrs Gandhi dismissed Pawar's PDF government in Maharashtra. Elections to the Vidhan Sabha were announced to be held in June 1980.

The Sena again entered into an agreement with the Congress-I. The deal was that the Sena would not contest any seat in the state but use all its machinery in support of Congress, and the Congress in turn would nominate three Sena members to the Legislative Council.

The Janata Party suffered a humiliating defeat, getting 17 seats, and Pawar's Samajwadi Congress, whose tally was second highest, managed to win no more than forty-seven. The Congress-I obtained a clear majority, with 186 seats. A.R. Antulay became the new chief minister of Maharashtra.

The Sena pramukh had an excellent rapport with Antulay, and when the latter contested the Assembly election from Shrivardhan after being chosen chief minister, the Sena canvassed for him and ran his campaign. Thackeray even addressed a joint rally in the constituency with Congress leader Ramrao Adik to solicit votes for Antulay.

The deal was carried out scrupulously: for the hard work done by Thackeray and his party before and after the polls, the Congress nominated Manohar Joshi, Pramod Navalkar and Wamanrao Mahadik to the Council.

17

TEXTILE TRAGEDY LEADS TO DIVORCE

A.R. Antulay's tenure as chief minister was fraught with difficulties, with labour unrest swelling in Mumbai's mills and industries in 1981 and allegations of misuse of power being hurled against him.

The Shiv Sena turned a blind eye to all this and backed the Congress chief minister, who was a chum of Bal Thackeray.

What it could not ignore, however, was the increasing assertiveness of the city's textile industry workers fighting for bonus and wage increase. Sensing their mood, the Sena's Girni Kamgar Sena (GKS) on 12 October 1981 gate-crashed into the Mill Owners Association's (MOA) office and submitted a charter of demands.

Thackeray called a one-day strike on 1 November and demanded a wage hike of not less than ₹ 200 per month. If it was not granted by mid-November, he said, he would call an indefinite strike.

Practically all workers participated in the stir. But the Sena's posture became less rigid in the next few days, and no indefinite strike was called.

Dissatisfaction among mill workers was growing, and the wind needed to fan the flames was provided by Dr Datta Samant, a trade union leader known for his militant ways. Founding a new textile union, the Maharashtra Girni Kamgar Union, Samant too threatened an indefinite strike from mid-November if his demands were not met and took on a more belligerent attitude as the days went by. Apart from higher bonus, his demands included wage increase of ₹ 200 to ₹ 400 per month.

Antulay appointed a high-powered committee (HPC) on 11 November to study the problems faced by mill workers, and Samant postponed a general strike to await its findings. But he took no steps to end the ongoing strike in eight mills and asked workers to be prepared for a strike which textile owners would themselves welcome.

After the Mill Owners Association pulled out of the HPC's proceedings pointing to the inability to end the ongoing strike, Samant called a one-day token strike on 6 January 1982, which paralysed the textile industry.

The HPC's proceedings collapsed owing to lack of cooperation from the parties concerned, and the situation was made worse by Antulay's exit as chief minister.[106]

On 18 January 1982, one day before Babasaheb Bhonsle replaced Antulay as chief minister, the indefinite textile strike, involving nearly 2.5 lakh mill workers, began.

The Sena opposed the strike, saying it would affect the workers' dependant families.

Whether Samant's demands were fantastic or not, the Sena would not have supported a campaign spearheaded by him because its animosity with him went back to September 1972.

Samant had shot into prominence as a union leader that year after he clashed with the Sena. When workers at Godrej's Vikhroli factory went on a strike to demand a higher bonus, he held rallies in the area and employed militant tactics to prevent disapproving workers from resuming work. One Shiv Sainik was battered by Samant's men, and when the Sena decided to despatch Manohar Joshi to take stock of the situation, tension in the factory's vicinity was aggravated and police bandobast strengthened.

Joshi first went to the injured Sainik's home and then proceeded towards the factory, with emotionally charged Sainiks. As he entered the factory's premises, stones and soda-water bottles were hurled in his direction. Samant's followers and Sainiks were soon engaged in a violent battle, and the police escorted Joshi out of the factory in their van. Samant's followers then ran amok, stoning to death a police officer Chandgude and holding him 'responsible' for escorting the Sena leader away. Two havaldars were also killed in the violence.

Samant was sent to jail for nearly a year after this episode, but the incident established his reputation for militancy.

From the very day the 1982 strike began, Thackeray and other Sena leaders blamed Datta Samant for taking labourers up a blind alley.

Yet the workers listened neither to the Sena nor to their official representative union, the Rashtriya Mill Mazdoor Sangh (RMMS). They stood by Samant.

The new chief minister declared the strike illegal and said as the RMMS was the sole representative union, talks with Samant were out of question.

A month into the strike, Thackeray said he would not allow lives of thousands of Marathi mill workers to be destroyed.

He said the Sena would launch its own 'struggle' for the workers. 'Our talks with various persons are on. The Sena is making all efforts to give justice to workers. Give us your trust and confidence.'

But so great was the workers' disillusionment with RMMS and so big the hopes generated by Samant's promises that workers thought the doctor would have his way.

The strike lingered on.

Thackeray met Chief Minister Bhonsle in April 1982 and suggested he give workers an interim raise of ₹ 50 to end the stir, but nothing came of the talks.

The 1 May deadline given by Thackeray to the government to find a solution to the issue – he had said he would not consider the Congress his friend if the matter was not sorted out by then – passed, and no end to the strike seemed to be in sight even two months after that.

The voice of Thackeray and Dattaji Salvi got shriller; now, both Samant and Congress-I were targeted. All along, the Sena chief had maintained that mill workers' problems had been exacerbated because of Samant's intransigence. Now, with friend Antulay too no longer the chief minister, the Congress-I became equally blameworthy.

In mid-August, the Sena suggested a solution. The monthly raise of ₹ 45 given by the earlier Pawar government and the sum of ₹ 30 conceded by the Union labour minister, it said, should be incorporated in the workers' salary, and ₹ 1,500 to ₹ 2,000 given as advance.

If this was not accepted, the Sena threatened, it would take a morcha to Vidhan Bhavan in September, when the state legislature session was slated to begin.

The solution was unaccepted, and the government was blamed by all parties for its inertia. Both at the state and national levels, the government refrained from intervening and preferred to wait and watch.

Thackeray now had no option but to snap ties with the Congress. Continuing to side with the Congress despite government inaction would entail huge losses for the party in the worker-dominated areas of Lalbaug, Parel, Worli and Kalachowki.

On 9 September, Thackeray held a rally at Kamgar Maidan and, dissociated his party from the Congress-I after nearly seven years.

He reiterated the strike would destroy the *Girni Kamgar* (mill worker), but the Sena would always stand behind the labourers. 'The Kamgars are Marathi, they'll be destroyed. The policemen who rebel (there had been a police strike in 1982) are Marathi. And those who fight on the border issue are Marathi. The Sena is concerned about all of them,' he stressed.

There was speculation at the time that Bhonsle would be replaced soon. Thackeray ended his address by saying the man to replace him would be Sharad Pawar.

On 28 October, when the Sena held its annual rally on the occasion of Dussehra – the festival known for crossing frontiers – the party crossed frontiers of a different kind. Lok Dal leader George Fernandes and Congress-S helmsman Sharad Pawar came on to the Sena platform that day and jointly addressed the rally. All three slammed the Congress-I and Samant and threatened action if the strike was not resolved within a week.

George Fernandes said:

Mumbai was never in such a sorry state on the auspicious day of Vijayadashmi. Circumstances not only in Maharashtra but in India have brought the three of us together. Balasaheb has played an important role in this. We, the leaders of three different parties, are going to sit and think of solutions to the crisis gripping the nation.

Pawar said:

People aren't sure if we'll stay together. But the circumstances pointed out by George demand such a unity. Go anywhere in India, you'll find the pre-poll promises given by Congress have not been fulfilled. We must overthrow this regime...

Thackeray said:

I had declared at a meeting at Sena Bhavan that I would perform a miracle on Dussehra day. I have done that. People are fed up of

Congress-I's rule. The only policy that matters to Indira Gandhi is, "How will my Rajiv grow?" ... Bal Thackeray doesn't ask for any seat of power. But I wish to guarantee that the Congress won't be in power in 1985... My friendship with Pawar is intact. When he was chief minister, he gave an unprecedented raise of ₹ 45 to workers. Now we need to arrive at a consensus.

But the promised action 'if the strike wasn't settled in a week' never came, and the strike ended only after eighteen-and-a-half months, in August 1983. The results were disastrous: large-scale retrenchment and unemployment for tens of thousands of workers.

The overwhelming majority of the textile mill workers stood behind Samant when the strike began, but this diminished to a minority as time passed.

Most workers lost heart after six months of staying off work; the strike leadership knew this but ignored it. Nearly 80 per cent of workers had believed the strike would be over in two or three months; that was not to be.

Almost 75,000 strikers, most of them sole breadwinners, lost their jobs. Instead of giving workers a bonus and wage hike, the strike caused losses in terms of jobs and wages and sapped the workers' fighting spirit.

Thackeray did not miss any opportunity to criticise Samant all through the latter's career and often referred to him as a *keed* (worm). Even after Samant was sprayed with bullets near his Chembur residence on 16 January 1997, the Sena leader's language for him remained the same. Addressing a rally at Shivaji Park in February 1997, Thackeray, rubbishing the demand for dismissal of the then Sena-BJP government in the wake of Samant's killing, said: 'They say the neta of the workers is dead. But he died because of his karma.'

18
SWAYING TO THE SOCIALIST SONG

he sluggish wandering of the Shiv Sena wasn't to end
too soon after the Congress cover had been cast away.
It continued to meander in the morass of uncertainty till
1984, going this way and that and getting nowhere.

In this period of incertitude, Bal Thackeray had a fleeting flirtation
with socialism.

Nilkanth Khadilkar, editor of the largest-selling Marathi daily
Nava Kaal, and a friend of Thackeray's, visited the Soviet Union
in 1983. On his return, he wrote a book *Practical Socialism*, based
on his experiences in the USSR and the application of socialist
principles there. He mentioned how the introduction of a permit
system had provided an effective solution to the problem of outsider
influx in Moscow.

Thackeray, eager to stop the inflow of outsiders into Mumbai, found
the idea of a permit system fantastic and was attracted to socialism.

Khadilkar recounts:

> When I put forward the concept of practical socialism, Balasaheb
> liked it so much that he accepted it for the Shiv Sena. He called
> his associates and told them he was going to proclaim it as the Sena
> ideology at the Dussehra rally. He said even if all of them deserted
> him, he would embrace the ideology alone. And he enthusiastically
> launched a campaign for practical socialism. But after a few months,
> he called me and said, "It's not possible to implement this ideology
> unless one is in power. At the Dussehra rally, I'm going to begin the
> fight for Hindutva. Can't this idea be presented as Hindu socialism?"

In early 1984 (21 January), Thackeray, in the grip of socialism,
praised it at the Sena's *adhiveshan* (convention) held at Savarkar
Smarak, Dadar.

Thackeray had, on this occasion, invited the guru of Indian Communists, S.A. Dange, to speak to Sainiks. He and Dange had been bitter political adversaries, but their respect for one another had been considerable, and each acknowledged the power of the other to mobilise masses. Dange responded with alacrity.

Bani Deshpande, Dange's son-in-law, who was present at the convention, told me:

> Seven thousand Shiv Sena delegates were present. And when Dange addressed them, such was the response he got that everyone was left to wonder who the real leader of the delegates was – Dange or Thackeray. I'm sure even Bal must have been surprised. Every now and then, Dange's words received tumultuous applause from the Sainiks. They had all heard him during the Samyukta Maharashtra movement. They were the same Marathi youngsters who felt and fought for Samyukta Maharashtra, and they were getting to hear one of the stalwarts of that movement again. They weren't Dange's enemies, it was just that they'd gone away from him.[107]

Thackeray had also invited trade union leader S.R. Kulkarni and D.V. Deshpande, an intellectual, to speak on 'Expectations from the Shiv Sena.'

Criticising all three the day after they had spoken, the Sena chief said: 'Nobody told us where we went wrong or guided us properly. They only tried to prove how clever they were. Dange didn't point out our mistakes, didn't show us the direction of revolution. He merely displayed arrogance by suggesting the Sena has no theory, and said an organisation can't survive without a theory. Then how has our organisation survived for 18 years? And how is it that despite a theory, your organisation is finished? We invited them and gave them an opportunity. But they only showed their extra-smartness.'

Thackeray, though, retains his admiration for the Communist leader, especially for his oratory. 'There was mischievousness in Dange's talk,' he says. 'And from the way he spoke you could also see how studious he was. The labour movement in Mumbai grew mainly due to his oratorical skills. Of course, he didn't give anything to the labourers, but on the basis of his oratory, he gave them the strength to fight'.[108]

19

OVER TO HINDUTVA,
AND BACK TO BHIWANDI

After having vacillated for some time, the Shiv Sena made a definitive shift to Hindutva in 1984. Its Hindutva appeal became salient in April and May 1984, when riots erupted in Bhiwandi, but when Thackeray first elucidated his idea of Hindu nationalism in January that year, it went largely unnoticed. Addressing a rally at Shivaji Park on 22 January, Thackeray mooted the idea of a confederation of Hindu organisations, the *Hindu Mahasangh*, and 'unveiled' a three-point programme:

> First, Muslims should, like Hindus, adhere to the one-marriage rule and resort to family planning. Because this was not done, the population of Muslims in India has risen from 2.5 crore in 1947 to 14 crore. Second, they should extend support to the ban on cow slaughter. Third, they should accept this is a Hindu Rashtra.

> Only those Muslims willing to accept these things have the right to stay in Hindustan. I do not acknowledge the term Bharat Rashtra. It has been coined to keep everyone happy and get votes. According to me, he who lives in Hindustan is a Hindu. I have decided to bring all Hindu organisations together and create a Hindu Rashtra Fauj. This fauj will be formed in February, and we will have 500 Hindu missionaries working to spread it. I have already spoken to organisations like the Patit Pawan, Arya Samaj and Hindu Ekta about this. All Hindu bodies should gather under one flag to root out Muslim fanaticism.

The call for a *Mahasangh* received no response from any major Hindu group.

Thackeray's second Hindutva posturing came in April that year, after Kashmiri militancy had claimed its first victim. This time round, he was not just heard, but a distorted version of his speech was disseminated, and the result was a riot.

Early in February, Ravindra Mhatre, assistant commissioner at the Indian High Commission in Birmingham, was kidnapped and shot by a group called the Kashmir Liberation Army (KLA), allegedly in retaliation for a crackdown on extremist outfits in Kashmir. The perception in India was that Pakistan was not an innocent bystander in all of this.

Reacting to Mhatre's assassination, Thackeray said at a rally at Girgaum Chowpatty on 21 April:

> If Indira Gandhi gives Khalistan to the terrorists, we won't forgive her. Terrorists in Punjab have the support of Pakistan and America. And as Bhindranwale has the blessings of Indira Gandhi, Hindus in Punjab have no one for them… All the people here should live as Hindus. Today, the number of Muslims in India has gone up from 2.5 crore to 14 crore. But Indira Gandhi still bestows favours on Muslims because they're a minority. If, by virtue of being a minority, they are going to be pampered in future, our Hindu Mahasangh will perform the necessary operation to weed out this cancer. All Hindus should gather under the saffron of the Mahasangh. Also, I reiterate, the Shivaji Jayanti procession in Bhiwandi will take place this year under any circumstances.

A ban had been imposed on the Shivaji Jayanti procession in Bhiwandi after the 1970 riots, and it had stayed in place for eleven years. The state lifted the ban in 1982, and the procession went off peacefully in subsequent years.

But Bhiwandi's communal troubles erupted again, soon. Though many felt Thackeray's language at Chowpatty was provocative enough to ferment trouble, some Urdu newspapers and magazines (among them *Bhiwandi News* and *Akhbar-E-Alam*) reported that he had made derogatory remarks against Prophet Mohammed, something he had not done. Some pamphlets too were distributed among Muslims to spread the word.

Muslims in Parbhani, 450 km from Mumbai, took out a morcha to the zilla parishad office on 11 May to register their protest against the 'insult'. It is rumoured that in this morcha, Congress MLA A.R. Khan publicly placed a garland of chappals around a photograph of Bal Thackeray.

Furious, Shiv Sainiks called a bandh in Parel in Mumbai on 17 May. Boards were put up at street corners and outside Sena shakhas across the city condemning the act. The next day, a bandh was called in Girgaum.

Some self-styled leaders of the Muslim community tried to exploit the situation, and Issa Azmi, editor of *Bhiwandi News* which had a good circulation in the communally sensitive township, wrote of how he was forming the Bharatiya Muslim Sena to give a 'befitting reply to Thackeray's remarks' and exhorted Muslims to avenge the insult to their Prophet.

On 17 May, when a group of Muslims in Bhiwandi's Ghunghat Nagar tried to plant a green flag higher than the saffron one placed atop a nearby Shiv Sena shakha, an altercation took place between youths of the two communities. And violence erupted.

Six persons, including two SRP jawans, were stabbed to death, two persons shot, and more than 100 injured till late evening. Hotels, shops and stalls were torched, and stones hurled at people's homes. Chief Minister Vasantdada Patil issued shoot-on-sight orders, but when that did not help, the Army was called in.

Curfew was imposed in Bhiwandi at 6 am the next day, but the conflagration spread to Mumbai after a Shiv Sena office in Govandi was burnt by a mob returning from a masjid. Police had to fire 8 rounds to stem the frenzy in Govandi, and clashes erupted between Hindus and Muslims in several other areas of the city. Stone-throwing incidents at Sion and Musafirkhana near Crawford Market forced police to lathi-charge mobs. Vegetables at Dadar market were destroyed by a group of 25 youths; a place of worship was stoned in Worli; Loha Bhavan at Karnak Bunder was attacked, and two huts were burnt near Ganeshpuri.

In all, 424 persons were arrested in Mumbai, and 300 in Bhiwandi the same day.

On 19 May, a house at Anur Fata outside Bhiwandi was torched, all 20 members of the family staying there burnt alive, and members of one community targeted homes of the other.

Hundreds were rendered homeless, and the violence spread to Thane and Kalyan, where five persons were stabbed to death.

In Mumbai's Nagpada, a sub-inspector, N. Gokhale, and a constable, Gulam, were killed by a mob; a police chowky was torched at Maulana Shaukat Ali Road, and cops were stoned by a mob near Null Bazaar. A police van was attacked at Musafirkhana, and seven policemen injured. At Kherwadi, police opened fire on rioters: 4 were killed, 3 hurt. Curfew was clamped in Nagpada, Dongri, Pydhonie, VP Road and Crawford Market late evening.

The chief minister said that he had received complaints that Thackeray had incited communal sentiments, and that he would look into them, and the Congress Minority Front chief, Javed Khan, demanded the Sena chief's arrest.

There was, however, no let-up in violence over the next five days, despite police commissioner Julio Ribeiro's statement on 21 May that reports of Thackeray's speech carried by Urdu papers were 'utterly false'. Instead, violence broke out in hitherto peaceful areas such as Girgaum and Kurla. Kherwadi in Bandra was worst-hit, with shops, buses and rickshaws torched and police having to open fire repeatedly. Eighteen incidents of stabbing were reported from the vicinity of JJ Hospital in a day.

The Army had to be called in, and nine areas of Mumbai had to be placed under curfew.

By 25 May, when both Bhiwandi and Mumbai limped back to normalcy, the death toll was 256. The area-wise toll: Bhiwandi-109, Mumbai-87, Thane and Thane rural-52, and Kalyan-10.

Prime Minister Indira Gandhi called the riot 'a blot on the history of India'.

A case was also registered against Thackeray for making an inflammatory speech at Chowpatty, but Police Commissioner Ribeiro said police had recorded that speech, and Thackeray had not been guilty of slander.

A couple of months later, Mumbai-based smugglers Haji Mastan, Karim Lala and 15 others were arrested under the National Security Act, and Ribeiro said their role in supplying Molotov cocktails, acid bulbs and other explosives to rioters in Bhiwandi and Mumbai had been confirmed.

Mastan and Lala were freed soon. Their release, and the fact that many Sainiks were still in prison for rioting, irked Thackeray. In an interview to *Hindustan Samachar*, he said: 'Ask Police Commissioner

Ribeiro, who arrested these smugglers and made loud proclamations about the action to be taken against them, how they were released. I smell something fishy. Their release could have been possible only if crores of rupees had changed hands.'

Ribeiro, criticising the Sena's 'goondaism and intimidatory tactics', shot back: 'Whose rule exists in Mumbai? That of the government or the Shiv Sena?'

Thackeray replied: 'If he wants to know, I'll show him how the Sena rules here. Then he will have no option but to come to us to save his job.'

When the issue of the riots was raised by BJP leader Jaswant Singh in the Rajya Sabha, Union Minister of State for Home P. Venkat Subbaiah told the House the violence was the result of misleading and inflammatory appeals made by the Shiv Sena, the Hindu Mahasabha and Urdu dailies.

The rioting was indeed horrible, but it brought the Shiv Sena, direction less for a while, back into the spotlight.

Tribute to Indira Gandhi

The assassination of Prime Minister Indira Gandhi on 31 October 1984, shocked and saddened Bal Thackeray. He had more than just sneaking admiration for her. He had supported the Emergency, and had, not too infrequently in his speeches, spoken of her firmness, her decision-making ability, and above all, her offer of a gubernatorial post to him. '*Balasaheb se kehna, unko main unche se uncha pad de dungi*' (Tell Balasaheb, I will give him the highest post), was her message he claimed to have received many times from her associates. He said he had turned it down because 'the post of Sena chief was the highest one could get on earth.'

He took to criticising her after the Sena snapped its ties with the Congress in 1982, but her death again brought to the fore the veneration. The editorial he wrote in *Marmik* in the aftermath of Indira's assassination is remarkable for the extraordinary praise he showered upon her. Headlined '*Rakshakach bhakshak banle*' (Defenders have turned destroyers), it said:

Indiraji is no more! Someone poured the news into our ears, and it felt as though the mind was stung at once by innumerable ants...

We initially did not believe it. Because we believed that even if Satan stepped into India – where, from time immemorial, woman has been revered as Mother – he wouldn't be able to perform the evil deed of killing a woman. But the belief was shattered. Humanitarianism, and humanity, were shattered... A demon born as a human cruelly and fatally attacked a woman. Indiraji had fallen a victim to the assault. She had prepared herself for it, but the national consciousness wasn't prepared to take the disaster... It was impossible for anyone to make sense of the incident, because the barbaric attack had been carried out by Indiraji's own bodyguards. The defender had turned destroyer! The person to whom Indiraji had assigned the job of providing her security proved treacherous. How did the bodyguard, who, in the 10-12 years of his proximity to Indiraji, had seen her greatness from close quarters, kill her? How was it possible for him to perform the inhuman act of killing the Maha-Mata, before whom even leading politicians, strategists and diplomats of the world would bend respectfully?

We do not believe in crying. But how long do we hold back our emotions? Life is the licence given by death to man. When this licence expires, everyone has to go... We can't hold back our tears because Indiraji left before that period was over... She has become immortal!... She faced death boldly. She did not fear death; death feared her. Finally, he attacked her like a coward. But Indiraji has climbed the steps of heaven with the courage of Yuddhistira. The honour that Yuddhistira didn't get was had by Indiraji. When he went to heaven, 105 Kauravas and Pandavas from this Mahabharat bid Yuddhistira goodbye. But when Indiraji ascended to heaven, 105 countries, along with this Mahabharat, bid her farewell with tears. Even the Gods musn't have had such honour when they went to heaven... But even if we envy heaven, we won't get Indiraji back. Never will there be another Indira. Such a personality is born once in ages. In future, there will be Margaret Thatchers and Golda Meirs, but there won't be an Indira, because she was a jewel of the earth, a gift of the Gods. She was born in the great Bharat, but she belonged to the world... There was no country on earth which was not made holy by the touch of her feet... She influenced the world. And gave it light. The world also showered its love on her. Politics for her was a journey. It wasn't her goal. As she chose Bharat as her vehicle for that journey, this country acquired the importance of Jayadratha. This Rath was converted into Chaitanya Rath. This country was faced with endless problems, but Indiraji never allowed the wheels of the Rath to be trapped in the earth. Fearlessly, she managed the nation's affairs. She loved every human being in this nation ... No corner of this country was left untouched by her sense of humanity.

The anti-Sikh violence that convulsed New Delhi following her assassination did not reach Mumbai. Thackeray has claimed he was complimented by then President Zail Singh for keeping the city quiet:

> When Zail Singh came to Mumbai after the anti-Sikh riots, he invited me to Raj Bhavan. Dattaji Nalavade accompanied me there. The president told me: "Sikhs in Mumbai have remained safe because of you. If only you had given a call, similar demonstrations, and the same frenzy, would have been enacted here. You didn't do anything of the sort".[109]

The Sena's critics said this was more a statement about the Sena's potential to create trouble than anything else, but Thackeray saw it as genuine appreciation which, 'inexplicably, till date, has not been published by any newspaper'.

20

JOINING HANDS WITH THE BJP

The Shiv Sena and BJP formed an alliance for the first time for the 1984 Lok Sabha elections called after Indira Gandhi's assassination. Efforts had been made in 1971 to fashion an alliance but had failed. This time, too, the BJP tried to forge a tie-up with the Janata Party till the day of filing nominations, and only after the negotiations derailed did talks with the Sena gain momentum.

They bore fruit mainly due to the efforts of BJP leader Pramod Mahajan. He was the chief architect of the tie-up, arguing that the BJP would benefit from a pact with the Sena. He stuck to his position despite opposition from within his party, and succeeded.

It was decided the Sena would fight two seats in Mumbai – south-central and north-central Mumbai – while the remaining four would be contested by BJP. In the rest of Maharashtra, the Sena would not put up any candidates but support those of the BJP.

In an article in *Saamna*, Mahajan recalled the early days, when he did the rounds of Thackeray's residence for negotiations:

> I wasn't the first person from Jan Sangh to extend the hand of friendship to Thackeray. He had taken up the cause of Hindutva. I told him: a Hindu votes as a Maratha, Mali, Dalit, Marwari, and as Brahmin, but never as a Hindu. How will our politics be successful? Without hesitation, he replied: "When I started the Shiv Sena, people said the same thing – that the Marathi *manoos* doesn't vote as a Marathi. But I proved this wrong. You'll see, I will make Hindus vote as Hindus." I hesitated to believe what he said. He proved his word in just five years.[110]

Thackeray took up cudgels on the BJP's behalf during the poll campaign.

Rajiv Gandhi's swearing-in smacked of dynastic succession, he noted, and added: 'After Indira, Rajiv, and after Rajiv, Rahul. Is the prime minister's seat a *paan-beedi* shop, that after the father dies, the son takes over?'

Along with A.B. Vajpayee, Thackeray held several meetings in Mumbai and suggested a Hindutva wave was about to sweep India. But the electorate weren't ready to buy the Hindutva rhetoric yet.

Rajiv got a mandate unprecented in independent India's history. The Congress-I got over 400 seats, and between them, the four national opposition parties had 19 seats. Maharashtra had played a vital role in creating this one-sided Parliament. Out of the state's 48 seats, the Congress-I had won 43.

The BJP could not win even one of the 20 seats it contested, and the Sena lost both its seats to the Congress.

The BJP's hopes in Maharashtra, pumped up by the alliance, had not been fulfilled. Many BJP leaders attributed the failure in Maharashtra on the tie-up with a 'disreputable' outfit like the Shiv Sena. Leading the pack was lawyer Ram Jethmalani.

The BJP's strength in the state had always been insignificant. Its highest tally in the Assembly polls had been 14, and in the Lok Sabha elections its high watermark was zero.

Still, the party's 'post-poll introspection session' cast all blame on the Sena, and the BJP decided to keep a distance from the Sena in the Vidhan Sabha elections scheduled for March 1985.

The BJP could not fight the polls on its own steam, so its leaders got locked in negotiations with Congress-S leader Sharad Pawar, who was trying to forge a front against Congress-I. The Janata Party and Left parties agreed to join this front, called the Purogami Lokshahi Aghadi (PULOD). The BJP too joined in. The Sena was kept away even from the process of negotiations.

Mrinal Gore, Janata Party leader in Mumbai, and the PULOD's Left constituents abhorred the saffron outfit.

Even when Thackeray expressed his willingness to join the front and said the task of seat arrangement should be left to Pawar, the latter, despite his friendship with Thackeray refused to respond.

Mahajan disagreed with the decision to keep the Sena out and, despite Gore and the Left's opposition, did not give up his efforts to rope the party in even after seat-sharing among front constituents was almost over.

He suggested a way out to Pawar: PULOD could have an understanding with the Sena in the same manner Antulay had in 1980. The Sena wouldn't contest any seats but support the front. The front, in return, would give it a few seats in the Council.

Pawar and Mahajan dashed off to Thackeray's Bandra residence to discuss this idea, but by then it was late. The Sena chief had already declared names of many Sena candidates, and he told the two he could not backtrack.

The Sena bagged a solitary seat in the Vidhan Sabha elections, its only winning candidate being Chhagan Bhujbal. The Congress-I got 162 seats, the Congress-S 54, the Janata Party 20, the BJP 16, and the PWP thirteen.

A young Bal Thackeray at work, before he had formed the Shiv Sena. Thackeray said a cartoonist needed to have intimate knowledge of human anatomy in order to be good.

Thackeray addressing a Shiv Sena rally in the 1960s, with the Sena symbol, a growling tiger, in the background.

Shiv Sena
chief Bal
Thackeray
tries his hand
at a game of
Cricket.

Bal Thackeray
with Meenatai and
Kishore Kumar.

By using the name of Chhatrapati Shivaji, Thackeray evoked the memory of the Maratha warrior tradition and thereby converted the Shiv Sena into a militant outfit.

One of Bal Thackeray's cartoons in the *Free Press Journal* on the duplicitous role of colonial rulers. He drew many cartoons on international affairs at the *FPJ*, depicting personalities such as Churchill, Hitler, Stalin, Roosevelt and Marshal Tito of Yugoslavia.

The Thackeray family: (Standing from L to R) Jaidev (Thackeray's estranged son), his wife Smita (since separated), Madhavi (wife of Thackeray's eldest son Bindumadhav), Bindumadhav, Uddhav and Rashmi (Uddhav's wife).
(Seated) Bindumadhav's children Neha and Nihar, Bal Thackeray, Uddhav's son Aditya, Jaidev's son Rahul and Meenatai Thackeray.

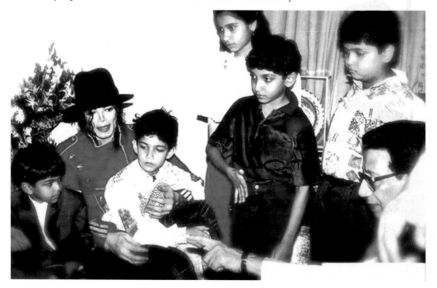

Thackeray and his grandchildren with Michael Jackson at the Thackerays' residence, Matoshree, in 1996.

Bhendi Bazaar's Muslims meet Bal Thackeray at Matoshree, after his wife Meenatai Thackeray's demise.

Thackeray being taught the tricks of the trade by his son, Uddhav, who is an avid photographer.

Thackeray and Amitabh Bachchan have been close friends. After Amitabh was injured on the sets of *Coolie* in Bangalore in 1982, it was a Shiv Sena ambulance which took him from the Mumbai airport to Breach Candy Hospital.

Another close friend, Dilip Kumar (with Hollywood action hero Steven Seagal to his left). Kumar and Thackeray would have '*chana* and beer' on the terrace of Matoshree.

With Anna Hazare, who had carried out an agitation against ministers in the Sena–BJP government in Maharashtra.

With Pranab Mukherjee, whom he supported in the 2012 presidential polls, going against the NDA nominee P.A. Sangma.

With nephew Raj, who quit the Shiv Sena in 2005 and formed his own party, the MNS. Raj has been among the people closest to Thackeray, and could not hold back his tears at his funeral at Shivaji Park.

With Lata Mangeshkar and Madhuri Dixit at a function on the occasion of Lata's father Dinanath Mangeshkar's 70th death anniversary in April 2012. In the aftermath of Bal Thackeray's death, Lata said that Maharashtra had lost a father figure.

21

MUMBAI POLLS 1985:
A FRESH LEASE OF LIFE

The defeats in the Lok Sabha and Vidhan Sabha elections were a severe setback to the Shiv Sena. Still, they weren't enfeebling in the extreme, because the party was restricted to Mumbai and Thane, and its aspirations to parliamentary and legislative representation were limited. The Sena had taken up the Hindutva plank to enlarge its base, but getting ten Vidhan Sabha seats and, at the most, five Lok Sabha seats was still its highest goal. After all, the party was non-existent outside Mumbai, Thane and a part of the Konkan coastline region.

Concrete action was initiated to spread the party's wings all over Maharashtra towards the end of 1985, but in the first half of the year, the most important thing for the Sena was the approaching BMC polls.

A defeat in the civic elections, scheduled for 25 April, would have a crippling effect on an outfit which had just climbed out of a rut.

But if the Sena had any doubts about its chances at the BMC polls, they were dispelled by its political opponent, Chief Minister Vasantdada Patil.

Factional fighting was rampant in the Congress-I, and the battle between BPCC and MPCC was ugly. To checkmate BPCC Chief Murli Deora, Patil helped spread a rumour that the Centre was 'planning' to make Mumbai centrally administered as it was India's richest city.

But by doing this, he literally handed the BMC to the Sena.

Any such suggestion of central administration was anathema to the Sena and also to a majority of Marathi-speaking voters, for whom the inclusion of Mumbai in Maharashtra was an emotive issue.

Chief Minister Patil went a step further and roused Marathi emotions by remarking that 'Mumbai may be in Maharashtra, but I don't see Maharashtra anywhere in Mumbai.'

The Sena had got its issue for the BMC polls.

No alliance was struck with the BJP, and Sena candidates fanned out across the city's constituencies with 'Marathi Mumbai' as their manifesto. The electorate was reminded that it was the Congress, which had made such conspiratorial moves possible. If voters voted for Congress, they'd give their consent for a Mumbai cut off from Maharashtra; if they voted for Sena, they were told, Mumbai could never be severed from the Marathi state.

The chief minister later tried to retract his statement, but the bogey of 'Maharashtra without Mumbai' had already drowned out other issues.

The Sena received huge support: it won 74 seats out of the 139 it contested. The second highest tally was the Congress-I's: all 170 seats fought, just 37 won. The PULOD, which included only Congress-S and Janata Party this time, failed miserably. The Congress-S got 9 of 63 seats contested, and the Janata, which earlier had 38 seats and had now put up 102 candidates, returned only 10 corporators. The BJP, which had fought 136 seats, won 13.

The Sena bird, which had slowly trudged forward and reached pre-lift-off speed, had taken flight. And its ambitions had acquired wings.

The Shah Bano controversy

Before the Sena entered the rural areas, the Shah Bano controversy gave it a chance to sharpen its Hindutva plank.

When the Muslim Personal Law Board (MPLB) objected to the Supreme Court judgement granting maintenance to Shah Bano[111] and rallies were held across India asking the Centre to undo the ruling by introducing a bill in Parliament, the Sena and BJP condemned this demand and resolved to extend all help to Muslim women in their cause for justice.

However, Muslim protests continued, even in Maharashtra. Nearly 35,000 Muslim women attended a conference in Malegaon and passed a resolution condemning the Supreme Court judgement. A meeting was organised by the Bhiwandi Muslim Personal Law Action Committee (Women) on 30 September to protest the ruling. On

13 October, a similar meeting was held by the Maharashtra Action Committee (Women's wing) of the All India Muslim Law Board in Mumbai to support Muslim personal law.

By now, a wave of anger was sweeping across progressive sections of Muslim society, but its fury wasn't half as great as that of the fundamentalist surge.

As Shariat was declared superior to the Indian Constitution and Indian laws, the Shiv Sena sent out warning signals to Hindus and underlined the so-called danger posed to the integrity of India.

Remarking that an 'Islamic bomb' was hanging over India's head, Bal Thackeray wrote in *Marmik:*

> Every nation has only one law. But in our country, laws and restrictions are for Hindus and all concessions are for Muslims. How long will we tolerate this? Some concessions can be given to minorities, but if they obstruct national interest and human rights, they must be withdrawn...[112]

After Syed Shahabuddin declared 'I do not consider the Government of India, the Parliament and the Supreme Court as competent to interpret the scriptures which lay down the essentials of Islam,'[113] the Sena chief's language grew more vitriolic. Now he did not just point to an Islamic bomb; he demanded that those who did not accept the Constitution be hanged.

Even as the protests against the Supreme Court ruling grew fiercer, Thackeray intensified his crusade. He wrote:

> Our politicians are mum because they want Muslim votes. Only Muslims are talking... Muslims in India can say "Mussalman" in every sentence, but Hindus can't utter the word "Hindu".
> Tomorrow Hindustan may be declared the largest Muslim country... What is Supreme in this nation? The Court, Parliament, or the Muslims of Bhendi Bazaar?[114]

In an interview to Marathi daily *Loksatta*, Thackeray was defiantly uncool.

> The Muslim demonstration was provocative. They were shouting slogans like "We got Pakistan easily, now we will seize Hindustan". These slogans remind us of pre-Partition days. We have gulped

the poison of Partition, we do not want civil war. There are large numbers of Muslims true to our country, but the handful of communal Muslims should be checked... All true patriotic Muslims must come forward to work for this... There might be many religions in the country, but there must be one Constitution, and one law applicable to all... Are there different laws applicable to Muslims in Russia or America?

22

INROADS INTO RURAL AREAS

So long as the Shiv Sena's agenda was restricted to an aggressive Maharashtrianism, there was no way it could go beyond Mumbai, Thane and, perhaps, Pune, to a limited extent, because the natives-versus-migrants issue was limited to these areas. In other parts of the state, Marathi-speaking people were in a comfortable majority, so the Marathi plank would not work there.

Having reached a saturation point in Mumbai and Thane, however, the Sena was feeling the need to expand its base. That was the reason it took up Hindutva in 1984-85. In the second half of 1985, that is, in the wake of attention it had gathered with its stand on the Shah Bano controversy, the Sena made its first foray beyond its metropolitan confines.

It organised its second statewide convention in November 1985 at Mahad, at the base of Fort Raigad, capital of Shivaji's kingdom – the heart of the Konkan region. Konkan had been chosen first for this experiment in rural areas because the region has deep socio-economic links with Mumbai, and most of Mumbai's mill workers come from here. So, the party's logic went, this part of the state, where families belonging to Mumbai workers knew more about the Sena than in other rural areas, should be tapped before venturing elsewhere.

The rallying cry for the *adhiveshan* was a martial *Aata Ghod-Daud Maharashtrat* (Now we go with a gallop into Maharashtra), and the days preceding the convention saw such drama that rural Maharashtra had to take notice of the Sena.

All the action revolved around the Maharashtra-Karnataka border issue, and it was in most part engineered by the newly-appointed mayor of Mumbai, Chhagan Bhujbal.

The Sena chose to organise a satyagraha in Belgaum on the border issue a few days before its Mahad convention, and it met with a rough response from Karnataka police. The Sena won sympathy from Marathi people across Maharashtra.

Addressing the convention, Thackeray vowed he wouldn't stop till the whole of Maharashtra had been conquered, and to lay the groundwork for such a conquest, the Sena appointed samparka pramukhs (communications chiefs) in all districts of the state.

The samparka pramukhs set themselves to the task promptly along with Bhujbal.

In mid-1986, still early days of the Sena's march into the hinterland, the party, in association with Congress-S and Janata Party, decided to organise another agitation on the border issue. Bhujbal's unique show of aggression in Belgaum this time worked as a publicity strategy for the party.

To circumvent the ban on entry into Belgaum, Bhujbal wore a disguise and gatecrashed into the border township with all the nonchalance of a Sainik flouting laid-down rules. Posing as one Mohd Iqbal Sheikh, he flew to Panaji and from there drove to Belgaum, also ensuring that there was a lensman around to record his most dramatic role for posterity. Pictures of a disguised Bhujbal, who had cocked a snook at authorities in Karnataka, were splashed in newspapers across Maharashtra, and his peculiar brand of dynamism became the subject of much curiosity.

Enjoying the confidence of Sena's lower ranks, Bhujbal marched into three of the state's four major regions: the Konkan, Northern Maharashtra and Marathwada (the fourth is Vidarbha).

Here was an earthy politician with mass rapport and good links with the rank and file of the Sena. His candour, by way of which he sought to wipe out the 'only-urban' image of the Sena, impressed them:

> The toiling farmers of rural areas need not be baffled when they look at Mumbai. Mumbai belongs to all of Maharashtra. Mumbaikars get water from the interiors of Maharashtra, they get vegetables from rural areas, and the electricity obtained by Mumbai also comes from other parts of the state. If the rest of Maharashtra doesn't supply all this to Mumbai, the city will collapse. Isn't this enough to prove Mumbai belongs to the whole of Maharashtra?

Running riot

When the Babri Masjid–Ram Janmabhoomi issue was dragged out of obscurity in 1986, the Sena, along with BJP, decided to organise a Rath Yatra in Nashik, because Nashik and Panchavati had a 'special significance' as 'Ram Dharti' (Ram, Sita and Laxman are believed to have stayed in Panchavati). They insisted the procession be allowed to pass through Muslim-dominated areas, but expecting communal trouble, the deputy superintendent of police refused permission.

The procession was nevertheless held on Gudi Padwa Day, which marks the Maharashtrian New Year, and Bhujbal defied the police ban by wearing a frame containing the image of Ram around his neck and leading the yatra.

The next major event in the town was to be the Shiv Jayanti procession on 10 May 1986. Two days before Shiv Jayanti, police authorities called a meeting of the Peace Committee, in which the Sena's local head Rajendra Bagul, members of the RSS, BJP, Congress-I and the Hindu Ekta Aandolan were present, along with some prominent Muslims. It was then decided the procession would pass through Muslim localities and be welcomed by Muslims with *sherbat* and cold water. Eventually, the only greetings exchanged by Hindus and Muslims turned out to be provocative slogans, and large-scale rioting resulted.

The police force proved insufficient, and only when reinforcements arrived could things be brought under control. Four Muslims and three Hindus lost their lives.

The same day, Hindu-Muslim clashes took place in Nanded (Marathwada), a town with a population of two lakh, of which nearly 70,000 were Muslims. Here too, provocative slogans were shouted when the Shiv Jayanti procession went past two mosques. Rioting began after the procession ended. Almost 40 shops, belonging to either community, were torched. One state transport bus and a municipal truck were also burnt, and two cops were stabbed.

The disturbances soon spread to Umapur village in Beed district and Aurangabad.

In Panvel too, the fire of communal frenzy burst forth on Shiv Jayanti day.

No trouble was expected in the procession by locals and law-enforcing authorities and the bandobast wasn't great either. But stones were thrown on the procession when it reached a narrow junction known as Muslim Naka Masjid. As the people leading the procession had already walked past the junction when the stone-throwing started, panic spread and participants in the march started running helter-skelter. A 22-year-old Hindu boy, who entered the side-lanes, was struck with a sword and somehow managed to walk back to the Naka, profusely bleeding. (He later succumbed to his injuries in a Mumbai hospital). The sight caused anger, and two Muslims were stabbed to death in the area the same evening.

In other instances of trouble too, the Sena assumed charge of the situation, pushing other parties to the background. One day after the murder of General A.S. Vaidya by Sikh terrorists at Pune in August 1986, an all-party committee called for a Pune bandh and organised a protest march. The Sena soon took control of the march and allegedly began shouting communal slogans.

Pawar games clear Sena's path
Bhujbal's whirlwind campaigning no doubt took the Sena to the interiors of Maharashtra, but the path for its rapid growth in rural areas was cleared by Pawar himself.

Popular opinion in Maharashtra had started swinging against the Congress from 1967, and if the percentage of votes secured by all opposition parties in successive Lok Sabha and Vidhan Sabha elections were to be taken together, it was evident that the Congress had managed to entrench itself in the seat of power chiefly because of a fragmented opposition.

The dominance of the Maratha-Kunbi caste was established in the Congress by Yashwantrao Chavan. However, it would be wrong to suggest that the Congress retained its grip on the state mainly because of the unity of various Maratha leaders and the solidarity shown by the Maratha-Kunbi caste with it. The politics of the Communist Party, the Peasants and Workers Party, the Lal Nishan or the Socialist Party had similarly been centered around the Maratha-Kunbi caste and the Bahujan Samaj. So not just the Congress, almost all parties in Maharashtra focused their politics on the same caste.

As the Congress was in power, it obtained greater support of the Maratha community and worked to further politicise caste affiliations. The Congress was also adept at bringing upcoming opposition leaders and workers into its fold, thus taking the wind out of the Opposition's sails from time to time. This was one of the reasons for the Congress' success and opposition parties' failure.

But among the Maratha-Kunbis too, disillusionment had gradually set in. They could see dynastic rule all around: the Patils of Sangli, the Naiks of Pusad, the Hires of Nashik, the Deshmukhs of Latur, the Mohite-Patils of Malshiras, and the Chavans of Nanded. And they knew how families ruled: the father as MLA, the son as chairman of a sugar factory, the brother as zilla parishad president, and sisters and wives as chairpersons of district banks.

Power was not with the caste, it was with feudal lords. And all those who were not part of the lords' vested interests, be they Maratha-Kunbis or other members of the Bahujan Samaj, were ordinary ryots.

So long as Congress protected the interests of the Bahujan Samaj, the latter had remained loyal to it. But after 1970, when feudalism became rampant, the Bahujan Samaj started looking for an alternative.

It tried the Janata Party in 1978, but the alternative proved nonviable. The first viable alternative was provided by Pawar after he left Congress and formed the PULOD.

Young, dynamic and ambitious activists, for whom the doors of the Congress had been slammed shut, found an opening in the form of his Congress-S and, by extension, PULOD. People upset with the high-handedness of local Congress satraps in sugar factories, credit societies, banks, the marketplace – just about everywhere – found in Pawar a leader they could relate to. Unlike the BJP and Janata Party leaders, he did not have an urban image. He was very much a man of rural Maharashtra. When he appealed to people to overthrow the Congress regime, Marathi people in rural areas gave him a good response. The 1980 and 1985 poll results showed that an alternative to the Congress had indeed emerged.

Pawar, too, then played Maratha politics, yet political workers belonging to all castes gathered around him.

But then he could not stay out of power for long. One-and-a-half years after becoming leader of Opposition, Pawar went back to the Congress-I in the last lap of 1986. Young activists nurtured by him, who looked at him with hope, got the shock of their lives.

Pawar had joined the same Congress, and courted the same Gandhi dynasty, which he had reviled and asked so many young activists across the state to fight. The activists of Congress-S did not know where to look. Nor did the rural populace, who had grown to support Pawar's front because they felt it formed a real alternative to the Congress.

Weren't there other opposition parties to make up for this loss? The Janata Party and the BJP didn't have any rural moorings, and the PWP had only a few pockets of strength in Raigad district. What was more, the leadership of the BJP, Janata Party and PWP had been riding piggyback on Pawar's party in rural Maharashtra. In the absence of Pawar, none had the confidence or credibility to portray itself as the sole alternative to the Congress. Pawar's decision to rejoin Congress shattered these parties and left a void in the state's politics.

Into this void stepped the Shiv Sena.

Target No. 1: Conquering the enemy's turf: Marathwada

The stunts of Bhujbal and the violence in Nanded, Nashik and Panvel had made the rural masses take note of the new 'Sena of Hindus' at a time when the majority community was feeling uneasy owing to the situation in Punjab and the overturning of the Supreme Court judgement in the Shah Bano case. The Rajiv Gandhi government's introduction of the Muslim Women (Protection of Rights on Divorce) Bill, perceived as a sellout to obscurantists, further helped the party gain political capital especially in the Marathwada region, where it had decided to concentrate immediately after its *adhiveshan* in the Konkan.

Marathwada, comprising seven districts – Aurangabad, Osmanabad, Beed, Parbhani, Nanded, Jalna and Latur – forms the heartland of Maharashtra. The region was the cradle of the Marathi language in medieval times: the saint-poet Dnyaneshwar and Eknath hailed from Paithan, Samartha Ramdas from Jamb, and Mukundraj and Dasopant from Ambejogai.

These saint-poets had brought about social cohesion in a caste-ridden Hindu society, but there was a perception that during the Nizam's rule, imposition of Urdu as the official language and the Muslim dominance in public life stifled the cultural growth of the Marathi people here. The legacy of the Nizam's rule, which ended in 1948, had a major influence on the political life of Marathwada, and a deep dislike of the feudal era haunted the locals.

The Sena's Hindutva avatar was welcomed by the people of this region. Before mid-1986, Sena had barely 50 followers in Marathwada, whereas most of Pawar's anti-Congress force came from here. Pawar's shift to Congress-I made erstwhile Congress-S supporters and sympathisers look to the Sena with hope and expectation.

The Sena also quickly picked up an issue which held out the promise of firmly lodging it in Marathwada soil and exploited it to the maximum.

Right in the middle of Aurangabad was an abattoir which, residents demanded, be shifted elsewhere.

The Sena decided to hold a *rasta roko* to push the plea. And like most Sena agitations, it turned violent. Almost 6,000 people, half of whom had come from neighbouring villages, participated, and 2,000 courted arrest. Some of the arrested youngsters somehow managed to unfurl the saffron flag atop the Aurangabad police station, and police had to use force to rein them in.

The abattoir was immediately shifted, and the Shiv Sena claimed credit for it.

The energetic and ambitious Congress-S activists, rendered directionless by Pawar's 'ditching,' now joined the Sena in large numbers. They sensed an opportunity to do political work in a party which went ahead full-steam, portraying itself as an alternative to the Congress.

This entry into Marathwada was significant because Chief Minister S.B. Chavan, a bitter critic of the Sena, hailed from the region, and making a dent here was tantamount to sending out warning signals to all parties across the state.

Following the abattoir episode, Sena branches were formed in almost every village in the region, and Sena boards and flags became common sights at the entrance to each village. In the villages, several shops and houses displayed Sena flags, and young boys moved around proudly with saffron kerchiefs around their necks. What was more, a plethora of Sena slogans, written on roads, pipelines, rocks and even trees in bold letters met the traveller's eye. The Sena presence in Marathwada had become distinct.

On a tour to Marathwada late in 1986, Chief Minister S.B. Chavan was shocked to see the spreading tentacles of the Sena.

At a training camp of the Bombay Regional Congress Committee held around the same time, Chavan and then Union Minister of State for Home Ghulam Nabi Azad voiced concern over the Sena's growth.

But even as Chavan made it known he was worried by Sena's rising clout, Thackeray's party gloated over its new-found importance in the chief minister's stronghold.

The economic backwardness of Marathwada, and rampant unemployment, were important factors in propelling the Sena forward in the region.

Economic indicators showed that even the least developed area in western Maharashtra was better than any place in the whole of Marathwada. In the early seventies, entrepreneurs began opening industrial units here in response to incentives offered by the state. It was expected the region would develop speedily, with local unemployed youths getting jobs and technically qualified young entrepreneurs being able to launch small units of their own.

But industrial units brought skilled workers from headquarters located in urban areas. The big industries put up forbidding conditions for small-scale industrialists wanting to manufacture accessories, thus killing the hopes of small entrepreneurs as well.

At the employment exchange in Aurangabad district alone, 62,000 persons were on the waiting list in 1986. In the six other districts of Marathwada, almost 3.5 lakh had registered themselves for employment.

This figure excluded farm-hands, robbed of their only means of livelihood by the chronic drought plaguing the region. In Aurangabad alone, nearly 2 lakh farm labourers and small farmers had filled forms to demand work on the Employment Guarantee Scheme projects. Among them were graduates and undergraduates. The situation in the other districts was no different.

When the Sena fanned out in Marathwada, its image as a sons-of-the-soil party which had given jobs to thousands of Marathi people created hopes among the educated unemployed. And as it was seen to have 'delivered' on the broader Hindu platform in the abattoir case and the riots, rural youngsters felt they had reason to place faith in it.

23

ROLLING OUT THE SAFFRON CARPET

The Shiv Sena organised a *Bhagwa Saptah* (Saffron Week) in November 1986 to mobilise public opinion in its favour across the state. Thackeray asked party leaders and corporators to tour the districts for a drive at organisation-building. He wrote in *Marmik*:

> The whole of Maharashtra has been waiting for us for the last 20 years, as people have lost their faith in every other political party... The flag of Hindu Independence, which Sant Ramdas (Shivaji's guru) placed on the shoulders of Shivaji, now needs to be carried on our shoulders in a triumphant march from Kashmir to Kanyakumari.

Manohar Joshi toured Raigad district; Chhagan Bhujbal was sent to Nashik; Madhukar Sarpotdar went to Aurangabad; labour front chief Dattaji Salvi toured Ratnagiri; Sudhir Joshi went to Pune; Subhash Desai toured Jalgaon; Wamanrao Mahadik was despatched to Sindhudurg; and Pramod Navalkar visited Satara and Sangli districts.

A membership drive was undertaken in Marathwada, Konkan and northern Maharashtra, and the party claimed the *Saptah* had led to the spawning of more than 20,000 shakhas. Most political observers called this an exaggeration but conceded the Sena was making advances.

The newly-appointed communications chiefs also were not standbys without a script. Congressmen initially looked at these Sena office-bearers as ciphers without a base in the districts assigned to them, but determination can be a force, and in the case of Sena samparka pramukhs, it carried them into unfamiliar territory with confidence.

Whether it was Diwakar Raote in Parbhani, Mo Da Joshi in Latur, Gajanan Kirtikar in Jalna, Suryakant Mahadik in Kolhapur, Gajanan

Thakre in Buldhana, Ramakant Mayekar in Osmanabad, Sharad Acharya in Dhule, Rajeshwar Raginwar in Amravati, Shantaram Barde in Beed or Mahadeo Mote in Solapur, all the communications chiefs employed techniques learnt in the Sena school of operatives to establish a foothold in rural Marathi soil.

The Sena set up its fortress-like branches in villages in extravagant style, Sainiks swathed head-to-toe in saffron clothes and bandannas splashing *gulal* all over the place and shouting slogans of *Jai Bhavani, Jai Shivaji* to the blowing of conch-shells and the accompaniment of leather-drums, kettle-drums and other instruments. If exposure is a source of political strength, the Sena used it well, pressing into service the paraphernalia of Maratha tradition for propaganda. It enlivened memories of the Marathi people's past, designating itself as the protector of Maharashtra Dharma. And it worked to convince the people of interior Maharashtra that it *felt* into the earth.

Violence in Vidarbha

Mere symbolism could not have taken the Sena far, though. Maharashtrianism had to be bolstered by the catalyst of action.

A lot of this 'action' was communal in nature. In Nanded, Nashik and Panvel earlier, the outbreak of violence had helped the party. In Vidarbha too, the Sena branched out in the wake of communal riots, which, opponents alleged, were sparked by the Sena.

Amravati district in the backward region of Vidarbha had a socio-economic environment which led to communal tension. There was poverty and rising unemployment, and growth of education, the relatively high percentage of literacy was not matched by jobs in agriculture, industry or trade.

Agriculture consisted almost exclusively of cotton, and absence of jobs meant the district had the largest number of agricultural labourers in India. Work for this force was inadequate. No new industries had come up, many old ones had shut, and those that remained were in bad shape.

Unemployment led to a rise in crime, and competition for odd jobs arose between Hindus and Muslims. For instance, in many towns earlier, Muslims had traditionally been drivers of horse carriages, with patronage from the Hindu community. Unemployment made Hindus enter the trade. There was also, increasingly, competition for plying autorickshaws.

In the Assembly, the Sena was accused by the ruling party and the Opposition of fomenting communal passions. Its opponents said tension arose in Vidarbha after the visit of Bhujbal, who had reportedly made provocative speeches.

The most serious accusation was that the Sena was trying to inflame sectarian sentiment *where none had existed before.*

The party's political isolation was clear when, during a calling attention motion on the Amravati riots, the Opposition watched as Bhujbal was placed in the dock by Congress MLAs.

During the same debate, Bhujbal made gestures on the floor of the House which were described as obscene and insulting to the minority community, and a motion to expel him was moved and backed by the Opposition.

This drew Bhujbal closer to the Sena rank and file, and his activities increased. After entry into one of Amravati's riot-hit villages, Warud, was banned, Bhujbal rode into the village, in dramatic fashion, on a scooter. He went to other parts of the state just as dramatically.

With his blustery, headline-hitting tactics, he made an impact in the Konkan, Marathwada, and northern Maharashtra. He received invitations from Sainiks from various areas and addressed many rallies. He was alienated from the upper-class and middle-class intelligentsia due to his image as a rugged activist, one who was headstrong and who needed to cultivate a bit of sophistication. His attitude also infuriated a few Sena old-timers, who saw him as slightly immature, but his tours and smart-alecky stratagems took the Sena message further into the heartland.

Bhujbal has since claimed that 'every Sena shakha pramukh outside Mumbai is my creation.'

'It was I who built up the party in the districts and took the Sena flag to places like Parbhani and Gadchiroli at a time when senior Sena leaders did not even know the road out of Mumbai,' Bhujbal told the *Indian Express* in 1996.

Clashes with Dalits

At the same time that it was inflaming religious passions in late 1986, the Sena began targeting Dalits in Marathwada. It launched a programme for converting encroachments on public property into 'public welfare endeavours'. The project was soon directed against landless Dalits and tribals who had been ploughing portions of untilled community lands for a long time, nursing hopes that the lands would in due course be legalised.

The Sena clashed with Dalits cultivating foodgrains on 'village grazing lands' (*gaavraans*) first in Ambegaon in Aurangabad; the clashes later spread to 35 villages. It was alleged that the Sena destroyed crops by leading cattle into the fields. Reports said the party was backed by landlords and rich, upper-caste peasants, who, resentful of the transformation of 'supplicants' into landlords, made use of its muscle-power.

Leaders of the Dalit Panthers and Lal Nishan Party protested the 'concerted attacks', but that did not stop Dalit youngsters from swelling the Sena's ranks. Why?

Because, it split the numerically larger neo-Buddhists from other communities in the Dalit fold. It highlighted the rise of these ex-Mahars through education and militant action, and called them Dalit avengers who had punished those from other sections of the Dalit community. And members of Dalit communities such as the Chambars, Dhors, etc. wishing to join the Sena were welcomed, regardless of the clashes over *gaavraans*.

Thackeray's attacks on Maratha leaders for their 'incompetence' also helped him exploit the discontent of Dalits and poor peasants against the concentration of power and economic privilege in the hands of a few Marathas.

Reservation of jobs and seats in educational institutions had then become another focal point for tension between Hindus and Dalits. The Sena opposed reservations. Its position was that quotas should be allotted on the basis of economic criteria.

The Sena and the Konkan

Did the Sena's influence in rural areas grow because of religious and caste conflicts alone? No doubt, the reorientation of its policy to Hindutva gave it reach, but only communal issues could not have helped. In many places, the Sena exhibited 'intent' and gained ground. For instance, in the Konkan region, the Sena looked at a major problem plaguing locals and formulated a strategy to tackle it.

Konkan, a linear coastal strip, has many rivers which crisscross its villages before finding their way into the sea. Some rivers even divide a village into two. In the absence of bridges, this means a local who wishes to get to the other side of the village, or into another village, has to traverse a lengthy, circuitous route, which in some cases may take hours.

Residents had for years demanded bridges, but the appeals had gone unheeded.

The Sena took up the issue and, soon as it entered Konkan, went on a bridge-building spree by pouring in its own funds. The bridges were not pucca. They were made of wooden planks, but they were a boon to villagers. Apart from those areas of Konkan which are near rail and road routes, the others are backward. Inhabitants of such areas saw the bridges as the beginning of progress. In south Konkan, in many areas of which a farmer barely manages to feed his family for eight months a year, and for whom even wood is not easy to get, the Sakavs – as the wooden overpasses are called – brought reassurance.

If, earlier, it took three hours for locals to cross a waterway, the same could now be done in five minutes. Roza Deshpande of the Communist Party told me:

> The Congress made big five-year plans which were failures. Socialist leader Madhu Dandavate is from Konkan, but he didn't realise the elementary problem of crossing rivers. The Sena didn't go to the people with big issues, but it took small problems, ignored by other parties, and solved them.[115]

The coastal belt's links with Mumbai too helped the Sena spread its wings there. The region, consisting of four districts – Thane, Raigad, Ratnagiri and Sindhudurg – has always been influenced by Mumbai, as the city provides employment opportunities to a huge section of its population. Forty-five per cent of the total immigrants from the rest of Maharashtra into Mumbai come from Ratnagiri district alone, and most people in Konkan live on the money order economy, i.e., remittances sent through money-orders by workers in Mumbai.

Socio-economic-political ideas from Mumbai permeate to villages of the Konkan owing to the cultural bonds maintained by migrant workers with the rural areas. The workers visit their villages during the Ganesh and Diwali festivals, and in Mumbai, they maintain their identity by organising groups of persons from the same villages. The cultural links are strengthened through festivities, dramas and bhajan mandals.

Developments in Mumbai thus have undercurrents in the Konkan. So when the Mumbai-based Sena decided to make inroads into rural areas, it got relatively easy acceptance from residents of this region.

Konkan's literacy rate too is high, making its people politically aware. Prior to the Sena's emergence, certain areas of Konkan had always backed the Opposition. This anti-ruling party sentiment further helped the Sena.

The party quickly opened over 500 branches in Raigad district alone and took on the Peasants and Workers Party (PWP) in its traditional strongholds, Raigad, Sindhudurg and Ratnagiri. Many clashes took place between Sena and PWP workers, the most notable of which was at the Reliance polyester plant at Patalganga, and the Sena soon captured a dozen trade unions in Raigad, including the ones at Reliance and Bharat Electronics Company.

The party raised the demand of 80 per cent reservation for locals in the area to gain support of youth who were unable to get jobs through competition in upcoming manufacturing units of big companies. This resulted in many youngsters switching allegiance from the PWP.

Plagued by infighting, the PWP had become a victim of its inability to move with the times. Earlier, it had organised agrarian folk and championed their case for compensation for land taken over for public projects like CIDCO, Navi Mumbai and Nhava Sheva, but it lost its appeal with time. The Sena took up the cause and launched an agitation for compensation for peasants' land acquired by the government.

The PWP also never had a labour wing. That vacuum was filled by the Bharatiya Kamgar Sena, which captured labour unions in many places, often by using strong-arm tactics.

The Congress covertly supported the Agri Sena in Thane and Raigad district to check the Sena's spread. The Agri community, comprising poor and middle-class farmers, has a sizeable strength in these districts, but despite the Congress's attempts, Agri youths deserted the Agri Sena and joined Thackeray's organisation in large numbers.

This was because, among other things, the Sena raised funds for temples, agitated for bus-stops in remote places and provided quick-fix solutions.

At Chowk, a small town with a population of nearly 10,000 located off the Mumbai-Pune highway, the Sena started a balwadi, provided an ambulance unit and unveiled plans to build a theatre within days of establishing its branch.

Its ambulances went to the far corners of the state; its balwadis were noticed; and it opened gymnasiums in towns and villages. Taking note of the water crisis in the state, it sent water tankers to many regions, especially to Vidarbha, where scarcity was most acute.

These tactics worked, as did the root cause of youth frustration in rural areas: skewed economic development and unemployment.

Maharashtra's economic development had created islands of prosperity and large numbers of poverty-stricken people. Education had spread in rural areas, and educated youth had become conscious that they were denied an opportunity to share power and wealth.

There were few opportunities for young graduates and technicians from the talukas. Polytechnics and colleges had sprung up and had raised aspirations, but the government had not created enough jobs. Colleges and polytechnics had also 'educated' these youngsters out of the traditional profession of farming, and frustration had set in.

According to the state government's 1986-87 economic survey, 25 lakh jobless youth were registered in the state's employment exchange.

The programmes of other parties did not attract these youths, because they expected quick results, which the Sena provided or promised to provide.

For instance, if a youth desired to open a small kiosk (tapari), he routinely became a victim of red-tape and corruption. The same happened if a youth wanted a loan from a bank or some other financial institution to start a venture. The Sena, when approached for assistance, asked the youth to go ahead with illegal construction of a kiosk and offered protection, often by pure physical belligerence. It also quickly arranged for loans from financial institutions for ventures.

Corruption and the Shiv Sena

The control over BMC gained in 1985 was said to have facilitated the Shiv Sena's expansion in rural areas. The BMC is the richest civic body in the country, with a budget bigger than that of many small states.

But the Sena's role in the BMC came under a cloud twice. The first time was when it refused to give permission to Municipal Commissioner S.S. Tinaikar to prosecute two civic engineers (both Maharashtrian) for their alleged role in a construction scam. Thackeray insisted a minister behind the scam be prosecuted first, and said the Sena was committed to protecting interests of Marathi speakers.

The second episode was grimmer. In October 1988, Rustom Tirandaz of the Opposition unearthed a taped address, allegedly of the then standing committee chairman, Sena's Diwakar Raote, to a group of 77 traders from Dadar.

The tape, which sought to implicate Raote as an extortionist, was first played at the Congress office before it was taken to the mayor's chamber. The then mayor Chandrakant Padwal apparently recognised the voice as that of his party colleague. Both Padwal and Bhujbal later asserted the cassette had nothing to do with the affairs of the civic body and was 'a Congress conspiracy,'[116] but it created a stir, and Tirandaz said it 'propagated the philosophy of the Sena'.[117]

Part of the controversial text of Raote's taped address to the traders, as reproduced by the *Telegraph*, ran thus:

> For 20 years we haven't demanded a single paisa from you. You all deserve goondas who will make you dance on sword and knife-point. You deserve people who extort money. Whether you pay me or not it won't make a difference to my work. I am here to serve the public.
>
> You still don't know... Diwakar Raote? I've carried you Gujaratis on my shoulders. Go to Thane and ask, the Gujarati community recognises me.
>
> You will remember us... Shiv Sainiks. Don't I have a wife or children? Why should I do all this? I look after the depressed because I am a Shiv Sainik and when it comes to Sena, I throw aside everything else.
>
> Our boys are ruined. Don't they have mothers or sisters? Don't they have their homes? When the real time comes you undervalue us. Businessmen... should help the organisation. I had sent my boys to your doorstep. You behaved as if you were throwing a 10 paise coin to a eunuch. This is how you value us? All right, I'm happy. Go.[118]

No action was taken by Sharad Pawar, who had taken over as chief minister from S.B. Chavan in June 1988, after he was given recordings of the conversation.

Well before this drama, however, a controversy in November 1987 over Dr Babasaheb Ambedkar's *Riddles in Hinduism* nearly caused a major clash between Dalits and Hindus.

Riddles of Sena's Hindutva

Riddles in Hinduism was an appendix in the fourth volume of the Maharashtra government's publication of Dr Ambedkar's *Writings and Speeches*. The Maratha Mahasangh, a caste organisation of Marathas, launched an agitation to protest against the inclusion of *Riddles* in the government publication, saying it denigrated Hindu deities Ram and Krishna. After a Mahasangh morcha, the state announced, on 16 November 1987, that it would delete *Riddles* from the volume.

All Dalit organisations and parties in Maharashtra expressed their disapproval. On 23 November, a massive morcha of Dalits was led by Prakash Ambedkar, R.S. Gavai, Ramdas Athavale, Namdeo Dhasal, Raja Dhale, and Arjun Dangle to Kala Ghoda. The gathering was so huge that if one end of the morcha was at Kala Ghoda, the other was at Azad Maidan, more than a kilometre away. Shaken, the state, on 25 November, revoked its decision and said the annexure would stay.

At this point, the Sena, sensing another chance to flaunt its Hindutva colours, jumped into the fray. Sena legislators Sudhir Joshi and Manohar Joshi held a dharna on the floor of the Assembly to condemn the state's 'surrender'.

The next day, Chhagan Bhujbal clandestinely brought into the House a banner folded in a newspaper, and as soon as question hour ended, unfurled it in dramatic fashion, so that everybody could see the words written on it: *Down with the government defaming Hindu Gods!* He raised slogans condemning the Congress and created an unruly scene, forcing the Speaker to call in marshals to remove him from the House. The Assembly unanimously passed a resolution suspending Bhujbal from membership for two days.

Himself an OBC, Bhujbal strained his vocal cords to the limit during the controversy. His suspension gave him greater impetus to raise an uproar. He growled: 'Do you know what is there in the *Riddles*? It claims Rama's birth to be debaucherous and says he never ruled the state. It says he spent his time with wine, women and eating prohibited food. It is alleged he drew Sita also into "evil ways." Even the virtuousness of Lord Krishna is questioned. What the hell is this? Hindus who tolerate abuses against their religion are regarded as "intellectuals" and "philosophers". Those who fight for Hinduism are labelled rabid communalists. In that case, I want to be communal.'[119]

At a function organised on the death anniversary of social reformer Mahatma Phule, Bhujbal said: 'We don't consider Dr Ambedkar and Gautam Buddha as bad. Then why do you publish something that gives a bad name to gods we revere?'

The chief minister called an all-party meeting on 7 January 1988 to try and resolve the issue, in which the Sena aggressively demanded deletion of *Riddles*. 'If, bowing to pressure from Dalits and so-called progressives, the government retains the controversial appendix, the Sena will launch an *aandolan* all over Maharashtra,' Manohar Joshi warned all gathered. The BJP, then trying hard to shed its image of a party rooted among the upper classes, supported retention of *Riddles* (so did the RSS and Patit Pawan). The ostensible reason for that was the possibility of the issue generating caste friction, but the BJP was clearly apprehensive of political implications.

Unlike the BJP, the Sena did not think alienation of Dalits would be bad political arithmetic. Though the Maratha Mahasangh had initiated the agitation, it was the Sena that continued the battle over *Riddles* almost single-handed in the latter phase.

The Sena argued that since it was the morcha of Dalits that had forced the government to backtrack, it would have to organise a morcha of its own to push its demand. Front-page ads were issued in newspapers urging 'pure-blooded Hindus' to join in, and according to Muslim scholar Asghar Ali Engineer, 'it is surprising that the major national dailies prominently carried such a blatantly communal advertisement'.[120]

The ad carried by the *Indian Express* on 14 January 1988, read:

Shiv Sena's Appeal to All Staunch Hindus! Friday, January 15, 1988 at 2 pm from Azad Maidan: CHALO MANTRALAYA! Beware! Should anyone insult the Hindu religion!

The government seems to be determined to reinsert Dr Ambedkar's *Riddles in Hinduism* appendix in the government publication. If this irreligious act is not resisted in time then these secular (!) rulers will not even hesitate to destroy the Hindu religion itself in the country in the specious name of secularism. It is, therefore, time that all Hindus rise to the occasion now and nip in the bud this nefarious act of the government.

Yes right now!

Only those Hindus who have unadulterated blood in them should join this morcha. Come from every direction of Maharashtra and join with saffron flags.

The morcha was massive. Volunteers from every district of Maharashtra, with huge contingents from local shakhas, marched from Azad Maidan to Kala Ghoda wearing saffron caps, waving the Sena flag and raising anti-government slogans.

Addressing nearly two lakh partymen who squatted along MG Road between Kala Ghoda and Hutatma Chowk, Bal Thackeray claimed half the battle had been won because the mammoth turnout had delayed a decision on the issue beyond the government deadline of 15 January. He warned of trouble if the government succumbed to pressure from parties who wanted *Riddles* retained. Finally, he added, 'Our fight is not with Dalits, and this morcha isn't against any caste or community. It's against the government which has consistently humiliated Hindus.'

Again, cutting across party lines, Dalits united and, on 5 February, staged a counter-demonstration bigger than that of the Sena. Almost half-a-million people had turned up. When the crowd reached Hutatma Chowk, it went berserk and damaged the martyrs' memorial erected by the BMC at the instance of the Shiv Sena. According to the local Sena corporator Dnyaneshwar Gawde, 22 bulbs were removed, names of the 105 Hutatmas (killed in police firing during the Samyukta Maharashtra movement) wrenched out and lamp-posts and marble slabs damaged.

Thackeray visited the spot the same night to see for himself the damage done. 'We won't tolerate any insult to the sacrifice of the Hutatmas,' he rumbled.

Tension, now rather high, was further heightened when Bhujbal, the next day, performed a religious ritual with Ganga *jal* at the Smarak, calling it a 'cleansing operation'. This came in for flak from other parties, but Bhujbal clarified the cleansing act was not done with the intention of expressing anger against Dalits. 'The Sena and Bal Thackeray do not believe in untouchability. The cleansing operation was merely done in view of the damage and defacing of the memorial by anti-social elements,' he said,[121] adding he couldn't forget there were Dalit leaders too with him when the Smarak was set up. 'If you're angry with me, attack me. Why do you defile the Hutatma Smarak?' he asked.

Dalit leaders including Prakash Ambedkar and R.S. Gavai then performed a puja at the memorial to invoke 'peace'. Ambedkar and Gavai said Dr Ambedkar and the RPI had played a 'leading role in the formation of Maharashtra, and the memorial isn't the property of any single party or organisation.'[122] They urged: 'One shouldn't make political capital out of it. There were Dalits too among the martyrs whose names were embossed on the memorial. But since it (the damage) happened during our morcha, we are morally responsible for the damage. We pay homage to the martyrs.'

A compromise formula was then worked out in four days. At a meeting called by Chief Minister S.B. Chavan on 9 February, where Dalit leaders as well as the Sena chief were present, a hitherto unthought-of solution was mooted and approved by both sides: the appendix would be retained, but with a footnote saying the government was not in agreement with the views expressed in it.

The riddle finally proved not such a brain twister, and curtains came down on the controversy.

24

AT THE CENTRE STAGE

The by-election to the Vile Parle Assembly constituency in December 1987 attracted much attention because of the Shiv Sena's blatantly aggressive Hindutva campaign, and its outcome showed in whose favour the scales of Maharashtra politics were tilting.

In the last four elections, the Shiv Sena had not fielded any candidate from Parle due to the dominance of non-Marathi speakers in the area. But to test its Hindu card, it put up Dr Ramesh Prabhoo as its candidate in 1987. Pitted against Prabhoo were Pranlal Vora of Janata Dal and Prabhakar Kunte of Congress. The BJP was then invoking the *mantra* of Gandhian socialism, and to ensure the Sena's defeat, it decided not to put up any candidate and extended support to Janata Dal's Vora.

To appeal to Hindu sentiments, the Sena also roped in film stars such as Mithun Chakravarty and Nana Patekar and called upon people to assert their Hindu identity. The slogan *Garv Se Kaho Hum Hindu Hain* (Say it with pride, I'm a Hindu) gained currency for the first time in this poll campaign, and banners proclaiming Hindu regeneration were put up not only in Parle but all over Mumbai. Hoardings were put up at strategic points saying *Dharmik Tethe Marmik* (meaning, where there is religion [Hinduism], there is *Marmik* weekly).

Thackeray openly adopted a communal line. He told voters: 'The Khalistanis are going to come at you. The Mussalmans are going to come at you. What are you, as Hindus, going to do? Neither the police nor the government are going to protect you'.[123] And he went so far as to say: 'There are nationalist Muslims and anti-nationalist Muslims. But to tell you the truth, I don't know how to distinguish between one and the other.' Dalits were also warned, in the wake of the *Riddles* row: 'If Dalit leaders ignited a controversy and threw a challenge, there would be arson in Dalit villages.'

Seeing the thrust of the Sena campaign, Chief Minister Chavan too made the by-poll a prestige issue and campaigned extensively for Congress candidate Prabhakar Kunte, adding to the contest's significance. Kunte, a former housing minister known for issuing 'photo passes' to slum dwellers during his ministerial stint, made slum improvement and city development the crux of his campaign.

The Janata Dal's Pranlal Vora had leaders like George Fernandes and Dr Datta Samant to court slum dwellers for him; he also attempted to woo the middle class and the 50,000-strong Gujarati community in the constituency with an appeal to end communalism.

The Sena courted the Gujaratis by getting Gujarat's leading religious spokesman Shambu Maharaj to campaign for its candidate, and took care to lay stress on the combination of 'the Saraswati of Maharashtrians and the Laxmi of Gujaratis'.

The BJP and RSS cadres initially threw in their lot with Janata Dal candidate Vora, but his secular credentials came under a cloud when Syed Shahabuddin came to canvass for him. A significant section of RSS cadres swung in favour of the Sena and actively began seeking votes for Dr Prabhoo. After all, Sena was contesting the polls on a single plank: Hinduism. Its only appeal was: 'Vote for the Sena to defend Hinduism'.

The result came as a shock to the Congress and Chavan: the Sena candidate polled 29,574 votes and had a winning margin of 10,791 over the Congress nominee. Janata Dal's Vora had secured just 13,928 votes.

The Sena's win was significant, because from now on, no party could underestimate the slogan of Hindutva, and no party could be complacent when fighting the Sena. It had won in an area in which Maharashtrians were not in a majority, and where it had not contested Assembly polls on the previous four occasions. For other parties, the Sena threat was here to stay.

'Boycott' of Sikhs
After Vile Parle, it was the turn of Aurangabad in the Marathwada region to paint itself saffron. But in the interregnum occurred an episode in which the Sena faced plenty of flak.

As terrorist trouble in Punjab accelerated, Thackeray gave a call for 'economic boycott' of Sikhs if the community's high priests did not issue a *hukumnama* ostracising all Khalistanis in India.

'We want a non-violent boycott of all Sikhs. No truck or business establishment owned by a Sikh, or even a Sikh-driven taxi, should be patronised,' he declared.[124] Once ex-communicated, the terrorists would be Sikhs no more and could not ask for a separate homeland, he argued. Asked if the boycott would widen the Hindu-Sikh divide, he said: 'I haven't thought of anything like that. I am in a different mood now. But this nonsense has to be stopped. How long can it be tolerated?'[125]

The nonsense, according to him, was that finance was flowing from Sikhs in Mumbai to terrorists in Punjab. He claimed to have information that Mumbai-based Sikh businessmen had collected ₹ 40 lakh in a day and handed it to Sikh separatists who had come to the city.

When a delegation of distressed Sikhs met him, he told them he would invite a few Sikh leaders to a public meeting at Shivaji Park, where they would have to tell the people they disassociated themselves from trouble-makers in Punjab. The decision on the boycott would then rest with the audience, he said.

Some Sikh leaders agreed, but others opposed the suggestion, saying there was no need for them to testify before Thackeray.

All parties 'denounced' the boycott call.

The Sena chief then said he was not against common Sikhs but Sikh businessmen who filled terrorists' coffers. Condemnatory voices, however, still came in.

Chief Minister Chavan said a case had been registered against Thackeray for inciting communal disharmony and asked the Sena chief to stop attempts to create a dangerous situation in Mumbai. However, the sentiment in the Sikh community, as expressed by one of the Sikh leaders, was: 'All this tamasha and embarrassment has been caused because the government is inept'.[126]

After all this, Thackeray one day suddenly announced he was withdrawing the boycott call and vowed that Sikhs in Mumbai and Maharashtra would be protected by his organisation 'at any cost'. He said he had changed his mind because a section had felt it would help pro-Khalistan elements and affect Hindu-Sikh unity.

Eyebrows were raised at this abrupt withdrawal, and allegations were made that the Sena had made a good packet by forcing Sikh businessmen to cough up extortion money. All in all, the affair gave ammunition to the Sena's opponents.

Key win in Aurangabad

The first elections to the Aurangabad municipal corporation (formed in 1982) were held in April 1988 on bitterly communal lines. Strong feelings of distrust among Hindus and Muslims were nourished by political parties to win the polls.

Keeping an eye on the Muslim votebank in the township (Muslims constituted 27 per cent of the population), the Congress had in all previous elections fielded only Muslim candidates. Before the corporation was formed, the civic council presidents had mostly been Muslims. A list of MLAs elected on a Congress ticket from Aurangabad also showed mostly Muslim names.

In 1988, the Congress put up 20 Muslim candidates, one of them a detainee under the National Security Act, Javed Khan. It also announced that if it won the elections, Aurangabad's first mayor would be a Muslim.

This gave the Sena an opportunity to exploit Hindu disenchantment. Chants of *Garv Se Kaho Hum Hindu Hain* rent the air, and Thackeray not only roused religious sentiments but declared his party would change the name of Aurangabad to Sambhajinagar, after the son of Shivaji.

His task was made easier by attempts to resurrect the Muslim fundamentalist thrust in Marathwada with the slogan 'Islam is in danger'. Apart from making the usual fanatical statements, the Itah-Ud-Deen Muslimeen – an organisation floated by the late Nizam to check popular struggle against his atrocities – released a list of 32 Muslim candidates and urged the 'faithful' to vote only for these Muslims, irrespective of their political affiliations. The organisation warned: 'Muslim supremacy of the past shouldn't be forgotten.'[127]

With things so stirred up, violence broke out at the time of the polls, leaving 27 persons with stab wounds and one dead.

The poll results, declared amid such tension, left the Congress and other parties shocked: the Sena had emerged the single largest party, capturing 27 of the total 60 seats.

The Congress had contested all seats but had won only 18. The Sena, on the other hand, had fought 40 seats.

The BJP and the Janata, the so-called national parties, were routed. They not only drew a blank but polled just a few votes. Ten of the 40 BJP candidates polled less than 100 votes.

'The Shiv Sena tiger is roaring. The way is now clear for our saffron flag to fly atop the Mantralaya,' Thackeray said.[128]

But the way still was not clear for the Sena to have its mayor. It had to sway three persons in its favour from among the RPI, Dalit Panthers, Muslim League and dissident Congress corporators to get its candidate elected. On 6 May, the day of the poll, both the Sena and Congress, which trailed by 17, came ready with their strategies.

The RPI, led by Prakash Ambedkar, had earlier announced it would be neutral, but at the last moment, it cast in its lot with the Congress, saying 'it is the lesser of two evils'.[129]

This made the Sena jittery, as it could no longer be sure of securing victory. Sena corporators created a ruckus and tried to subvert the poll process by demanding the poll procedure book – which was in English – be provided in Marathi. Later, they staged a noisy walkout.

Municipal commissioner, Narayan Phadtare, announced he was adjourning the meeting for the day.

The Congress seized this chance to get its own candidate elected. State Revenue Minister Vilasrao Deshmukh, deputed by the Congress leadership to ensure the Sena candidate's defeat, blasted the civic chief for having adjourned the meeting and forced him to reconvene it. When the corporators re-assembled in the absence of Sena men, the Congress scored an easy 'victory' with the support of five Muslim League corporators and three RPI corporators. The reward given to the Muslim League was the deputy mayor's post; the RPI got chairmanship of the standing committee.

The Sena challenged the mayoral poll results by filing a petition in the Aurangabad bench of the Bombay High Court. An estimated 3,000 Sainiks thronged the court premises when the plea came up for hearing. When the court postponed the hearing, they went on a rampage, attacking commercial establishments. When the violence spread to sensitive parts of the city, it acquired a communal colour, and inadequate police presence saw things get out of hand.

Chhagan Bhujbal was in Aurangabad when rioting began. He remarked: 'I can't control my men if injustice is done.' Apart from the

Sena and Muslim organisations, local Congress MLA Amanullah was also said to have played a role in the riots.

Next day, violence broke out in Bidkin, about 30 km from Aurangabad, and on 19 May, Hindu–Muslim clashes started in Paithan, 60 km from Aurangabad.

But the fact was that the Sena had jumped on to the centre stage of Maharashtra politics with the win in the Aurangabad civic polls and had become a source of worry for other parties. The *Free Press Journal* wrote:

> In a particularly depressing political atmosphere, where established political parties have not only failed to deliver the goods but have also ceased to express the feelings of the masses, people have been clutching to any party or group which appeals to their emotions and sentiments. The Shiv Sena fits into this role just as Telugu Desam did in Andhra Pradesh. One added advantage to the Sena is its brazenly aggressive Hindu appeal at a time when a similar appeal of the BJP is being diluted and the secular credentials of the established parties – more importantly that of the Congress-I – are wearing thin.[130]

Just how concerned the Congress was about the Sena's growth became obvious at the first Congress legislature party meeting under Chief Minister Sharad Pawar in July 1988. Pawar, who had succeeded S.B. Chavan in June, was bombarded with demands by Congress legislators to arrest the Sena's rise. The MLAs asked the government to deal firmly with the Sena.[131]

The chief minister declared his resolve to 'crush the Sena,' and as reports appeared in a section of the press about Pawar's 'success' in controlling it, Thackeray cried foul. He accused Pawar of using the police machinery to terrorise Sena activists and asserted the government would never succeed in finishing off his organisation.[132] 'Pawar knows this well, but if Congressmen desire a confrontation, the Sena is prepared to fight at every level,' he said.[133]

These statements, and the ones that followed, were proof that the Sena's strategy would be more combative in future. The party had become aware that it had come to pose a challenge to the Congress. And it knew its aggressive Hindutva would make it more conspicuous.

Pune convention

The Sena's third state-level convention, held in Pune on 30 and 31 December 1988 and attended by over 40,000 delegates, had the same purpose. The venue was carefully chosen. After the first convention in Mumbai in 1984, Sena had consolidated its hold on Mumbai and Thane; after the second one in Mahad, it had branched out into the Konkan and Marathwada; with this third convention in Pune, it was announcing its resolve to target the state's western and southern parts.

'We're not running after power, power is running after us, and we shall have it,' Thackeray told a mammoth gathering at Pune's SP College grounds.

He called the Congress *nalayak* (useless), and after doing a well-orchestrated job on the let-down by Congress governments, came to the moot point: 'Hold aloft the banner of Hinduism. If you fail to do this, Khalistanis and Pakistanis will pounce on you and divide India. There is no need to define Hinduism. I am proud to be called a Hindu. This is my definition. India was divided on a religious basis – Hindustan for Hindus and Pakistan for Muslims. My Shiv Sainiks are Maharashtrians in Maharashtra and Hindus in Hindustan. The Congress shouldn't stop me, otherwise the whole country will be on fire.'

The Sena also tried a reformist ploy in order to demonstrate it was not against Dalits. Anti-Brahminism was in full play in the citadel of Brahminism: attacks were made on the vegetarian habits of RSS Brahmins, and the cult of not drinking tea or coffee in RSS shakhas was derided. 'The Sena is not against Dalits. Hindus have never criticised the Buddha's religion. They regard the Buddha as their own,' Thackeray said.

At the same time, a conciliatory message was sent out to orthodox Pune Brahmins. Pune-based Sena man Shashikant Sutar, reading from a text prepared for him, said in his welcome speech, 'Our leader will realise Dr Hedgewar's dream of a Hindu Rashtra'.

At Thackeray's public rally, described by the *Times of India* as 'one of the biggest ever held in Pune',[134] 10 resolutions were passed. The most important: 'Rename India as Hindustan'. Others were aimed at the rural vote: demands for higher prices for agricultural produce, a ceiling on prices of five essential commodities, a government takeover of all holy Hindu sites and their upkeep at state expense, a pension scheme for industrial workers, a changeover to Marathi in all state matters, and an appeal to the state to pressure the Centre to solve the Maharashtra-Karnataka border dispute.

The paper tiger: the birth of *Saamna*

On 23 January 1989, Bal Thackeray gifted himself a paper tiger, the daily newspaper *Saamna*. As the Sena extended its reach, the need for a newspaper was being badly felt, because *Marmik*, being a weekly, could not disseminate its response to developments and criticisms with the speed and immediacy a daily would provide. *Saamna* was born to channelise party appeal into a force potent enough to dislodge the Congress regime.

Sena workers had been building up the atmosphere for the paper's arrival months in advance. Walls in Mumbai had been adorned with banners and colourful hand-drawn ads with the catchline *Dainik Navhe, Sainik* (Not a daily, but a Sainik).

Thackeray himself was at his most bellicose at the launch function at Savarkar Smarak, Dadar: 'We have begun the battle (Saamna means confrontation) by arming ourselves with the weapon of a newspaper. But if circumstances so demand, we'll fight with real weapons.'

The paper flaunted its Hindutva policy on its masthead, which announced it as 'the only Marathi daily which advocates the cause of fiery, militant Hindutva,' and Thackeray asserted its thrust would be to 'strengthen Hindu identity'.

Saamna's inaugural issue showed that with the Sena's growing clout, some of the party's bitterest adversaries were beginning to see virtues in it. *Blitz* editor Russi Karanjia, a trenchant critic of the Sena in its early days, headlined his guest article saying: 'Let the reins of power go to Balasaheb's hands'. Giving credit to the Sena for 'beautifying Mumbai' and asserting that 'a Sena in power would cleanse the city of anti-social elements', Karanjia predicted, 'Once the Sena comes to power, it will protect the principles of democracy and secularism!' George Fernandes wrote: 'I'm certain that one day my close friend (Thackeray) would prove to be the symbol of unity of all Indians.'

25

CROSS–VOTING AND THE BAN ON VOTING

In the midst of promising times for the party erupted a controversy that held the danger of blotting out all progress.

Mayoral polls were to be held in Thane in March 1989, and the Shiv Sena, with a majority of 30, thought it would sail through with support from the Janata Dal's one and BJP's two corporators.

What happened left the Sena with no sense of certainty. Its mayoral candidate, Prakash Paranjpe, lost to Congress' Manohar Salvi by one vote, and its candidate for deputy mayor lost by two votes.

Two Sena corporators had voted against the party diktat. The first cracks had appeared on the Sena's taut surface, and Sainiks in Thane quickly reached a pitch of pique against the 'traitors'.

Thackeray's outburst was severe: 'All the corporators took oaths the previous evening and then indulged in seditious activities. They have betrayed the party. I can't forgive them. Never in the history of the Sena has such a lowly act been performed. The persons who've done this dirty deed won't be forgiven by the Mother Goddess.'

To grind out the first traces of indiscipline, Thackeray ordered the resignation of all 30 Sena corporators, and when, on 21 March, all of them went to the municipal commissioner to quit, the corporation's headquarters were besieged by enraged Sainiks.

Anand Dighe, the Sena's Thane district chief, and party observer for the region Leeladhar Dake soon submitted a report to the party chief which was supposed to have contained the names of the turncoats. Sainiks were told Thackeray would declare their names after their involvement had been confirmed. Till then, they were asked to hold their patience.

The names finally did not have to be declared.

On 22 April, Sena corporator Shridhar Khopkar was stabbed to death by unknown assailants near his Louis Wadi residence. He had been facing threats to his life, and after the mayoral elections, his office had been attacked by miscreants. He escaped then, but the second attack proved fatal.

When he was returning home from Ghatkopar, he was attacked with swords and other weapons and stabbed all over the body.

Some Sena leaders had allegedly spoken of 'a death sentence on the traitors', and word spread that Khopkar had been bumped off by the Sena because he was one of the two 'rebels'.

Dighe was even arrested and charged with murder, conspiracy and rioting under Section 3 and 4 of the Terrorist and Disruptive Activities (Prevention) Act. He was later acquitted for want of evidence.

Congress leaders, including Mayor Manohar Salvi, Deputy Mayor Ramchandra Thakur and former mayor Vasant Davkhare were present for Khopkar's funeral, but not a single Sena activist or leader attended.

When the matter came up in the Assembly, Minister of State of Home Vilas Sawant told the House: 'After Thackeray's threat that traitors would be taught a lesson, security had been provided to Satish Pradhan, B. Tangdi, Bhaskar Pusalkar and Shridhar Khopkar. They didn't take it.'

Khopkar's killing gave the Sena's opponents a chance to hit out at the party. It was then surmised that the Sena would be isolated from the political mainstream and become 'untouchable', and nobody would be willing to have any truck with it. But predictions of political isolation were proven inaccurate.

The Sena chief knew his bravado on Hindutva had thrown up tangible benefits for his party, and he continued with his acerbic language in the belief that such an attitude would transform the wind of Hindu nationalism into a gale.

Even after Prabhakar Kunte challenged the election of Ramesh Prabhoo in the High Court by accusing him of corrupt electoral practices and of appealing to people in the name of religion, Thackeray made it plain he would proceed with his Hindutva campaign regardless of the verdict. The case dragged on for a long time, but that did not deter Thackeray. No court, no law, and no constitution could restrain him from protecting and propagating Hinduism, he said.

In April 1989, Justice S.P. Bharucha set aside Sena MLA Prabhoo's election, saying he had used religion to appeal to the electorate. The judge ruled Thackeray was a collaborator in the corrupt practices and pointed out sections of the Sena chief's speeches which he deemed offensive. Some of Thackeray's lines he objected to were:

> If the Sena comes to power, everybody will have to be converted to Hinduism and Christians and Muslims will have to implement family planning."
>
> "We do not desire Muslim votes."
>
> "I'm unable to understand how to distinguish a nationalist Muslim in the community."
>
> "We must dig up every mosque, and beneath it there is bound to be our temple."

In 1999, the Election Commission ruled, on the basis of complaints received about the Parle by-election and the court verdict on it, that Thackeray would not be allowed to vote for a period of six years.

26

ALLIANCE WITH THE BJP, AGAIN

The Shiv Sena's widening base and its strident Hindutva propaganda not just making 'secular' parties uncomfortable, but was also giving BJP the jitters. Members of many Sangh Parivar constituents, like the RSS, the Vishwa Hindu Parishad (VHP) and Bajrang Dal, were finding Thackeray's rantings more attractive than the BJP's 'Gandhian socialism'. The BJP had begun to get a queasy sort of feeling: what was supposed to be its own job was being done by Bal Thackeray.

After the Ram Janmabhoomi issue grabbed national attention, the BJP had tried to shake its hands off the matter, saying it was the VHP's concern, but its own cadres thought otherwise. They wanted BJP to cast off the garb of Gandhian socialism, which had paid little dividends, and champion the Ayodhya – and by extension – Hindu cause.

Most BJP leaders had raised their voices against Muslim fundamentalism in the wake of the Shah Bano issue and thereafter, but its now-on, now-off and hesitant Hindutva suffered due to its hobnobbing with Janata Dal. Its campaign for Janata Dal candidate Pranlal Vora in the Parle by-election at a time when Shahabuddin was soliciting votes for him, and its opposition to Thackeray's Hindutva in the same poll, its own activists felt, gave its claims to Hinduness a hollow ring.

When the party drew a blank in the Aurangabad civic polls, its MLA from the township, Haribhau Bagde, had served a notice on the BJP leadership. He had said: 'The BJP's brand of Hinduism has become too soft. People are convinced only the Sena can keep Muslim arrogance from growing.'[135]

Plus, the BJP had reached a dead end in Maharashtra. It had hitched its fortunes to Sharad Pawar's Congress-S till 1986, but Pawar's return to Congress-I had left it without anyone it could ride piggyback on.

It did not have the strength to fight on its own in the state, though it was concentrating on spreading its network, and badly needed a political partner to make headway. The Janata Dal could only bring it more losses.

All this caused a rethink in the BJP: Thackeray was in form, and even the Sangh Parivar found his declamations to its liking.

Hindutva fervour was building up across the nation. The Ram Janmabhoomi issue had triggered a nationwide debate, and the VHP was campaigning for 'liberation of the shrine.' It was impossible for BJP to keep a distance from Hindutva anymore. Speaking on the political resolution at the party's Agra convention in April 1988, Pramod Mahajan, with the consent of L.K. Advani and A.B. Vajpayee, suggested the BJP throw its weight behind the Ayodhya campaign. The suggestion received a huge welcome from the delegates.

The Sena had gone to the people with the same issue, so the thinking in the BJP went that an alliance with the former would boost the party's prospects. Thackeray had also gone on record saying that if there was one party he could join hands with, it was the BJP. Pramod Mahajan, the strongest advocate of a tie-up and in-charge of Maharashtra BJP, held meetings across the state then to gauge the mood of BJP cadres. He found most were in favour of a Sena-BJP alliance.

The shift in the BJP's perceptions about the Sena, whether born out of opportunism or a genuinely fresh fondness, was reflected in an article *In Defence of Shiv Sena* written by BJP leader K.R. Malkani in the *Indian Post* in May 1989.[136]

The BJP, in its national executive at Palampur, Himachal Pradesh, in June 1989 passed two vital resolutions: it demanded that the Ram Janmabhoomi site be handed over to Hindus either through negotiated settlement or legislation, and it approved its Maharashtra unit's efforts to enter into a seat adjustment with the Sena.

The Janata Dal, which had an understanding with BJP in northern states, reacted sharply. Its Maharashtra unit chief Mrinal Gore said the party would have no truck with BJP if it entered into adjustments with the Sena. The Dal's position in Maharashtra was precarious, and not having an understanding with BJP was sure to come with a heavy cost. But Gore stuck to her stand that Janata Dal would not hold talks with the BJP due to its links with the Sena, and her position was endorsed by Dal President V.P. Singh.

Gore told me:

> I knew the Dal's existence in Maharashtra was at stake at the time, but I made it clear to the BJP leadership that we couldn't join hands with a party with which we had zero similarities. The Sena and the Dal represented as diametrically opposite political poles as one could think of, and never the twain could meet. I also told the BJP leadership that they wouldn't get along well with the Sena, but except for Ram Kapse, nobody else listened.[137]

In Punjab, the Dal was wooing the Akalis. In Kerala, it had tied up with the Left Front, and in Tamil Nadu, it was not just dependent on the DMK, it was also in alliance with the CPI(M) and the Muslim League. And in Andhra Pradesh, it was seeking to have adjustments with the Telugu Desam. But it was firm on opposing the Sena in Maharashtra. Commenting on the Dal's stance vis-a-vis the Sena, K.R. Malkani said:

> Political commentators would like to know from the Dal leadership why they are willing to deal with the Muslim League and not the Sena?... Why is the Janata Dal willing to deal with the communal Akalis and the parochial DMK and not with the Sena? ... Because that will displease some Muslims. The Janata Dal has similar apprehensions about the BJP; but since it cannot hope to defeat the Congress without the latter's support, it has to swallow its reservations. When it comes to the Sena, however, the Dal leadership is of the opinion that it can afford to keep it out because that party is confined to one state and cannot, therefore, disturb the Dal's all-India calculations.[138]

Seeing the Dal's stand, the Sena chief too adopted a tough posture against it. He said his party would be willing to cooperate with all opposition parties 'except Janata Dal' for the Lok Sabha polls scheduled for November 1989 and the Vidhan Sabha polls scheduled early in 1990.

The Sena had not been able to win more than two seats in the Assembly all these years, but it could now afford to be unyielding because it knew its threat to the Congress regime could no longer be dismissed as mere bluster. On its own, it would still have difficulty in getting close to power, but the tie-up with the BJP, which was working to spread its base in rural areas of the state, gave it added confidence.

The Janata Dal found itself isolated, because except for a couple of small pockets, it was nowhere in the picture. The PWP, once a claimant of grassroots support next only to Congress, had shrunk badly. And the two Communist parties had only tiny areas of influence. In such a scenario, the Sena, backed by BJP, VHP and RSS cadres, presented a formidable challenge.

The accord between Sena and BJP was that the former be the junior partner in the Lok Sabha polls, and BJP would play second fiddle to Sena in the Assembly elections. Accordingly, the Sena granted most of the parliamentary seats to the BJP. But in the poll campaign, it was Thackeray who played the senior role and got the tag of 'Hindu Hriday Samrat' attached to himself. He cast a shadow across Maharashtra, from Nagpur, Amravati and Akola in the Vidarbha to Solapur in western Maharashtra and Sindhudurg in the Konkan.

Accompanied by Mahajan, he attracted huge crowds and unabashedly played the Hindu card. Voters were told by both leaders that the Sena-BJP alliance was not just electoral but a 'unity of hearts, of minds, of programme and a unity to serve the Hindu cause'.

Thackeray's Hindtuva was, of course, more brazen than what Mahajan and other BJP leaders dared to project. 'Why should elections in India depend on the votes of the Shahi Imam and Syed Shahabuddin? To honour their emotions, why are the sentiments of 60 crore Hindus trampled upon? To hell with your secularism. In this country, Hinduism and Hindus should be respected first. This is our birthright, and if the government denies it to us, we know how to get it,' he bickered bluntly with 'anti-Hindu forces'. And he appealed to youth: 'Hindutva is not a wave. It's the breath of our life. If a Muslim is thrown out of any country, there are other Muslim nations where he can take refuge. Where will Hindus go? That's why we have to protect our Hindu land, and if need be, sacrifice our lives to save Hindutva. Destroy the forces who have converted the Lok Sabha into a Bhog Sabha.'

The attack on Muslims would usually be preceded by praise for Muslim cricketers. 'We need nationalist Muslims like Kirmani, Azhar and (Arshad) Ayub, who play for the country and help it win. Islam's first principle is that one should be loyal to one's country. But what are you people (pro-Pak Muslims) doing?' And when he said he could not tolerate closure of markets following deaths of Pakistani leaders and condemned those who burst fire-crackers after Pakistan's victory over India in a cricket match, he seldom failed to touch a responsive chord.

The results of the Lok Sabha polls were a pointer to the extent of popular response: the Sena won 4 seats, and the BJP romped home in 10 constituencies. Two of the 4 seats won by Sena were from Mumbai, the other two were Aurangabad and Parbhani in Marathwada.

Fourteen seats against a firmly entrenched Congress's 28 was good performance indeed.

With some puff, Thackeray told a gathering at the Sena-BJP's victory rally at Shivaji Park: 'I appeal to the new Prime Minister, V.P. Singh with folded hands not to appease Muslims. If he doesn't listen, we'll rouse Hindus and bring a Sena-BJP government at the Centre.'

But if the Centre was a long way away, the Sena chief certainly was in no doubt about his party's chances at the Assembly polls. 'The path is now clear for us to unfurl the *Bhagwa* atop Maharashtra,' he claimed.

Elections to the Assembly were declared to be held in March 1990, and a confident Sena-BJP got down to organising the campaign immediately.

For fighting a poll on such a large scale and capitalising on Thackeray's appeal, the Sena needed a well-oiled election machinery. Sudhir Joshi's Sthaniya Lokadhikar Samiti (SLS) provided it. It got together a force of nearly 1,000 activists, organised sessions to impart training to them in the running of a poll campaign and sent them across the state to spread the Sena message.

Thackeray was in full flow, promising to give Maharashtra not Lokshahi but Shivashahi, the benevolent rule of Shivaji.

The Shivashahi he promised was one in which people would be provided necessities like food, clothing and shelter, 40 lakh slum dwellers rehabilitated, cops and government servants given permanent homes after retirement, and 40,000 villages provided with water.

Political analysts then criticised the Sena chief for not having any economic programme, but Thackeray would retort: 'What has the Congress's economic programme given to people? What have all the five-year plans given to the common man? They (the people) don't even have basic necessities. Our only programme will be to ensure basic needs are provided.'

After this, he would proceed to attack Congress and other secularists and absorb attention with his oratory and his cheeky method of lashing out at opponents. Thackeray's speech at the Sawantwadi Assembly constituency, delivered on 11 February 1990, is an example of his refrain during the poll campaign, couched in peculiar language:

> In ten years they (Congress) have changed six chief ministers. How can the party give you a stable government, when it can't give you a stable chief minister? I'm talking of the Congress-I hathwale. If they have a *haath* (hand), we have a leg and we're going to kick them out.

> "Leg" an impolite expression. It is one of the body's organs. People are accusing me of using bad words, but what is bad in them? I'm a cartoonist and therefore I'm satirical.

> We have contested the Lok Sabha elections. The idea was to have some representation from Maharashtra. Congress-I MPs from Maharashtra don't open their mouths, and if they do, it is to yawn or put in some chewing tobacco. Our problems don't get solved until someone who belongs to us goes there (Lok Sabha). That is why we have formed an alliance with BJP. The purpose of the alliance is not power. It is not that Bal Thackeray was frustrated and wanted to be chief minister, and so he asked his wife to make a list of what she wanted, where she wanted plots, and where her relatives wanted plots. I do not dream like this, because I myself do not contest elections.

> This country, which we call Hindustan, is called by another name, Bharat, which we accept. We do not accept India, it was given by the British whom we drove out. If power comes to me, if I become prime minister, which I won't because I don't contest polls, I will change the name of our country to Hindustan, and have it put on the world map.

> Muslims in the Konkan are our people, unlike in Mumbai. They speak good Marathi, like A.R. Antulay. We accepted him as our chief minister. If you see him, he looks like a Chitpawan Brahmin. Once Indira Gandhi took Antulay to Uttar Pradesh for campaigning. Antulay told me this anecdote, after which he told me not to tell anyone (which he always does). He was introduced as Antulay, chief minister of Maharashtra, to the crowd. Mrs Gandhi pulled the tail of the Nehru shirt of the man introducing him and said: "Don't say just "Antulay," say "Abdul Rehman Antulay", so that Muslims in the audience realise he is a Muslim. Is this not communalism? But in this country it is a crime if you utter the word Hindu.

> In Kashmir they (Muslims) burnt the tricolour, hoisted the Pakistani flag and shouted slogans like Pakistan Zindabad. I'm talking about pro-Pakistan Muslims. Where are these traitors? You should find them.

We have fielded Alim Khan in Mumbai. He is a Muslim by birth, a Muslim in practice. We have fielded Anjum Ahmed, a Muslim lady (Nagpada, Mumbai). We asked her opinion on the common civil code and she said it should be enacted. What is wrong with fielding such a woman with nationalistic beliefs? This proves we are not anti-Muslim.

Those Muslims who live in India and side with Pakistan have no business to be here. They should leave the country. We are prepared to pay their travelling expenses. What will the result be? We won't get their votes. That is okay. Here we have our young Hindu brother who is going to win and under any circumstances enter the Assembly.

In Marathwada, houses were washed away by floods, and the collector would not give permission or land to rebuild them. But when a group of Muslims met Chief Minister Sharad Pawar for land for a burial ground, he gave land and offered to bear the funeral expenses. There is land for the dead, but none for the living.

See this chief minister. His hands are smeared with shrikhand from 555 *bhookhands* (plots). And after licking it, he says his hands are clean, but it is time to tell him the smell of shrikhand is still there.

There is a new prime minister who does not go for Ganpati darshan. He goes instead to the Imam and bends his knees in front of him. Mufti Mohd Sayeed is home minister, but he did not go to Kashmir or Punjab, he went to Malegaon to get Muslim votes.

You have tolerated these people for 42 years. Tolerate us for 5 years. You have nothing to lose.

After having addressed 65 meetings for the Lok Sabha polls, the Sena chief held 144 meetings across the state for the Vidhan Sabha elections. And though his glib prediction that the saffron flag would fly atop Mantralaya did not come true, the results showed the Sena–BJP had, astride the Hindutva horse, made serious inroads into Maharashtra.

The Sena representation in the Assembly leap-frogged from one in the earlier House to 52, and that of its ally, the BJP, rose from 16 to forty-two.

As against 94 MLAs of the Sena–BJP combine, the ruling Congress ended up with 141 seats, three short of a majority. The Sena had emerged as a big challenge to the Congress, and it owed its success to Thackeray and the SLS.

A study of the 1990 results showed the Sena's wooing of Hindu Dalits had paid it dividends. Of the state's total population, the Scheduled Castes accounted for 13 per cent, of which neo-Buddhists accounted for 8 per cent. The Hindu Dalits, belonging mainly to the Matang, Charmakar, Dhangar and Dhor castes formed 5 per cent of Maharashtra's population. Realising it could not afford to isolate them, the Sena chose to wipe out its anti-Dalit label and appealed to Dalits who were 'proud to be Hindus' to join cause with it. It took advantage of the Hindu Dalits' traditional antagonism towards neo-Buddhists and also of the former's failure to profit from reservations as much as the neo-Buddhists.

A caste-wise break-up of victorious Sena candidates in the 1990 polls shows how most of them came from the lower castes. Of the 52 elected candidates, 6 came from the so-called upper castes (Brahmin, Prabhu and Saraswat), 27 were Marathas-Kunbis, 13 were OBCs, one belonged to the Scheduled Castes, one to the Scheduled Tribes and 3 belonged to the 'Others' category.

27

BHUJBAL SULKS, QUITS SENA

When Manohar Joshi was elected leader of the 52-member-strong Shiv Sena legislature party, the largest opposition group in the House, Chhagan Bhujbal, whose performance as the lone Sena MLA since 1985 had been aggressive, felt cheated and sidelined.

The Bhujbal camp felt one of the reasons for the party's good performance in the elections was its cornering of OBC votes, for which Bhujbal, a prominent OBC leader, deserved credit. But Bhujbal was sent back to the corporation as mayor, while Joshi headed the Assembly group.

The subterranean tension generated by Bhujbal's sulking came out into the open over the issue of the Mandal Commission recommendations.

The BJP supported the reservation policy, but Thackeray voiced his opposition to it. This he did at the risk of estranging nearly 70 per cent of Sena supporters, who were OBCs. He also issued a warning to BJP that he would have no problem in initiating 'divorce proceedings' over the Mandal issue.[139]

But even before Thackeray had expressed his view, Bhujbal had gone ahead and publicly voiced his support for the National Front government's decision. Thackeray chastised him severely for his statements.

Most other second-rung Sena leaders were also in favour of supporting reservations, because they thought opposition to the quota policy would be politically suicidal for the party. But all attempts to convince the Sena chief failed.

At around the same time, V.P. Singh toured Maharashtra and extended an open invitation to Bhujbal to join the Janata Dal.

Bhujbal was finding it increasingly difficult to reconcile himself to the Sena's stance on Mandal, but he was in no mood to walk out of the party just then. To show his disappointment, he stayed away from a rally organised by Sena and BJP to welcome the BJP's Somnath-Ayodhya Ram Rath Yatra when it reached Mumbai.

Soon, his frustration at being sidelined found a more direct expression. In March 1991, he hit out at Manohar Joshi, saying 'Joshi has failed as Opposition leader and needs to be replaced'.[140] Bhujbal further said he was not interested in another term as mayor and would only welcome being made leader of Opposition.

This 'open revolt' did not sit well with the Sena's reputation as a monolith under one man's control, and Thackeray summoned both Bhujbal and Joshi to settle matters. He apparently also succeeded in ironing out the differences, and Bhujbal was reported to have profusely apologised for going public with the dispute.

But Joshi and Bhujbal continued to be at loggerheads, and Bhujbal finally decided to call it quits in December 1991.

When December dawned, it became clear that the Shiv Sena was headed for a split. Bhujbal had been sulking for quite some time, and his whimpers had become the talk of the town.

On 5 December, a group of 18 Sena MLAs submitted a letter to Assembly Speaker Madhukarrao Chaudhary asking him to allow them to form a separate group – Shiv Sena (B). The leader of the group: Chhagan Bhujbal.

The Speaker formalised the split in the Sena by recognising the breakaway group on 11 December, and on the 20th, 12 of the defectors led by Bhujbal joined the Congress-I.

The Sena had been dealt a body blow. One of its top-rung leaders, who enjoyed a mass base, had deserted it. Bhujbal justified his decision to say good-bye to the Sena thus: 'I have learnt from Manohar Joshi how to politely stab someone in the back!'[141]

The BJP then rubbed salt on the Sena's wounds by grabbing the post of Opposition leader in the Assembly. Just when the Sena was reeling under the shock of the split, the BJP staked its claim to the post which is on par with that of a cabinet minister.

The originally 52-member Sena group in the House had now been reduced to 34, and the BJP with its 41 members had become the single largest Opposition group. Taking this stand at a crisis-ridden moment for its alliance partner, the BJP got its MLA Gopinath Munde elected as leader of Opposition.

The two jolts left the Sena shaken, and though party leaders put up a brave front saying the split would not affect the Sena at all, the sudden baring of chinks in its armour had a demoralising effect.

The Sena was once again written off as a political force, and this time, the assertion of the doomsday prophets was more vociferous than ever before.

The BMC elections held in February 1992 lent vigour to such voices.

Talks between the Sena and BJP over sharing of seats floundered, and they decided to part ways. The Congress profited: it succeeded in winning control of the civic body after a gap of 14 years. The Sena won 70 seats, the BJP retained 14.

The Tiger had lost his stronghold. The defeat on home turf was humiliating, and it looked as if the Sena's progress had come to a grinding halt.

The questions now being bandied about were: Had the Tiger been tamed? Had he lost teeth? Above all, would the Sena be able to rise again?

Gandhi's assassin: A hero or villain?

For a short period however, the differences between Bhujbal and Joshi were temporarily pushed under the surface owing to drama generated by the Sena over two issues: one, the assassination of Mahatma Gandhi, and two, Pakistan's proposed cricket tour to India.

Thackeray stirred things up when, during the campaign for the June 1991 Lok Sabha elections, he praised Nathuram Godse, the assassin of Mahatma Gandhi. Addressing a rally at Alka Talkies Square in Pune on 17 May the Sena chief said:

> Nathuram wasn't a hired assassin. He was infuriated by Mahatma Gandhi's betrayal of the nation. The killing of any person is an evil act and should be condemned. But we must find out the reasons behind such incidents. Mahatma Gandhi betrayed the nation. He had said he would lay down his life before allowing division of the country. But ultimately he did nothing to stop the partition. Moreover, he insisted on giving ₹ 55 crore to Pakistan at a time when the country was ravaged by the trauma of partition. It was anger at this that led Nathuram to do what he did. He avoided any further partitioning of the country. His motivation was nationalistic pride. There was no selfish motive.

The topic had been broached by Congress leader Vithalrao Gadgil, who had said: 'They (Sena-BJP) speak of Ram but harbour Nathuram.' Thackeray swallowed the bait and paid the price for it. The Nathuram factor, along with the sympathy wave in the wake of Rajiv Gandhi's assassination, brought down the Sena-BJP's tally of Lok Sabha seats in the state to nine.

In October 1991, Thackeray turned arbiter of India and Pakistan's cricketing relations. He announced that the Pakistan team, which was to play a one-day game with India at Wankhede stadium on 28 October, wouldn't be allowed to step into Mumbai, and if the Mumbai Cricket Association went ahead with the match, 'Wankhede would be burnt.'

'India is playing cricket with Pakistan at a time when they are disturbing this country and fomenting terrorism. A cricket match with Pakistan at this stage is as bizarre as Nero, the Roman emperor, playing the fiddle while Rome was in flames,' the Sena chief said.[142]

Thackeray was accused by the media of mixing sports with politics. His answer: 'These buffons advise me to keep sports above politics, but they do not know what a nation is and what should be above what. It should be even above your sports. If you are going to keep sports and arts above politics, I say the nation is above everything. No one should teach me sportsmanship. It should not be at the cost of the nation. We must stand somewhere as one nation. Our enemy must know here is a Hindustan, where people are alert and sentimental as far as national spirit and pride is concerned.'

Well before the match was held, Shiv Sainiks implemented the chief's order to disrupt the game. On 22 October, a band of Sena activists led by Shishir Shinde damaged the Wankhede pitch. They tricked 60 policemen standing guard inside the stadium into believing they were construction workers, walked on to the wicket, dug it with sickles and old stumps and poured oil on the pitch.

The Shiv Sena and the media

One thing led to another. Soon after this act of vandalism, Nikhil Wagle, editor of the Marathi eveninger *Mahanagar* — which Thackeray had accused of trying to create a rift in the Sena after rumblings of discontent in the party erupted on to its front pages — wrote an editorial condemning Sena's strong-arm tactics. For months,

Mahanagar and Thackeray had been going for each other's jugular, but the flashpoint was reached when Wagle called the Sena chief a '*Veda* (Mad) Mohammed' for his stand on Indo-Pak cricket. The editorial in which he flayed Thackeray was titled '*Balbuddhiche Pratap*' (Exploits of a Bal's [literally, child's] mind).

Stung by criticism of their leader, Sainiks stormed Mahangar's Mahim office on 25 October, attacked its staff members and smashed the telex machine.

The media, whose relations with the Sena had always been uneasy, was aghast. A protest dharna was organised by The Mumbai Union of Journalists, Gujarati Patrakar Sangh and Urdu Journalists' Association, and 300-odd protesters, including politicians like Dr Datta Samant, Sharad Yadav and Rustom Tirandaz and writers like Vijay Tendulkar marched from the Mahanagar office to Sena Bhavan, shouting slogans like '*Bal Thackeray Murdabad*' and displaying placards saying 'Down With Shiv Sena Fascism'. CPI and CPI(M) leaders, besides members of other Left groups, also participated in the march.

No untoward incident took place during the procession, but when the participating journalists returned near the Mahanagar office after the protest, they were attacked by Sainiks with sticks, stones and rods, and serious injuries were inflicted on four scribes, two of them women. Manimala of *Navbharat Times* sustained a skull fracture requiring an operation; Milind Khandekar of *Dopahar* suffered concussion; Sheela Rawal of Gujarati *Femina* sustained back injuries, and Rajesh Chauhan of *Ekmat* suffered a deep gash on his left temple.

The Sena's terror tactics invited condemnation from across the nation, and though some journalists such as Govind Talwalkar (then editor of *Maharashtra Times*) pointed out how odd it was that Communists, who justified the shackling of the press in all Communist-ruled countries and states, were championing the cause of a free press, nothing could take away from the fact that the Sena's assaults were abhorrent in the extreme.

Raj and Uddhav

After the loss in the BMC elections of 1992, it was uncertain whether the Sena would rise again. But what was certain was that Bal Thackeray's nephew Raj, and son Uddhav, had risen in the party over the last few years.

Raj had been elected president of the party's youth wing, the Bharatiya Vidyarthi Sena (BVS) in 1988 and had since come to have a major say in political matters. It was reported that the appointment of new vibhag pramukhs and shakha pramukhs after the Sena's BMC debacle was supervised by Raj, who conducted interviews of all the aspirants.

The low-profile Uddhav had, on the other hand, taken upon himself the administrative and managerial responsibilities of *Saamna*.

But discontent was fuelling against both Raj and Uddhav among top-rung Sena leaders, who grudged the junior Thackerays their status.

Voice was given to this resentment by a man who had been completely sidelined in the party, Madhav Deshpande. Deshpande had been appointed observer by the Sena for the 1968 BMC polls, but with the passage of time, his position in the party had changed: in 1992, he was a nobody in the Sena scheme of things.

Whether out of frustration or due to prodding by someone in the Sena, the 'former Shiv Sainik' held a press conference in Mumbai in July 1992 – a time when reports on 'resentment over dynastic rule in the Sena' had started appearing in the press – and urged Sainiks to 'cleanse the party of dynastic rule'.

Deshpande accused the Sena chief of turning the party into a personal fiefdom and called for collective leadership and inner-party democracy. He was also learnt to have written a booklet citing specific instances of Thackeray's favouritism. 'By pandering to the whims of his son and nephew, Thackeray is bent on destroying an organisation faithfully built by Shiv Sainiks,' he alleged.

There was no doubt that Thackeray would be annoyed by these charges, but what irked him more was the fact that top-rung Sena leaders stayed tight-lipped even as Marathi newspapers front-paged Deshpande's statements.

The commander-in-chief was furious that his brigade had let him down in this hour of crisis, so he devised a ploy – similar to the one used in 1978 – to silence his detractors, show the other Sena leaders their place and re-establish his hold over the party.

The *Saamna* of 18 July 1992, sprang a surprise on Sainiks. There was a cryptic two-line announcement on page one of the paper, titled '*Akhercha Jai Maharashtra!*' (The Final Jai Maharashtra). The boxed item, which also had a photograph of Thackeray folding his hands for a farewell namaste to his admirers, said: 'Balasaheb Thackeray, along with his family members, says a final Jai Maharashtra to the Shiv Sena!'

Thackeray's decision to sever ties with the party rattled Sena leaders and Shiv Sainiks, and several hundred Sainiks rushed to Matoshree to join a well-orchestrated chorus of '*Balasaheb Zindabad, Awaaz Kunacha, Shiv Senecha*'. But they were told their leader was firm on his decision.

The next day, Thackeray wrote an editorial in *Saamna* with the same title – *Akhercha Jai Maharashtra* – and lambasted Deshpande and all newspapers which had carried reports on squabblings in the Sena triggered by Raj and Uddhav's growing clout. Tugging at the emotional strings of Sainiks, Thackeray wrote:

Even if one Shiv Sainik stands against me and my family and says "I left the Sena because of you", or "You hurt us", I'm not prepared to continue as Shiv Sena chief for one more moment. But this has never happened. I have never hurt anyone. Those who left us did so due to squabblings at the local level or to grab the spoils of power. Of course, they all repented! Where does dynastic rule figure in all this? All I want to tell those who say the Sena has suffered due to our dynastic rule is that the Sena was born to fight for the Marathi *manoos*. To bring good times for Maharashtra, we did not care about our home and health. We did not harbour any desires. By ensuring the respect of Marathi in Maharashtra, we have today spread Hindutva in Hindustan... We were firm on such a stand right from the Sena's birth. In our path to progress, we did not allow dynastic rule to even touch the Sena. We did not get properties for ourselves. We didn't amass wealth for our children. They won their spurs for themselves. By taking loans from banks. We never allowed them to use our position as Shiv Sena pramukh. But if as a father, we have encouraged them, it should not be surprising. But why and how do banner-lines like "Discontent among Sena leaders over rising influence of Raj-Uddhav" and "Raj's leadership unacceptable to MLAs" appear at all? Did the two go anywhere or do anything to establish their leadership?

The Shiv Sena is not our or our family's private property... Still, at the time of saying goodbye, it appears as if innumerable ants have bitten the head. Though the eyes are filled with tears, the mind has made up the decision. It is unavoidable. We loved all our Shiv Sainiks as a mother loves her children. The children are today angry.

We are not angry with anybody. Does a mother ever get angry with her children? It is the children who do... So far, we lived for lakhs of Shiv Sainiks. On the strength of their affection, we moved about in pride. We never harboured any enmity. We never resorted to treachery. That is why words are not enough to express the state of our mind at this moment of farewell. It is as if a child who had been so far walking through a huge crowd by holding his mother's hand has suddenly left the hand.

By employing such language and whipping up hysteria, Thackeray returned to centre stage the very next day.

The resignation drama ended with a compelling display of histrionics at a public meeting outside Sena Bhavan, which left a lakh-odd Shiv Sainiks delirious. Playing to the gallery with characteristic elan, the Sena chief let himself be persuaded by his party workers to stay back, but not before exhorting the faithful to shed sweat and blood for the party. 'If you're going to live like burning coals, then only for your love, I'm going to lead the *Mard* (manly) Shiv Sainiks. Those who are not men should get out of the Shiv Sena,' he said.

Thackeray's theatrics worked the assembled Sainiks to such a frenzied state, some even threatened to immolate themselves if he did not withdraw his decision to quit.

The slogan '*Ekach Neta, Balasaheb*' had reached a crescendo at the time of Thackeray's arrival at the hurriedly-erected stage itself. The lesson was driven home to other Sena leaders, who were suspected to have triggered this crisis, with telling effect. They were heckled and abused by the crowd, and even Thackeray's arrival on-stage did not pacify the agitated Sainiks. They continued to hoot the other party leaders present on the podium, angrily gesturing them to leave.

It took another thespian's act from the Sena chief to quieten them. When his appeal for peace went unheeded, Thackeray made a dramatic turnaround and started climbing down the stairs. There was pin-drop silence in a moment.

Resuming his speech, Thackeray scolded the Sainiks for insulting party leaders. He told the crowd he would not tolerate this affront to the leaders, because they had after all helped build the Sena. But by then, the other leaders had borne the brunt of the Sainiks' wrath. Some of them had also been assaulted by the crowd.

With a thespian's ease, Thackeray had proven who was the boss; the Sainiks had re-sworn their loyalty to him; and other leaders had been cut down to size.

The bond between the Sena pramukh and the Sena worker had become stronger at the end of the drama. So long as this bond remained firm, it was not going to be easy to dismiss the Sena as a spent force.

28

THE 1992–93 RIOTS

In the post-Babri demolition riots that rocked Mumbai in two phases – December 1992 and January 1993 – the Sena reinforced its position as 'protector' of Hindus. During L.K. Advani's *rath yatra*, the Sena had kept itself at a distance from the Toyota-chariot extravaganza. Thackeray said there would be hell to pay if the Ram temple was thwarted, and the battle cry of *Mandir Wahi Banayenge* was chanted at Sena meetings, but Sainiks weren't too enthusiastic about the *yatra*. After all, for them, both Ram and Advani had to compete with another deity – Thackeray himself. But as the Ayodhya issue turned explosive, so did Thackeray's posturing, and he chose to be one up on the others when matters came to a head.

When the saffron clan planned a 'decisive' *Kar Seva* at the disputed site on 6 December 1992, Thackeray decreed that his men be at the head of the Hindutva hordes. *Kar Sevaks* had started gathering in large numbers in Ayodhya from 1 December, but the Sena contingent from Mumbai made a move only 24 hours prior to the chosen day of action. Sena MP Moreshwar Save had proceeded with some Sainiks from Delhi and Uttar Pradesh to Ayodhya on 4 December, but the Mumbai batch of 100 Sainiks led by Manohar Joshi left on 5 December. This meant it would reach Ayodhya at the very last moment, and if the Hindutva parties had their way, the *Kar Seva* would have actually begun by then. Yet Thackeray wanted his team to lead *Kar Sevaks*.

In a front-page editorial in *Saamna* (6 December) entitled '*Ayodhyekade*' (Towards Ayodhya), he wrote:

> A sea of Ram *bhakts* has descended on Ayodhya, and now it is being joined by our brave Shiv Sainiks... The time has come to decide if this country should be identified with Maryada Purshottam Ram

or the intruder-aggressor Babar... This blot (Babri) now has to be wiped out. Return as victors in the Ram Janmabhoomi struggle. This is my appeal to my staunch Hindu Shiv Sainiks.

When the wave of Shiv Sainiks reaches the battlefield of Ayodhya, those opposed to the Mandir will tremble in fear. The Shiv Sainik will act as a warrior in the actual battle. He has not been born to clash cymbals and sing bhajans and kirtans. The only thing I expect from VHP President Ashok Singhal is that the Sainiks' courage will be appreciated... You fought all the previous wars without Shiv Sainiks. Now give them weapons and see. Their experience in waging struggles on the battlefield will help clinch the *Dharma Yuddha* in Ayodhya.

There was a warning too: 'If *Kar Sevaks* are fired upon, Hindustan will go up in flames.'

On 6 December, the Babri was razed. *Kar Sevaks* stormed the shrine at 12:15 pm and started pulling it down. By 5 pm, the deed was done.

Kalyan Singh immediately resigned as chief minister of Uttar Pradesh; the state Assembly was dissolved, and president's rule imposed.

In a bid to shrug off charges of unconstitutional behaviour, the BJP sought to distance itself from the demolition act. Advani and Murli Manohar Joshi denied the BJP had anything to do with it.

Thackeray proudly accepted his share of the responsibility. 'If the Babri has been demolished by my Shiv Sainiks, I'm proud of them,' he said.

In fact, the Sena contingent led by Joshi arrived in Ayodhya after the structure had been pulled down, but the Sena rushed to take credit. It said that Sainiks from Uttar Pradesh had led the *Kar Sevaks* atop the structure and claimed the first assault on the domes had been made by a Sainik from Vidarbha.

Thackeray's reaction came at a time when all other Hindu leaders were trying to disown responsibility, for fear of being labelled as heads of unruly hordes perpetrating a gross act of vandalism.

After BJP leader Sunder Singh Bhandari attempted to palm off responsibility on a 'non-BJP-RSS outfit', Thackeray said, 'Everybody had gathered in Ayodhya as a Hindu, so it is improper to make such a (partywise) differentiation. But if Bhandari and other leaders feel Sainiks were involved, I'm proud of my men. When the Babri fell, the BJP found itself perplexed. The *Kar Sevaks* did what they wanted.

Our Sainiks from Mumbai did not reach there, but those from other parts of India, especially Uttar Pradesh, were present.'

As pictures of the onslaught on Babri were flashed on BBC's hourly news broadcast all through Sunday, 6 December, the situation in Mumbai turned uneasy. Violence had already broken out in several parts of the country, with Muslims venting their ire to protest 'the betrayal' by law-enforcing authorities. Thousands of Muslims in Mumbai, too, gathered in the gullies and mohallas of Muslim-dominated areas of the city to discuss the outrage, and soon, distraught Muslim mobs went on the rampage, targeting government property and the police. Knives, swords, acid bulbs and soda bottles made their appearance on the streets, and police were forced to open fire to disperse mobs in areas such as Pydhonie, Nagpada, Bhendi Bazaar, Dongri and Umerkhadi, the inner-city Muslim-dominated pockets through which the huge Mohammed Ali Road flows.

The first vehicle to be attacked was a police wireless van near Minara Masjid. It was smashed with an onslaught of stones at 11:30 pm on 6 December. The same night, a policeman became the first casualty of the riots. Constable Vilas Kadam was stabbed to death at Pydhonie. Another cop was fired at in the same area, but the bullet bounced off his helmet and he escaped.

By the morning of 7 December, violence had so convulsed Mumbai, one body was being carried into the state-run JJ Hospital every minute. More weapons were brought into the open, and where there were no bullets, showers of bulbs, stones, and tube-lights rained down on police and the Hindus.

Bus-stops were ripped out of pavements and flung on to the roads, traffic signals were smashed, vehicles were set ablaze, shops looted and torched and police outposts attacked. The Lakshminarayan temple at Dongri was burnt. In Pydhonie, police had to fire to prevent more damage to a Jain temple, and at Crawford Market, one person was killed in firing when two temples were attacked by a mob. Many Hindu shrines in Kalbadevi were damaged.

At Bainganwadi in Deonar, two constables protecting a Datta Mandir were killed by a mob. The idols were smashed, petrol and kerosene was poured in and around the temple, and it was set afire. At Nagpada, a Kashi-Vishweshwar temple was damaged and then torched.

Reports of rioting came in from the suburbs as well, and police at Malwani, which is on the banks of Manori creek in northern Mumbai, had to deal with a 5,000-strong crowd at Jumma Masjid hurling stones and soda bottles.

Police opened fire to quell rioters, and their bullets found many victims, but the chaos continued to spread. The Army was called in the evening. The Fourth Gurkha rifles began patrolling the streets of Dongri and Byculla by 7 pm, reinforcements from Deolali's Artillery Centre too sped towards Mumbai. Curfew was declared in eight areas in central and north Mumbai.

By the end of the day, 43 persons had been killed and 94 injured.

The 8 December edition of *Saamna* had a front-page editorial by Bal Thackeray. Titled *'Deshdrohyana Chirdaa'* (Crush the traitors), it said:

> Babar was not a victor, but the Hindus who, after 450 years, fought for the Ram Janmabhoomi in Ayodhya and regained it have proven themselves to be victors. Muslims should learn a lesson from this and stop the poisonous upsurge they have once again resorted to, else they will suffer the same fortune the Babri's domes had to... The moment the domes fell, anti-nationalist Muslims unleashed an orgy of violence throughout the country. We warn them again, and for the last time, that they should understand the sentiments of Hindus and join the national mainstream. If you follow selfish leaders who are determined to push you into hell and make an onslaught on the Hindus, beware!

As a bandh was called by Left parties and the Congress on 8 December to protest the Babri demolition, the turmoil continued. The bustle and activity of Mumbai was nowhere to be seen. All that was visible was smouldering vehicles, smashed shrines, destroyed shops, roads turned into multi-coloured glass mosaics, and armymen staging flag-marches.

The losses of BEST alone were put at ₹ 1 crore, and government property came in for attack, along with policemen. Outside Dharavi police station, 13 cars were burnt to scrap, and 50 others parked on the streets had their windscreens and lights smashed. Roadblocks were put up in different areas to prevent police reinforcements from arriving, and the hail of tubelights, soda bottles and boulders continued to rain on residential colonies and shops.

After word spread in Jogeshwari that a pandit had been killed, a Muslim funeral procession was attacked. Seven persons died in the subsequent police firing. In Kurla, Hindus retaliated for an attack on a temple by targeting a mosque and a madrassa.

Police had to open fire at 18 places that day, and the police commissioner said the violence was shifting to the eastern suburbs. According to official figures, the death toll in the two days of rioting had gone up to 94, but unofficial figures estimated the figure to be upwards of 150.

Curfew was clamped in five more areas – Chembur, Kurla, Nehru Nagar, Kherwadi and Nirmal Nagar – and it was clear that calling in the army had not helped, because nowhere had the men in olive-green been given control of the situation.

By early evening, news of the arrest of BJP leaders L.K. Advani, M.M. Joshi and Uma Bharati and VHP general secretary Ashok Singhal trickled in, and in protest the BJP and Sena called a bandh the next day.

On 9 December, entire clusters of huts at Saki Naka and Asalpha village were set afire by mobs, and more than 1,000 families rendered homeless. Fifteen persons were killed in Dharavi, 25 seriously wounded, and 15 shops were set ablaze. On VP Road, Shivneri building adjacent to a masjid was fired at from within the mosque amid cries of 'Masjid Wahi Banayenge'. And mobs led by the Sena torched entire timber-yards and scrap-yards, mostly owned by Muslims.

The official figure of the dead went up to 136, and Chief Minister Sudhakarrao Naik, who had rushed to Mumbai from Nagpur after having adjourned the Assembly's winter session, was hard-pressed to answer a barrage of questions.

Soon as he arrived in Mumbai, the chief minister held a meeting with the Sena chief. The writings in Saamna during the three days of rioting had gained nationwide notice. Asked about the paper's belligerence and the talks between him and Thackeray, Naik said: 'The government is thinking about the aggressive writings in Saamna. As for other things, I spoke to Thackeray and told him what is necessary.'[143]

The 'necessary' admonition, if any, appeared to have no effect. For, in his editorial in the 10 December Saamna edition, Thackeray wrote:

The government is trying to stem the rise of the public wave with the help of the Army. But it should first stop the religious fanatics. It should confiscate the huge piles of their weapons... It should find out where these illegal weapons, which have been aimed at the government itself, came from... All we say is that no obstacle can stop the Hindu sea of strength. This fire which is blazing is needed by the nation. It won't extinguish itself before consuming those traitors who have sprayed the ground with the mother's blood... the Hindu will no longer allow himself to be attacked... The words of the Hindu success story have started reverberating throughout the universe.

This is the beginning of an era of retaliatory war. In this era, the history and geography of not only this country but the world is going to change. The dream of the Akhand Hindu Rashtra is going to come true. Even the shadow of fanatical sinners will disappear from our soil. We will now live happily and die happily... 85 crore Hindus are making loud acclamations of revolution, and the fanatics have started spilling blood all over Hindustan. No revolution is possible by shedding tears. Revolution needs only one offering, and that is the blood of the devotees! During the last two days, Hindus have given the Goddess of Revolution the offering of their blood. What next?

That morning, though, there appeared to be comparative calm in Mumbai. Fifteen areas were still under curfew, but half the BEST fleet was back on the roads, and trains were full of office-goers.

The calm did not last long. By noon, all shutters had been downed and all activities had come to a halt as rumour spread that the Sena chief had been arrested. Police despatched vans equipped with loudspeakers to scotch the rumour, but people hurried home, unwilling to take chances. The city came to a standstill again.

Nearly 500 slums in Mahim's fishermen's colony were torched that day, and thousands rendered homeless. A Mariamma Mandir in Dharavi was damaged and burnt, and a timber mart near Mahim fort was set ablaze.

The authorities now put the death toll at more than 160 and the total losses at ₹ 100 crore. Losses in terms of production were estimated in the region of ₹ 300 crore.

When 11 December dawned, it brought along with it a great sense of uncertainty, because the relative calm of the earlier morning had proven short-lived.

Luckily, the day passed off without any major incidents. But evening showed up with a big blot. At 5:20 pm, two persons fired indiscriminately at some youths playing cricket in Azad Maidan. The assailants came on a scooter, opened fire and escaped. Nathuram Mohite, a resident of Mangalwadi, Girgaum, was killed in the firing, and three others seriously injured.

What made the day – a Friday – politically more significant was that it marked the beginning of the Shiv Sena's *maha-artis*, intended as a 'Hindu reply' to the Muslim namaaz on the streets.

Muslims in Mumbai had asked for lifting of the curfew and the ban on assembly in various parts of the city to enable them to hold their weekly namaaz. Police relaxed curfew for the few hours needed for the prayers, and the Friday ritual went off peacefully.

The Sena, which had regularly criticised the Friday congregations for the 'traffic bottlenecks' they created, took objection to this concession allowed to the minority community in the midst of riots. And decided to register its protest by holding a sort of counter-ritual.

'If curfew can be lifted for namaaz, why not for us too?' asked the Sena leadership, and demanded its relaxation for a *maha-arti* it wanted to organise at Gol Deool, located in the heart of south Mumbai. Gol Deool was a carefully chosen shrine because it was close both to the Muslim-dominated areas and to the Sena's Hindu-majority bastions.

The authorities allowed the *maha-arti*, and amid heavy army presence, more than a thousand Hindus led by Sena MLA Pramod Navalkar performed prayers on the streets.

That night, a police chowky in Dindoshi, Malad, was attacked by a 1,200-strong mob of Muslims, and armed hordes set upon a Shankar temple at Chincholiphata and set it afire. The temple's priest was dragged on to the road and stabbed. In a chawl nearby, 19-year-old Pralhad Shinde, who was watching television at home, was stabbed to death.

The next day, 12 October was relatively quieter. Except for one incident in which four persons were burnt to death in Asalpha village, there were no major markers of madness.

On the 13th, curfew was lifted during daytime, and it appeared as if Mumbai had had enough of blood-letting. Tension slowly abated over the next five days, and the city limped back to normalcy.

There were two brief flashes of insanity later that month, when bombs went off in local trains at Kandivli and Chinchpokli (18

December) and a Mathadi Kamgaar was stabbed to death in Dongri (27 December). Yet the worst was *apparently* over.

The final death toll in the violence was pegged at 227. Nearly 1,800 riot-related cases had been registered; 79 places of worship had been attacked; and 161 incidents of arson reported.

The Sena had, however, realised that its *maha-arti* at Gol Deool had clicked. It had met with the approval of even those Hindus who had scrupulously stayed away from the party so far; and it had provided a platform for mobilisation of masses.

The party now decided to hold *maha-artis* at all important temples across the city. The first of these was held on 26 December, and by 6 January, when violence erupted afresh, a total of 33 such *artis* had elicited massive response from the Hindu community.

There were demands that these *maha-artis* be banned, but the state government could take such a step only at the risk of inviting charges of minority appeasement. Having suffered a blow to its image already, it was not prepared to take any chances.

Little did it know that whatever was left of its image was also soon going to be shattered by another, bloodier, phase of rioting.

Two ghastly incidents coalesced conditions for a second round of rioting.

The first one was at Dongri. In the early hours of 6 January, Vishnu Kadam, one of the Mathadi workers employed in the docks came out of Vijay Transport Company's godown, where his brothers were sleeping along with two friends, to answer nature's call. Soon as he stepped out of the warehouse, he was attacked by a mob of 10 persons and killed on the spot. The assailants then entered the warehouse and slashed Vishnu's brother Rajaram Kadam with swords and choppers. Rajaram's screams awakened his other brother Tukaram and two other friends; when they rushed to his rescue, they too were stabbed.

News of the stabbings spread through Mumbai quickly, and the attack was seen as one on Hindus in a Muslim-majority area.

Efforts were made to explain the killings as arising from inter-union rivalry, but there were no takers for this theory.

Next day, the Maharashtra Rajya Mathadi Transport and General Kamgar Union declared a bandh in Dongri area, and Mathadi Kamgars came out on the streets in full strength to protest. Tensions had aggravated by now, and reports of stabbings and arson had started filtering in from many areas. The blaze of violence had enveloped flashpoints like Dharavi in no time at all.

The morning of 8 January brought with another piece of news.

Early that morning, the home of a Hindu family in the predominantly Muslim Radhabai Chawls in Jogeshwari was torched. Five people died on the spot: Rajaram and Sulochana Bane, the couple who had been staying there for nearly 30 years, Kamlabai Batlu, her 16-year-old daughter Laxmi and a 20-year-old disabled girl Meenakshi Narkar. One Vandana Kondalkar succumbed to her injuries two days later, but her two kids, aged 5 and 11, managed to escape.

Bane, a worker in a paint factory, was a supporter of the Shiv Sena, though he was not an active party worker. When Jogeshwari witnessed communal violence for the first time in 1973, the Bane family had been advised to shift out of the Muslim-majority chawls. Unlike other Hindus staying nearby, who then took advantage of a Sena offer and moved to Hindu-majority areas, the Banes did not do so. Riots rocked Jogeshwari the second time in December 1990 and January 1991, but the Banes still refused to move because they had not been affected.

The third time, they were not so lucky. As they slept in their one-room tenement, hoodlums spread kerosene around it and set it ablaze.

The entire city got wind of the incident by late afternoon, and the Sena posted its blackboards at street corners to announce the grisly event.

Anger swelled as reports came in that Muslim youths had established a garrison in the madrassas around Hindu chawls in Imamwada and were hurling petrol bombs at the chawl residents, and word spread that attacks were being mounted on Hindus in various areas by armed men sheltered by burkha-clad women.

Restless Sena cadres had begun assembling in the 221 shakhas across Mumbai, as if waiting for a nod from their leader to hit back. Looting and arson, meanwhile, spread from south and south-central Mumbai to central Mumbai, and large-scale destruction was wrought by rioters in Agripada, VP Road, Kalachowkie, Bhoiwada, Dadar and Mahim.

On page one of the *Saamna* issue of 9 January was an editorial headlined '*Rashtra Jivanta Theva*' (Keep the nation alive). In it, Thackeray laid out his case against 'anti-national' Muslims and gave a clear signal to his 'boys' to retaliate:

Fourteen harmless citizens were burnt alive by traitorous fanatics. Even small children were set ablaze. Entire lives were annihilated. Even after all this, the government, police and the shameless minister of state for home (Babanrao Pachpute) are going around in the localities of the fanatics carrying green handkerchiefs. We don't blame the cops. They too are being badly burnt in the blaze. They too have fallen victims to fanatics' bullets. Sudhakarrao, your peace committees are doing nothing. Your Congress leaders, who are going around as messengers of peace, have all circumcised themselves. How do the majority of Hindus live? Why should we watch silently, when arrogant animals are sprinkling blood on all streets? When the blaze of violence is burning the soul of the city, the government is busy chewing Chikni Supari at Varsha... The gunshots of fanatics are making people writhe in agony. Whose job is it to establish peace?

We can't be messengers of peace when our Hindu brothers and sisters are being tyrannised and trampled upon. The government may have gone down on its knees to Muslims who have separated themselves from the national mainstream and those who are out to mortgage the nation, but we don't want to release doves of peace... Anybody gets up and admonishes Hindus. As if we incited the riots. What do we have to ignite?... Weapons brought from Pakistan and Bangladesh are wreaking havoc in Bhendi Bazaar, Dongri and Behrampada. These arms have cruelly targeted and killed everyone, from infants to the aged. Mundkur and Khan, who showed what religion they belonged to when they attacked unarmed Hindus in Dharavi and Kurla, should stop the dirty dance of their own brothers in Bhendi Bazaar. Your true colours, and your loyalties, have been exposed. Our prediction has also come true. A Muslim, regardless of which nation he lives in and what position he enjoys, is a Muslim first and foremost. For him, the nation is subordinate to his religion and his brothers belonging to the Muslim religion. The attacks on nationalist citizens during the last two days have been assaults on the nation... The ones who were burnt in the Jogeshwari blaze and those who were stabbed on the streets of Bhendi Bazaar represent the agony of all nationalists. Even cops are now openly saying, "This government is inept". Around their waists are their service revolvers, but the government has assigned the cops only one responsibility – that of counting the bodies of people killed and thrown on the streets by anti-nationals. Police, too, are agonised. Everything has gone beyond patience. When dark clouds of danger loom large over

Hindustan, the government is telling us not to fight the danger. We have clamped curfew. Sit at home. Even if traitors burn your homes, don't hit back. Burn like camphor and die, we're told. We spit on such an impotent government! The people of Hindustan and Maharashtra are openly spitting on the face of the rulers! Even if the government is wearing a green burkha and standing on a street corner of Bhendi Bazaar with bangles in hand, lakhs of Hindu youths will keep this nation alive. Even if the sun and the moon exhaust their energy, human beings will now burn in anger! This is not provocation, this is simmering anger. If there's no wound on the body, a victory is meaningless! The next few days will be ours!

The next three days saw unprecedented violence in Mumbai. Defence Minister Sharad Pawar had arrived in Mumbai on 8 January, but his arrival sparked a game of one-upmanship between him and Chief Minister Naik, and as they busied themselves fighting political games, Thackeray's boys ran riot. Mumbai was scalded.

Attacks on Muslim establishments took place between 9 and 12 January. Hordes of Sena youths attacked Muslim homes, offices and shops. Municipal records were checked to find out where Muslim enterprises were located. Goods were pulled out of shops, piled up on roads and set afire. Nothing was too insignificant to invoke the wrath of the mobs – not even cycle shops, tea stalls, paan shops or cobblers' wooden planks. Footwear shops, most of which belonged to Muslims, were looted, and till the end of January, shoes and slippers looted during rioting were being surreptitiously sold all over Mumbai for half the price.

Criminal elements sensed in these riots a chance to have a field day, and they made the most of it. (On 12 January, when Thackeray appealed to his men to stop the violence, he admitted criminals had taken over the arena).

Mumbai's largest timber market at Reay Road was torched, and mobs roaming the streets stopped vehicles at will and set ablaze passengers of the 'other' religious persuasion.

As the cauldron of hate bubbled over, police were accused by Muslims of being partisan and not only assisting Hindu attackers but also attacking the minority community. There was more than a grain of truth in the charge, because in most areas, cops remained mute witnesses to the activities of Hindu mobs.

On the other hand was the accusation of the cops: the police force, armed with inadequate and antiquated weapons, had found itself besieged and targeted for assault in Muslim areas, and even Police Commissioner Shreekant Bapat had narrowly escaped a bomb attack when trying to quell a Muslim mob.

Armymen held flag-marches in over 30 areas of the city, but they had no clear-cut orders from their boss, Pawar, who appeared more interested in seeing Chief Minister Naik's reputation bite the dust than in restoring peace to a burning city. When the rioters realised the men in olive-green wouldn't get down from their vehicles, they began taking advantage of the situation. It was as if rioters had been given a free hand.

The state had withered away.

In the *Saamna* of 10 January, Thackeray wrote:

> Mumbai is burning. This is a spontaneous outburst. The arrogant belief of traitorous fanatics that they are victors is going to be reduced to ashes in this blaze. The traitors remember their own exploits. But Hindus have made them bite the dust on many fields of battle. Hindus have started burning the separatist tendencies harboured by Muslims. Only if past mistakes are corrected in the present does the future become bright. The brilliant history of the Hindus will be written by the same Hindu blood that was spilled at Bhendi Bazaar yesterday. Now we won't be crushed to death. Samartha Ramdas has said *Maarta Maarta Marave* (One should go down fighting). When the Hindu becomes aggressive, even mini-Pakistans start burning. Those who fondle the beards of Mullas and Maulvis should bear this in mind. The Hindus have opened their Third Eye.

As violence continued to rage, the shadow of fear stalked the streets, triggering rumours and panicky reactions. Commando squads from Islamic countries were supposed to be heading towards Mumbai with sophisticated arms, and warnings were sent out about nocturnal attacks on housing colonies by gangs of the 'other' community. Squads of young men were set up in various areas to stand alert for any sign of approaching danger. In middle-class Hindu localities, 'weapons' like soda water-bottles, iron rods, tube lights, stones and boulders were stockpiled to ward off attacks, and youngsters stood awake all night in anticipation of trouble. Cable TV operators too made mischief by flashing on-screen messages that mobs had begun launching attacks on buildings serviced by the network, and that the raiders were fast moving forward.

In the JJ Hospital area, passers-by were stopped and asked for their names. Not satisfied by that, mobs forced them to drop their trousers for incontrovertible evidence before giving them 'the treatment'.

On 11 January, patrolling armymen stopped Sena MLA Madhukar Sarpotdar when he was passing through Nirmal Nagar in Bandra. A search of his car revealed two revolvers, two choppers, two hockey sticks and two stumps. When the army handed over Sarpotdar to the cops, he was let off for want of adequate evidence (he was detained in February under the National Security Act). Sarpotdar later claimed he was carrying the weapons only for 'self-defence' and was on his way to answer a call for help.

The same day, Thackeray made an announcement in *Saamna*: 'Enough is enough. The fanatics have been taught a lesson. Now stop this violence.'

Shiv Sena boards displayed this message all over the city, and the attacks on Muslim property ended on 12 January. But Mumbai continued to witness incidents of violence for three or four days more, as anti-social elements fished in troubled waters, especially in the north-eastern suburbs. The involvement of criminal gangs in the violence was indicated by the unusually high incidence of 'private firings'. Around 67 cases of discharge of firearms by members of the public were reported in January, nearly twice the number in December. Petty criminals made more hay than gangsters, settling old scores and keeping cops occupied.

The last explosion in the second phase of rioting took place in Behrampada. Muslim slum dwellers occupying the land along the railway tracks here said Hindu occupants of the Housing Board buildings across the road had hurled firebombs at them and set a row of huts on fire. The Housing Board residents, on the other hand, pointed to bullet holes in the windows, claiming shots had first been fired at them from the slums.

All lines of communication between Hindus and Muslims had snapped during the December and January riots. The division was complete.

When the madness levels dipped and the fires were finally doused, the death toll was pegged at 557. Most of the affected persons in January had been Muslims.

Economists estimated that the orgy of violence had cost nearly ₹ 125 crore every day. An Indian Merchants' Chamber panel said loss of production, sales, export and trade came to ₹ 750 crore. Labour-intensive small-scale industries were badly hit, and the Mumbai Stock Exchange was said to have lost ₹ 35 crore for each day it was shut.

The state government announced on 5 January that Justice B.N. Srikrishna of the Bombay High Court would probe the circumstances surrounding the December and January riots.

The Sena's role in the violence led to demands for Thackeray's arrest, but the chief minister refused to hold the Sena directly responsible. 'I'm in regular touch with Thackeray on the phone,' was all that Naik said when the media posed questions.[144]

After the Ayodhya incident, BJP leaders like Advani and Joshi were arrested, but not even the fingernail of the law touched the Sena chief, who not only owned up to the Babri demolition but also the Hindu backlash in January (later, in the year 2000, the rebel Sainik Chhagan Bhujbal got Thackeray arrested for inflammatory writings in 1993, but the court threw out the case, calling it time-barred).

Thackeray became the focus of global media attention during the riots, and the unwillingness of authorities to touch him gave his larger-than-life image among Sainiks a still-bigger dimension. And in a polarised polity, the Sena won much political capital as the self-proclaimed defender of Hindus – a position that helped it immensely in the run-up to the 1995 Assembly polls.

29

THE PATH TO POWER

T he Shiv Sena continued its political climb all through 1993 and 1994, with Thackeray easily rifling through the alleged misdeeds of the Congress regime.

The regime's infirmity had come into focus during the riots, and when a series of bomb blasts ripped through Mumbai on 12 March 1993, the enfeebling of the state was no longer talked about, it's complete failure was. The ordinary citizen's resilience saw the city jump back to normalcy within 24 hours, but attempts by the new Congress Chief Minister Sharad Pawar to hog credit for resumption of normal life did not succeed. The government was seen as incapable of dealing with the threat posed by terrorism.

Pawar was sent by Prime Minister P.V. Narasimha Rao back to Maharashtra to revive the flagging fortunes of the Congress in the aftermath of the riots. But as time passed, Pawar found himself at the centre of what the people perceived as the Congress government's venal ways. Thanks to a series of crises – the blasts, the Jalgaon sex scandal, the Latur earthquake, the Govari massacre – and a volley of accusations hurled at him, it became harder for the Maratha leader to make the case that the Congress was the only party that would provide good governance.

Pawar's second term had been controversial due to: a) the deletion of 285 city plots from the development plan, b) the throwing open of the Vasai-Virar belt for development, c) his alleged association with smuggler Bhai Thakur and propping up of TADA detenus like Pappu Kalani and Hitendra Thakur, and d) donation of a plot of land at Malabar Hill to a housing society floated by IAS and other government officials. The third term turned out even more controversial, with more charges of corruption and nexus with criminals being flung at him and his party.

Thackeray attributed all the state's ills to the new chief minister. By the time the Sena chief began his campaign for the Vidhan Sabha elections scheduled for February 1995, he had a dossier on Pawar ready. As he travelled the length and breadth of Maharashtra, he listed his charges at all public meetings:

> He (Pawar) is Shakuni Mama, the harbinger of evil. See what happened after he returned as chief minister. On March 12 the blasts; then the earthquake in Marathwada; then the plague; the stampede in Nagpur that killed 128 Gowari tribals; and unseasonal rain that destroyed standing crop.

> He had vowed to give up politics and go to the Himalayas if he ever had to rejoin the Congress. What happened? He's atop a Himalaya of a different kind today, of currency notes. He's the richest politician in India.

> On being appointed defence minister, the first decision Pawar took was to sell defence land, especially to two Pune builders. This was strongly objected to by the army, navy, air force and many MPs. The decision had to be cancelled.

> Then vegetable oil: the defence contract was given to Baramati Oil Mill owned by his nephew Ajit Pawar. The oil was adulterated, and the army rejected the supply.

> On behalf of the Thalassemia Foundation, Pappu Kalani gave ₹ 30 lakh to Pawar's trust, Vidya Pratisthan. Thus the connection of Pawar and Kalani is clear.

> Telephone calls were made by some ministers to Dubai. The agencies have recorded them, but no investigation has been done. And INTUC has been captured by the Arun Gawli gang.

> The Sharma brothers involved in the JJ Hospital shootout travelled with the defence minister on a defence plane! What's more, Dawood's brother, Noora, said in an interview to the *Telegraph* that his family had good relations with Pawar!

His militant Hindutva pitch, too, continued. When, in 1994, he was asked on a television programme what message he would like to give Indian youth, he replied: 'Be militant. Hindus will have to bring militancy in this nation'. The Sena thus staked claim to greater militancy of thought and action than BJP and RSS, whose Hindutva was seen as less combative.

Thackeray's saffron clothes, the *rudraksha mala* in his hands and his act of unsheathing swords at rallies further drove home the symbolic content of Sena's message during the build-up to the 1995 elections.

This was accompanied by anti-Muslim rhetoric. On 12 March 1994, the first anniversary of the serial blasts, Thackeray warned: 'If the Election Commission allows burkha-clad women of the minority community to exercise their franchise in the ensuing elections, the Sena won't allow elections to be held, not only in Maharashtra but the whole of Hindustan.'

The demonising of 'anti-national' Muslims was one of the vital constituents of Sena's Hindutva. 'If their heart is in Pakistan, and their body is here, we don't want Muslims here. There is no compromise on this issue. I will not tolerate any traitor belonging to any caste or religion. But Muslims must prove their credibility,' the Sena chief said.

The issue of 'pro-Pak leanings' was intertwined with the problem of infiltration of extremists and illegal immigration of Pakistanis and Bangladeshis. 'Suppose there are Pakistani extremists living in their (Muslims') neighbourhood, I want the Muslims to tell the police. I do not want these spots to be known as mini-Pakistans. It is the duty of those Muslims to prove they are not Pakistanis. Take Bangladeshi Muslims. I will kick them out. They have got to be chucked out. I cannot forget one thing, that the Partition of this country was done on communal lines. Muslims asked for their own nation. Then leave us alone,' Thackeray said.

Film personalities also became a target. The Sena declared it would boycott A.K. Hangal's films after he attended a Pakistan Day function in Mumbai in 1993. The irony was that Hangal had participated in the agitation to make Mumbai a part of Maharashtra in the 1950s. Shabana Azmi came in for criticism with her comments in the wake of the 1993 riots.

However, unlike many other constituents of the Hindutva Parivar, the Sena did not make too much of the entry of multinationals in the wake of the liberalisation programme, saying that if it was a 'two-way traffic', the entry was justified. By two-way traffic, the Sena meant India would have to benefit as much as MNCs would on entering India.

During the Enron episode, the Sena's opposition was centred on three things a) the ill-effects of the project on Konkan's ecological equilibrium; b) overpricing; and c) the wrong procedure of awarding a contract without open bidding.

'We don't want to stop the project but we will have to look into all the issues that have raised their head,' Thackeray said. 'There are two sides to the Enron issue. One is local. The Konkan belt is blessed with beauty – mountains, beautiful trees, all kinds of fruits, cashew nut and coconut. The locals too are hard nuts, and you cannot crush their protests. They are not concerned with the deal as such; they are worried about the degradation of their environment, and I agree with them on this. On the other hand, we must look into the manner in which land was granted and find out why tenders were not invited.'

The Sena's Hindutva was thus a mix of militancy, religious symbols and acidic attacks on 'pro-Pak' Muslims. And it was soft-shelled by an endorsement of the economic reforms programme.

In the post-riots and post-bomb blasts scenario, the Hindu community in Mumbai and Maharashtra was easily susceptible to its appeal.

More attacks on the media, and more populism

Part of the Sena's organisational machinery was the party organ *Saamna*, whose circulation was in 1993-94 in the region of 1,50,000 to 3,00,000. Thanks to its strong distribution network, *Saamna*, which was also expanded into a Hindi edition in 1993, gave the party control over a vital mode of popular communication.

In August 1993, Nikhil Wagle, editor of *Mahanagar*, said he did not regard *Saamna* as a newspaper. On 18 August, a group of Sena workers, including three shakha pramukhs, assaulted him at a seminar on religious fundamentalism organised by the Hindi Patrakar Sangh. The same day, activists of the Bharatiya Kamgar Sena ransacked the office of another Marathi eveninger *Aaj Dinank* and beat up its reporter. The paper had published a report a day earlier on the imminent removal of BKS President Dattaji Salvi from his post.

Over 500 journalists from across the country staged a dharna outside Shiv Sena Bhavan on 11 September 1993, to protest the attacks on the media. Among the journalists assembled were N. Ram, editor of *Frontline*, Nikhil Chakravarty, editor of *Mainstream*, Prabhash Joshi of *Jansatta*, Dileep Padgaonkar of the *Times of India*, Prabhu Chawla of the *Indian Express* and noted Hindi journalist

Mrinal Pande. Also lending support by their presence were Medha Patkar and Shabana Azmi.

Even after this, the Sena carried out one more attack on journalists in Aurangabad in early 1994.

For its part, the Sena mouthpiece, *Saamna*, received a boost when the Bombay High Court dismissed in September 1994 a public interest petition filed by J.B. D'Souza and Dilip Thakore asking for a court direction to the Maharashtra government to prosecute Bal Thackeray and Sanjay Raut, executive editor of the paper.

In January 1995, the Supreme Court too dismissed the special leave petition against the High Court order, and *Saamna* continued to go from strength to strength, its language unencumbered either by state institutions or the courts.

The Sena's populist programme also continued, and as in its initial years, it benefited by the system's failure to deliver.

When serial blasts rocked Mumbai, Sena workers were among the first to reach affected sites and help victims. Sena ambulances rushed the injured to hospitals and also offered help in hospitals which were experiencing a shortage of support staff in the emergency.

Similarly, after the earthquake in September 1993, a Sena team led by Dr Dipak Samant rushed to Latur, distributed free medicines and adopted a village, Limbala, for rehabilitation work.

The Sena's alleged use of coercion to gather funds, and the presence of criminal elements in the shakha network came under attack from across the political spectrum. Yet its populist measures worked in its favour, and it was perceived as less corrupt than the ruling Congress.

The party built Ramadham, a home for the aged, at Khopoli. It organised blood donation camps and medical camps all over Maharashtra, initiated a literacy programme in some villages of Nashik district in 1994 and launched cooperative credit societies for villagers. It also 'adopted' hundreds of students statewide and provided them educational facilities, besides distributing free notebooks and other stationery to needy school children. It also conducted agitations on local issues and succeeded in getting electricity and water connections for many villages.

In the event of any price rise or artificial scarcity of essentials, Sena activists raided godowns of traders, seized the hidden commodities and sold them at low rates in the shakhas, thus winning the appreciation of people hit by an inflationary spiral.

As usual, the focus was on local problems, not national ones, and that paid dividends for the party in the 1995 polls. The poll campaign showed that issues of everyday living occupied centre stage in the minds of the electorate. For instance, newspaper reports vividly described how, in Worli, Mumbai, the fight between the Sena and Congress was about who had done more for the area by way of spending funds for housing, beautification and opposing the sale of mill land.

The Sena's reputation for providing jobs too was vital, because the State Directorate of Economics and Statistics had recorded that the number of job seekers registered with the employment exchange had shot up from 2,50,000 in 1985-86 to 3,30,000 in April 1994. Besides, the proportion of educated unemployed in Maharashtra was higher than in most other urban areas of India.

Against the set-up of the saffron party was a Congress in disarray, faced with charges of corruption and mal-administration. Even its blank vote-bank cheque was in danger of being bounced: Muslims were alienated from the Congress due to the Babri demolition, the riots and the allegedly draconian use of TADA, and the backward communities moved away from the Congress in Maharashtra following the Govari deaths in Nagpur.

Conducting a whirlwind tour across the state ahead of the 1995 Assembly elections, the Sena chief unlocked a wave in favour of the saffron alliance.

'I won't give you *Lokshahi*, I'll give you *Shivshahi*,' he promised the people of Maharashtra, selling the dream of a state as just as the one that Shivaji had established.

Voters were angry about rising prices, unemployment and corruption. So he went on a promising spree: free houses would be provided to 40 lakh slum dwellers, the price line of five essential commodities – jowar, rice, dal, sugar and groundnut oil – would be fixed for five years, and 27 lakh jobs would be provided to the unemployed.

Ministers in the Sena government would be sacked if they were corrupt and unresponsive. 'I will decide who the chief minister will be, and the remote control will be in my hands. If a single allegation of corruption is proven against my chief minister, he will have to leave his chair. And if someone goes to a minister or an MLA with a grievance and the response is, "OK, I'll see later, I'm busy at the moment," I'll kick them out. Even if it's the chief minister, I'll kick him out,' he said to applause in all his meetings.

For a people irked at being pushed around in the corridors of power, there were more welcome words: 'I won't tolerate piling up of files in the Mantralaya. If I find people's complaints and requests for help are pushed into red-tape-bound files and there's a pile-up, I'll go to Mantralaya, pour petrol and set it ablaze. What's the use of a Mantralaya that doesn't solve people's problems?'

Government expenditure would be slashed so that funds could be utilised for developmental works, and dead departments like the one on prohibition and a few government publications would have to go. 'What is the need for a prohibition department when everyone, including ministers, drinks, and when you have swimming pools filled with liquor?' Thackeray asked.

The surprise in the package was the offer to withdraw TADA, which had almost come to symbolise state terror. The Sena's opponents alleged that this promise was being made to save actor Sanjay Dutt, who had been held in the bomb blasts case for buying a weapon from two of the blast accused. In the course of the election campaign, the Sena chief clarified his stand. Asked why he was backing Sanjay Dutt, Thackeray said: 'Because I'm sure he has nothing to do with the blasts. Plus, I'm not sympathetic to Sanjay Dutt, but to the film industry as a whole. I'm concerned about the film industry and the thousands of workers in it. Because of Sanjay's arrest, the industry is in the doldrums, and work on 20 films featuring him has come to a standstill. Thousands of workers are without work! I'm not saying the case against Sanjay should be withdrawn. All I'm saying is, release him on bail!'

The Sena government would study the issue of TADA atrocities, he said, and if it found that innocents had suffered, they would be released.

Then there would be separate police stations for women, with a woman police commissioner, ACPs, DCPs, and inspectors. Pilferage would be stopped, and corruption in octroi would be wiped out.

What about an economic programme? 'Providing food, clothing and shelter is my economic programme,' Thackeray explained. The Congress could not even provide water in 35 years, he said, but the Sena government would make Maharashtra tanker-free in five years. And it would build 55 flyovers in Mumbai and a six-tier Mumbai-

Pune Expressway which would reduce the distance between the two cities by two hours.

Thackeray's campaign meetings attracted huge crowds and led to a surge in Sena's popularity. Pawar and the Congress could do little to stop the Sena in its tracks.

Maharashtra registered an all–time–high 71.87 per cent turnout of voters in the Assembly polls of February, and when the ballot boxes were opened on 11 March, it was clear that Thackeray had won.

The victory rally

In the evening of 14 March 1995, a sea of humanity converged at Mumbai's Shivaji Park to see the Sena's Manohar Joshi take oath as chief minister.

This oath–taking function made a departure from the norm. Since 1960, all chief ministers had been sworn in at Raj Bhavan, the place of the state's constitutional head, the governor. This was the first time a chief minister was taking oath in the presence of lakhs of people.

Thackeray had wanted it so. 'If we come to power, the swearing–in ceremony of the Sena chief minister will not be at Raj Bhavan. It will be at Shivaji Park, under the statue of Chhatrapati Shivaji Maharaj, and the entire city will be invited,'[145] he had declared beforehand. After all, Shivaji Park was in Dadar, the heartland of Sena support, and the party had claimed 30 out of the 34 Assembly seats in Mumbai.

The electorate's verdict had been clear: the Sena–BJP combine had won 138 seats (Sena–73, BJP–65); the Congress had managed to get just 80. The saffron combine's performance in all regions of the state had been top–notch. In Mumbai, it had all but wiped out the Congress; out of the 65 seats in the Konkan region, a recognised Sena bastion, the alliance bagged 51, while the Congress had to be content with four; and considerably improving on its 1990 showing in the other three regions – northern Maharashtra, Vidarbha and Marathwada – the alliance had this time bettered its tally by 50 per cent. In the three regions together, the combine won 24 more seats in all; the Congress, on the other hand, got 30 seats fewer.

Newspapers all over Maharashtra emblazoned their pages with the Sena's performance, and front–page editorials in dailies, while expressing astonishment at the transfer of power in a state considered an unassailable Congress bastion, waxed eloquent on Thackeray's charisma and leadership qualities which had won the day for his party. Rather than throw its hat into the ring in disregard of the electorate's wishes, the 80-member Congress legislature party led by Sharad Pawar, which had emerged the largest single party, decided not to stake a claim for power.

On the morning of 13 March, a joint legislature party meeting of the Sena-BJP was held at Sena Bhavan, the Sena's headquarters opposite Shivaji Park. Presided over by the Sena chief and BJP leader L.K. Advani, the meeting elected Manohar Joshi as leader and Gopinath Munde as deputy leader of the Sena-BJP's 138-strong legislature grouping. Following this, Thackeray and Advani met Governor P.C. Alexander to submit a formal letter staking claim to form the government. They also informed him that a group of 10 independents had offered to support the alliance, thus taking its tally to 147, two more than the majority mark.

The debonair Sudhir Joshi was originally tipped to be chief minister, but the Sena chief had sprung a surprise by appointing Manohar Joshi to the post for his managerial savvy and administrative skills. Sudhir Joshi was perceived as more charming among the two, and far more dearer to Shiv Sainiks, but his maternal uncle Manohar, it was felt by the party boss, would tackle the bureaucracy and political adversaries better.

After the nearly three-lakh-strong crowd at Shivaji Park had witnessed the swearing-in of the chief minister and the deputy chief minister, Thackeray asked the triumphalists, at the very beginning of his speech: 'Is this a dream?'

He said nobody had believed him when he had said they would come to power, but the seemingly impossible had happened, and now, it was up to the Sena–BJP to give the people of the state a good government. He spoke of how providing water to people would be his priority, how the weight of schoolbags needed to be reduced, how a programme would be launched to provide a push for new industries, and how ex-army officers would be posted at octroi collection centres to curb corruption. He repeated his promise of reviewing the Enron project and of providing free houses to 40 lakh slum dwellers and asked illegal Bangladeshi and Pakistani immigrants to leave 'before we chuck them out of here'.

And he explained his 'remote control' concept of governing. 'I am not an advocate of Hitlerism, but the promises made by the Sena-

BJP shouldn't remain on paper. Hence I'll "remote control" the government to ensure the people's wishes are fulfilled.'

Thackeray was, indeed, in command. His Shiv Sena, often dismissed by political pundits as a non-serious factor in Maharashtra's politics, had captured power.

30

THE SENA GOVERNMENT

The Shiv Sena's record in power (1995 to 1999) left a lot to be desired. It was in this period that Maharashtra began to slip in economic terms from its number one slot nationally (the slide has since continued under the Cong-NCP regime). The saffron outfit did not deliver on most counts: its free housing scheme for 40 lakh slum dwellers came a cropper, its zunka-bhakar scheme to create outlets that would provide (Maharashtrian) food at affordable rates went bust, and on the development front, there was not much to show except 55 flyovers in Mumbai and the six-lane Mumbai-Pune Expressway, perceived not so much as the Sena's achievement as that of BJP man and then PWD Minister Nitin Gadkari. The majority of Sena's voters travelled on BEST buses which were not allowed to ply on the flyovers but had to take the congested roads below instead.

The party's voter base saw transformation it had not hoped for. 'Preferential treatment for locals' stayed on paper, as did 'job creation for the bhoomi-putra'. The number of new jobs promised was 27 lakh, but the Sena leadership itself complained the government had hardly done anything in this regard. Mill land gave way to high-rises, and mill workers' families, mostly Maharashtrian, had to shift from Parel, Lower Parel and Lalbaug in central Mumbai to the distant suburbs as the builders' lobby started establishing its grip over the city. Marathi-speaking people living in two other Sena-dominated areas, Dadar and Girgaum, too saw a growth in real estate in which they had little or no role and which would alter the Maharashtrian character of these areas forever; and no aspect of Marathi culture – language, food, theatre, films, music – was seen to have received any fillip from the state government.

Much as the Sena spoke of promoting the Marathi language, the number of Marathi schools reduced, and allegations flew that the Sena government was in a hurry to hand over land where these schools were located to the original owners so they could construct towers there.

Graft charges were made as Sena legislators and ministers changed their lifestyles overnight from plain to flashy and ostentatious. Equally significant was the fact that Gujaratis, Marwaris and Jains were no longer the only real estate developers in the city; prominent Sena leaders had stepped in there with their entrepreneurial acumen, and the ordinary Marathi *manoos* was displaced.

To begin with, the Enron muddle, for which the Sena had excoriated Sharad Pawar's government, grew worse. The Sena–BJP government first scrapped the deal and then renegotiated it. In the midst of these negotiations unfolded a drama that witnessed the first of many clashes between the Sena chief minister, Manohar Joshi, and his party chief.

Enron executive Rebecca Mark, who was supposed to meet the chief minister to try and save the power project, first went to Bal Thackeray's Matoshree residence to meet the Sena chief. Because of this, she could not keep her appointment with Joshi. The chief minister, waiting for her at the state headquarters at Nariman Point in south Mumbai, flew into a rage and cancelled the appointment.

Thackeray was furious when he learnt that Joshi had lost his cool because Rebecca Mark had chosen to meet him first, and tempers cooled down only after the chief minister informed him that was not the case. He told Thackeray he had been unaware that Mark was at Matoshree, and said he had been angry only because she had failed to arrive on time.

Then, the zunka bhakar scheme ended in a mess. The Sena government helped to set up zunka bhakar stalls, many of them on prime properties owned by the state, but the scheme became an avenue for corruption, and the stalls were such that the term Zunkha Bhakar Kendra was a misnomer: most of them were turned into fast food joints. Finally, the government ordered most of the stalls shut, decided that no new ones would come up, and announced that it would 'analyse' if the scheme had been truly beneficial to the poor or had been misused.

A project to provide free housing to 40 lakh slum dwellers, too, faltered from the start. It was criticised by the Sena's ally, the BJP, as unrealistic, and seeing that it was getting nowhere, the Sena government not only changed its housing minister but even gave up its role as facilitator and became an active player by forming the Shivshahi Punarvasan Prakalp Ltd (SPPL), a government-owned company, for rehabilitation of slum dwellers. However, even that did not help, as only a few thousand slum dwellers got free homes.

On the government's failure to provide jobs, one of the Thackerays, the Sena chief's nephew Raj, berated it. He said, 'Ever since the alliance came to power, I have been asking them to give me information on steps taken on employment generation and self-employment programmes, but the response has been poor.'[146]

Raj said Manohar Joshi had initially headed the Sena government's specially created Employment Department for one-and-a-half years. Later, Pramod Navalkar took charge of it, and Diwakar Raote took over from him. 'On many occasions I asked for information from both Joshi and Navalkar, but there was no response. I could get the status report only after Raote took over,' Raj, who in 1998 established the Shiv Udyog Sena to provide jobs to youth, noted.

Raj, for his part, was at the centre of the controversy that marked the first serious crisis for the Sena during its rule.

Early in the second half of 1996, Chhagan Bhujbal, erstwhile Sainik who was now leader of Opposition in the Legislative Council, called a press conference and introduced Sheila Kini, who alleged her husband Ramesh had often been called in at the *Saamna* office by Raj's men and asked to vacate his Matunga flat. She said her husband had left home on 23 July, saying he was going to the *Saamna* office. The next day, he was found dead in a Pune theatre. The Congress said the Sena, and Raj, were involved, and demanded a CBI probe.

As the state asked its Crime Investigation Department to investigate, Raj denied he had ever met Kini but confirmed he knew Laxmichand Shah, the man who wanted Kini's flat vacated. He called the charges a 'plot' hatched by Pawar and 'Lakhoba' Bhujbal.

Bal Thackeray demanded to know if Kini was a Mahatma Gandhi, and *Saamna* pulled no punches in blaming Kini's widow for the death. When the CID sent its report to the Bombay High Court, from where it was to be given to CBI for further investigation, the paper said the report had in fact established Sheila Kini's involvement in the case.

Later, the CBI absolved Raj of the charges, but the episode marked the first major attack by the Opposition on the Sena government.

In November 1996, social activist Anna Hazare accused two ministers – Agriculture Minister Shashikant Sutar of the Sena and Finance Minister Mahadev Shivankar of BJP – of corruption. The government set up a one-man inquiry committee under Justice H.W. Puranik to probe the matter. The committee absolved Shivankar but held Sutar guilty.[147] However, Puranik said that for action to be taken against Sutar, it was necessary to give him a chance to present his case. So another committee was set up to probe the charges, and its report gave Sutar a clean chit.[148] But before that, Sutar had to quit for the embarrassment the episode caused the government.

Hazare then also pointed an accusing finger at Social Welfare Minister Babanrao Gholap of the Sena and was sued for defamation by Gholap. The court freed the minister for want of evidence and sent Hazare to jail for defamation. The alliance government then cleverly used its special powers to release the social activist, thus blocking any surge of support in his favour.

While the Kini episode was fresh in memory and while Hazare's anti-graft agitation was on, the Sena got into poll mode. Elections to the BMC were to be held in February 1997. Bal Thackeray ran the poll campaign as if winning the elections was a matter of prestige to him. I remember him holding even street-corner meetings during this time, defending the Sena government, attacking Hazare and generally painting the elections as a referendum on his own record as Sena pramukh and not so much a referendum on the Sena government. His efforts worked, and the Sena captured the BMC with 103 seats. As a thank-you gesture, Thackeray did a *saasthang namaskar* before the crowd at Shivaji Park at the victory rally.

Barely had this win been celebrated, when Sainiks got their government into trouble. Ten Dalits were killed, and 26 injured, after a police officer Manohar Kadam ordered his men to fire on a crowd protesting against the desecration of a statue of Babasaheb Ambedkar at Ramabai Nagar, Ghatkopar, in north-east Mumbai in July 1997. Bhujbal again went on the offensive and called the Sena government 'the killer of Dalits'. The Sena alleged Bhujbal himself had masterminded the desecration, but Sainiks did not stop at that: they stormed his official bungalow at Nariman Point, situated in a high-security area, and tried to 'find' him. When they could not, they smashed the furniture and left. Bhujbal escaped narrowly by somehow managing to hide in the house.

This act of violence nearly brought down the Sena government. The Opposition's demand for imposition of Article 356 was eventually rejected, but those in the Sena government had no defence to offer, especially when the party proudly owned responsibility for the attack.

Increasingly, it became clear that Thackeray himself was none too happy with the government, and especially with the chief minister he had appointed.

He and Joshi had already had a spat over Rebecca Mark's visit. Another disagreement took place when, during a visit to the US, Joshi suggested the state sign a MoU with the Hinduja Group for building an airport. The Sena chief told his chief minister there were more important things to be done for the people: an airport was not the most elemental necessity, food, clothing and shelter were.

All through 1995-97, the tone of the Sena mouthpiece *Saamna* suggested Thackeray was pressing for greater compliance with his orders as 'remote control'. Through the pages of his mouthpiece, he slammed the government, and Joshi in particular, for the bureaucracy's 'intransigence' and for its inability to implement welfare steps. He expressed displeasure that 'pro-Pawar' bureaucrats were not being reined in despite instructions to do so. But even as he hit out at the government, Thackeray ensured, in the first two-and-a-half years at least, that his impatience did not cross a certain limit.

That limit was crossed after the Sena's debacle in the March 1998 Lok Sabha elections. The Congress won 40 seats in Maharashtra, and the Sena-BJP, which earlier had 33, got just 8.

Thackeray said the 'arrogance' of some of his people, meaning those in government, had led to the defeat, and in an interview to *Saamna*[149] went all out against the chief minister.

What seemed to have particularly riled him was that soon after the poll defeat to a Sharad Pawar-led Congress in the state, Joshi had praised Pawar and said he was fit to be Congress Parliamentary Party leader. Further, Joshi had patted himself on the back and said no corruption charges had been made against him.

By this time, complaints had apparently reached Thackeray that Joshi was encouraging the builders' lobby, and he had also heard of the existence of a 'mini-chief minister' who, apparently, in league with a builder, was extorting money in Mumbai. Referring to Joshi's statement that Pawar would never launch an attack on him, Thackeray said:

> How can you give this guarantee? On what basis?... Should one be close to such people? He (Joshi) should ask himself: Is this proper? It means I should accept enmity. You will keep your companionships intact. The companionships still exist. I know that. I don't live in darkness.

Despite Joshi's claim that no graft charges had been made against him, the fact was that allegations had been hurled at him and his son. On this, Thackeray said:

> The chief minister should answer these charges. Why should I enter into it? When charges were being flung at me and my family, no one came forward to defend us. I won't interfere in the matter. Because only he must be having answers to the accusations.

Not stopping at this, Thackeray went on to make corruption charges himself:

> I know for a fact that someone called Raj Dadarkar is causing havoc in the name of the chief minister. I don't know if Joshi knows him, but he has gone berserk. This man can prove costly for the chief minister. Countless stories have come to my ears. In certain cases, this man has taken money but not done the work for which he was paid. He has in some cases taken ₹ 40 lakh. Some of the persons who paid him met me and complained... The chief minister should himself see the kind of persons he's close to.

About Joshi's perceived closeness to Pawar, he said:

> If my chief minister is pro-Pawar, he'll have to pay for it. I'm saying this frankly. If my chief minister is pro-Pawar, I'll have to do a rethink on him. I won't spare anyone. After all, you have friendship with those who're out to finish us. How can this be

possible? I work here day and night, and you strut around and get close to the enemies.

Thackeray went on to the criticise the government for its inability to take the Sena agenda forward and announced he had decided to take sanyas from active politics for a while. During this period, he petulantly said, those in government could do what they wanted.

Sainiks immediately rushed to Matoshree in large numbers, saying, '*Saheb havet, Sarkar nako* (We want Saheb, not the government)' and heckled, abused and even manhandled Sena ministers and legislators who had come to the Thackeray residence to request the Sena chief to revoke his decision.

In mid-1998, the Srikrishna Commission report on the 1992-93 Mumbai riots was tabled in the Assembly. The Commission, set up in January 1993, had been disbanded by the Sena-BJP soon after the alliance came to power but had been revived following the intervention of Prime Minister A.B. Vajpayee during his 13-day rule in 1996.

In his 700-page report, Justice Srikrishna had indicted 31 policemen and many top leaders, including Bal Thackeray. 'Thackeray,' the report said, 'acted like a veteran general commanding his loyal Shiv Sainiks to retaliate by organised attacks against Muslims.'

Joshi called the report 'biased and anti-Hindu' and defended his political mentor and the Sena (the BJP differed, with Deputy Chief Minister Gopinath Munde saying the party did not believe the report was biased). This, however, helped to keep the peace between Thackeray and Joshi only for a short while.

In September 1998, Thackeray, indicting his government again, said investments into the state had decreased, and fresh investments were going to Andhra Pradesh. He also gave Joshi an unkind cut by remarking that Chandrababu Naidu, chief minister of Andhra Pradesh was 'moving like a typhoon'. Joshi tried to clarify that someone must have given Thackeray wrong information, and added that he would call on the Sena chief to explain the correct situation, but by now, the schism between him and his mentor was too deep.

When a case was filed in the Bombay High Court alleging that a Pune plot reserved for a school was illegally de-reserved to accommodate the multiplex of the chief minister's son-in-law Girish

Vyas, Thackeray made it clear that any strictures by the court against the chief minister would lead to his ouster.

Joshi was eventually removed early in 1999, Sena style: Thackeray sent a two-line letter with an emissary to the chief minister's official residence, Varsha, asking him to submit his resignation to the governor.

Apart from the Thackeray-Joshi conflict, other tensions had also been brewing in the Sena government all through 1998, and embarrassments were piling up all the time.

A few days ahead of a Cabinet reshuffle in May that year, Joshi asked Ganesh Naik, the Sena's minister for environment and forests, to resign. What Naik did then was unforgivable in the Sena: he questioned the directive. Three days later, he was sacked.

Naik soon floated the Navi Mumbai Nagri Vikas Aghadi with the help of 24 Sena corporators, who severed ties with the party to support him. When the Aghadi put up its candidate for the mayoral election and took control of the Navi Mumbai Corporation, Thackeray called a stop to quarrying in Navi Mumbai to cut Naik down to size. The Sena leadership reasoned that by breaking Naik's grip over quarries in the Navi Mumbai belt, it would hurt his source of strength. But within days of imposing a ban on quarrying operations, Joshi had to revoke the decision. The ban had cost thousands of youngsters their jobs, a majority of them Sainiks.

Naik later joined Pawar's Nationalist Congress Party.

Soon after this, the Sena government had to face the embarrassment of Sena legislators cross-voting during Rajya Sabha elections in favour of two Independent candidates. It soon emerged that the Sena's own member, Mukesh Patel, was instrumental in inducing some Sena MLAs to flout the party diktat. Patel was let off with a 'warning'. The Sena took no action against him.[150]

To make matters worse, two Sena ministers, Suresh Navale and Gulabrao Gawande, alleged they had received threats from Sainiks who felt they were about to desert the party. Both Navale and Gawande later joined Ganesh Naik's camp.

In July 1998, the Sena government had to eat humble pie after it decided to deport 28 allegedly illegal immigrants from Bangladesh. A team of Mumbai police was on its way to the Bangladesh border with these immigrants, when a mob swooped down on the train in which they were travelling and rescued the people being deported. West

Bengal's Communist regime informed the Maharashtra government that 'prima facie it transpired that some of the deportees brought by Maharashtra police were Indian citizens belonging to some districts of West Bengal',[151] and Home Minister L.K. Advani told Parliament that the Jyoti Basu government had 'advised the Maharashtra government to ensure proper co-ordination with West Bengal police while deporting immigrants'.[152] Chief Minister Joshi protested, but the Calcutta High Court, acting on a petition filed by some deportees, restrained the Centre from deporting them.

The one success for the government seemed to be in its fight against gangland. The year 1998 witnessed an explosion in underworld activities in Mumbai. Extortion killings, inter-gang rivalry and disputes settled with the bullet produced an all-time record number of shootouts. The government for some time insisted the law and order situation was fine and that the common man was safe, and later brought in a legislation, the Organised Crime Control Act. Along with that, it approved of the policy of police encounters. The maximum number of encounters took place during the Sena's regime, and the encounter specialists were seen as heroes for a while (most of them were discredited later when it was revealed that many encounters were fake and allegations were made that various cops were acting on behalf of individual gangs, wiping out members of rival gangs).

Sainiks outside the government, meanwhile, had not stopped short of creating trouble for their party's government ever since Thackeray had expressed his desire to take political sanyas in March 1998.

In April that year, they had disrupted Pakistani ghazal singer Ghulam Ali's concert at Hotel Centaur in Mumbai. The Sena government came in for flak for this attack, but Thackeray's son Uddhav defended the Sainiks, saying, 'Indian soldiers are guarding our borders under adverse conditions. Pakistani troops are firing. And some people want to enjoy an evening of ghazals with a Pakistani artiste.'[153]

In December 1998, two major 'agitations' took place: one, against Deepa Mehta's film on homosexuality, *Fire*, and the second, against Pakistan's proposed cricket tour to India.

Attacks on theatres screening *Fire* and Sainiks' half-Monty outside Dilip Kumar's house for his endorsement of the film and his role in a petition filed in Supreme Court for the film's screening led to accusations that the Sena was using its power to define what was culturally agreeable to society. The government found the party's position difficult to explain, more so the disruption of shows and destruction of property.

Among the worst acts of Sena vandalism was the attack on the Indian cricket board's headquarters in Mumbai. Sainiks entered the BCCI office, smashed the furniture and damaged the Prudential World Cup that India had won, for the first time, in 1983. Uddhav denied Sena's involvement in the attack, but the alliance government got 14 Sainiks arrested for the incident.

Early in January 1999, Shiv Sainiks in Delhi dug up the pitch at the Ferozshah Kotla stadium.

Differences between the Sena and BJP were also coming to a head around this time. A BJP functionary had questioned the financial viability of Thackeray's pet project, the free housing scheme; the Sena had opposed the ban on the Marathi play *Mee Nathuram Godse Boltoy*, a defence of Gandhi's assassin, while the BJP had felt it was in order; the finance minister (from BJP) had written a letter to the chief minister (from the Sena) warning him of the state's perilous financial position, but the chief minister had claimed the state was not on the brink; the chief minister and deputy chief minister had stopped addressing joint press conferences; and Sena MP Sanjay Nirupam had blamed BJP leader Pramod Mahajan for the grounding of the Tata Airways project, charging that Mahajan bent the civil aviation policy to protect the interests of Jet Airways, and an agitated Mahajan had responded by saying, 'I have been trying to restrain myself despite provocations, but I must admit that for one reason or the other, relations between the alliance partners have turned sour'.[154] Then there had been a spat over providing free power to farmers: Thackeray had 'directed' the chief minister to provide free power to 24 lakh farmers in the state 'at any cost', but Munde, who held the energy portfolio, had opposed it, saying it would add a burden of ₹ 2,380 crore to a nosediving economy. Thackeray had then accused the state power board of corruption.

The worst game of one-upmanship took place over Pakistan's proposed cricket tour. While Thackeray said he would not allow Pakistan to play in India, the deputy chief minister, Munde, and Prime Minister A.B. Vajpayee assured security to the Pak team. Vajpayee was so categorical as to say that 'no individual or organisation would be allowed to obstruct the Pakistan team'. Thackeray finally withdrew the 'agitation' after deputy prime minister and Union Home Minister Advani met him in Mumbai to persuade him.

On 12 March 1999, the Bombay High Court made damaging observations against Manohar Joshi in the 'Girish Vyas land scam' case.[155] Joshi was found to have misused his executive powers as chief minister and urban development minister to illegally de-reserve a school plot in Pune for the multiplex of his son-in-law and to have tried to 'mislead' the court during hearings. The ruling came as a blow to the Sena-BJP government, but the blow would have been even bigger if Joshi had still been chief minister.

In the ultimate analysis, though Thackeray had said he wanted a *gati sarkar* (government of speed) and not just a *yuti sarkar* (alliance government), the government did few things as speedily as changing the name of Bombay to Mumbai or that of Sahar airport to the Chhatrapati Shivaji airport. The change in nomenclature of the city it brought about in its first year in power, but on the whole, the government's progress on various fronts was slow while the conflict between the government and its 'remote control' kept on increasing, and the Sena continued to embarrass it with its activities beyond the pale of the law. For the first time, Maharashtra appeared to be in danger of becoming a revenue-deficit state, the massive Krishna Valley Development Corporation irrigation scheme came under scanner for financial mismanagement, the announcement of a 'tanker-free Maharashtra' remained on paper, like so many other announcements, and the result was that in the 1999 Assembly polls, the Sena lost power even though the Congress and the Nationalist Congress Party, formed that year by Sharad Pawar, fought the Assembly elections separately.[156]

The Sena also lost two subsequent Assembly elections, in 2004 and 2009, though the Congress-NCP's performance in government was far from satisfactory. In 2009, the Sena even lost the status of the main Opposition party and the position of Opposition leader to the BJP, which got more seats.

31

RAJ VERSUS UDDHAV

When Uddhav and Raj Thackeray were born in the 1960s, the Thackerays lived as a joint family at their ground-floor residence at Dadar. Bal's father Prabodhankar was around then, and Bal and his brother Shrikant, a musician, got along well.

Right from childhood, Raj, whose real name is Swar-raj, given to him by his musician father Shrikant, was as close to his uncle as any of the Sena chief's own children: Jaidev, Bindumadhav and the youngest, Uddhav. He was early attracted to the tools of his uncle's trade, the brush and colours, and seemed to have a natural aptitude for sketching. This endeared him to his uncle and made the uncle a source of constant encouragement. Thackeray would show him the works of noted cartoonists, especially his all-time favourite, David Low, and would provide tips on cartooning.

An incident from Raj's school days illustrates the closeness between the two. Both Raj and Uddhav studied at the Balmohan Vidyamandir, a reputed Marathi school situated close to their residence. One day, Thackeray was returning home from a rally when he saw Raj leave the home with his father, Shrikant. On entering the house, he asked Raj's mother where the two had gone. They had gone to Raj's school, she said. The principal had summoned the father for some mischief the boy had done. Thackeray, who had just about taken off his chappals, put them on again and headed straight to the school, a disturbed look writ large on his face. 'You can imagine what happened once he reached the school,' Raj said later, recollecting the incident.

The closeness remained intact even after Balasaheb's family shifted to Matoshree in the late 1960s. Raj now began to spend a lot of time at the Bandra bungalow. What became evident soon was that he had not merely taken up the brush, he had also begun to model himself on his uncle. He had the uncle's looks; his mannerisms too soon started resembling Thackeray's. He discovered as he grew up that he had the uncle's deep baritone voice as well.

In childhood, Raj had begun accompanying Bal Thackeray to some of his public meetings. By the time he had completed schooling and studied at the JJ School of Arts after that (Uddhav too studied at JJ), his interest in the Shiv Sena, in politics and in public affairs was much developed.

In 1988, Raj became president of the Bharatiya Vidyarthi Sena (BVS), the party's youth wing. That was the time elections were allowed in colleges affiliated to the University of Bombay. Raj took on the Congress's National Students Union of India (NSUI), the Sangh Parivar's Akhil Bharatiya Vidyarthi Parishad (ABVP) and Left-wing student groups. He was an extrovert and assertive. Uddhav, who at this point had little interest in politics, was, on the other hand, shy and reserved. He liked his own company and his camera, which he had taken to.

Raj made sure the BVS was seen as an aggressive outfit, and it was part of clashes that would then erupt among rival student groups in Mumbai's colleges. This was also the period in which the Sena, having embraced Hindutva, was growing rapidly, so a lot of youth were driven towards its youth wing and towards the adrenalin rush that Raj represented and advocated.

The year after Raj took control of BVS, Thackeray launched his newspaper, *Saamna*. Raj began drawing cartoons and sketches for the paper and also took up a corner on the first floor of the paper's offices at Prabhadevi in central Mumbai.

Raj participated in his uncle's campaign for the state polls in 1990, and his participation was even greater in 1995, when Thackeray's persistent attacks on the Congress brought the Sena to power. Uddhav preferred not to be in public view in 1991, busy as he was with photographic pursuits. In the years leading up to the 1995 poll campaign – in particular, after 1993 – he carried this pursuit into the political arena: he began accompanying his father to rallies in order to perch himself at vantage points and take pictures. He almost never sat on the dais during this period, happy instead at clicking away and recording all the action on-stage.

During the 1995 campaign, his interest in politics seemed to have awakened, but even then, he chose to remain mostly in the background. After the Sena came to power, however, he started playing a role in the action backstage. After his mother Meena-tai died in September 1995 and his elder brother Bindumadhav (a film-maker, he produced the Bollywood film *Agneepariksha* starring Manisha Koirala and Nana Patekar) passed away in the first half of 1996 in a road accident, Uddhav grew especially close to his father. Now he was consulted on many matters and willingly offered suggestions.

Within a year of the Sena coming to power, Raj got embroiled in a controversy over the death of Ramesh Kini (*see* pg 219). Chhagan Bhujbal, erstwhile Sainik who was leader of Opposition in the Council during Sena rule, took up the issue and tried to put the Thackerays on the defensive.

Thackeray Sr responded belligerently, saying Raj was being framed, and during a by-poll campaign in Kurla in the midst of the controversy (the Sena lost that seat), even angrily asked, 'Who is this Kini? Was he a Mahatma?' A CBI inquiry later cleared Raj, but the controversy had an effect on his political career.

Another controversy that came up soon after complicated matters further. Raj decided to organise a Michael Jackson concert in Mumbai, in association with event organisers Wizcraft, to raise funds for the Shiv Udyog Sena, an outfit he had floated after the Sena came to power to provide jobs to Maharashtrian youth.

The Sena came in for much criticism. Bal Thackeray openly derided westernised Indian youth and had even ridiculed the practice of cutting cakes on birthdays. The Sena's critics said his party was welcoming a pop star, an icon of western culture who represented everything the Sena railed against.

The Sena chief was defiant – to the point of playfully voicing pride over Jackson's use of his toilet. He is still much quoted on that one, but he said one more thing at the time that has since been forgotten. Asked by the media if he thought Jackson was a man or a woman, Thackeray said, 'He's somewhere in between'.

An old family feud proved to be another irritant ahead of the concert. The venue, Andheri Sports Complex, had earlier been granted to Thackeray's estranged brother Ramesh for a programme. When the Jackson concert got the go-ahead, Ramesh threatened to immolate himself, but was arrested. Close family friends then stepped in to work out a compromise.

The police said 70,000 people attended the concert held on 1 November 1996, but the organisers Wizcraft said they had sold only 16,000 tickets. The Shiv Udyog Sena was supposed to raise ₹ 4 crore from the programme, but Raj said they got nothing except criticism.

Raj then organised a Lata Mangeshkar concert, at the same venue, in 1997, to raise funds. It was a success, but these high-profile events in effect marked the beginning of the cold war between Raj and Uddhav. Having involved himself in party politics since 1995, Uddhav by this time had a camp he could call his own; and Raj, already de facto number two in the party, had his own band of followers. Uddhav's camp disapproved of the high-profile events which, it believed, had not led to success for the Shiv Udyog Sena in delivering on its promise of jobs; and Raj's camp did not like its leader's status in the party challenged by the rise of the son.

They quickly drifted apart, and by the time the Sena lost power in 1999, there were two openly competing currents in the party – one that favoured Raj as the successor to Balasaheb, and another that backed Uddhav.

The two did not merely represent disparate groups; their style of functioning was radically dissimilar. Raj relied a great deal on his oratory, his charisma and his ability to hold crowds; Uddhav was spoken of more as the quiet administrator and the low-profile organiser. These approaches need not have been conflicting, some Sena insiders said. The two could complement each other, they argued – one could deal with the masses while another could strengthen the organisational network; but their ambitions clashed.

There was a third current too, represented by Smita Thackeray, estranged wife of Thackeray's eldest son Jaidev. Smita lived at Matoshree when the Sena was in power and became quite a power centre herself, making a successful foray into production of Hindi films and, for a while, even wielding influence in party affairs. But with Uddhav steadily gaining the upper hand both in the house and within the party, she remained a serious challenge within the party fora only for a while. Sometime in 2009-10, she spoke of her desire to join the Congress, saying she had faith in Sonia Gandhi's leadership, but there has been no response to her overtures from the Congress.

Raj had, from 1998-99, been privately complaining to his uncle and to close friends that he no longer had much of a voice in party affairs. In the year 2000, he began to feel marginalised further, and in the next two years, he felt he was being deliberately kept out of the loop and, more worryingly for him, not allowed to appoint his loyalists as party office-bearers. His followers, he felt, were being sidelined in order to undercut his influence. He began to spend more and more time in Nashik, which he sought to develop as his stronghold, having got the impression that the way things were going, he would soon be left without a constituency if he did not work to develop it himself.

In 2002, he went public with his complaint for the first time, saying he had had no say in granting party tickets for the Mumbai civic polls scheduled in February that year. That was the first election in which Uddhav called the shots and decided almost each and every candidate, an ageing Thackeray having quietly made up his mind to hand over the reins to him. Hardly any Raj follower got a seat. The Sena won a thumping victory at the elections, and Uddhav was hailed as the new cub who ruled over India's financial capital.

In truth, the win of the Sena, whose mass base had been fast eroding ever since it lost power in the state and ever since Thackeray's involvement in public life became limited as a result of the age factor, could be attributed to the simple logic of the Mumbai civic election. Mumbai has 227 electoral wards, each with a voter count of around 40,000. Of these, 20,000 voters never vote. So the party that could take 5,000 of its loyal voters to the ballot box often emerges the winner. The Sena's organisational network and dedicated cadre could do this. In fact, the party had been successfully exploiting this logic for three decades, and it worked in 2002 as well. But Uddhav was given credit for leading a victorious campaign and for his choice of candidates, many of whom were freshers.

The Sena sought to play down the rivalry between the Thackeray cousins after the civic elections, but early in 2003 carried out a much-publicised exercise in which Uddhav was officially anointed successor to Bal Thackeray. At a Sena conclave held in Mahabaleshwar, a hill station more than 200 km away from Mumbai, Raj himself proposed the name of Uddhav as the party's executive president in front of a crowd of Sena followers and office-bearers, and the crowd, taking the cue, responded resoundingly in the affirmative.

Thackeray Sr has, to this day, maintained the episode was not an orchestrated one. He shared, 'When I went on to the dais later in the evening [that is, after the crowd had endorsed Raj's proposal], I asked my colleagues who so many of the garlands kept there were meant for. They told me Raj had asked for Uddhav to be appointed executive president, and that Sainiks gathered there had approved. I said, "How could you do this without letting me know?" and then addressed the crowd directly. Does this appointment have your approval, I asked. Have you said yes under duress? If you have, I will cancel the appointment rightaway. The crowd said, "No, no, nobody has forced us, we said yes of our own accord; of course, we approve of it." It was only then that I said okay.'

Raj later called his appeal to the crowd the biggest mistake of his political career and described it as similar to the act of hurling a stone on to one's own feet. The distance between him and his cousin grew wider after this incident, and Raj perceived that he was, increasingly, becoming more an outsider.

Meanwhile, Uddhav's leadership was beginning to court controversy too. In 2002-03, he floated a campaign called '*Mee Mumbaikar*' (I am a Mumbaikar) in an attempt to bring North Indians, by then a sizeable vote bank in Mumbai, into the Sena fold. This alienated the Sena's traditional mass base and was called ill-defined even by those who were clear that a pluralistic outlook was the only way to do politics in India. The party youth wing headed by Raj did its bit to pucker the campaign: activists of the Vidyarthi Sena attacked a group of North Indian youths at Kalyan railway station, where they had gathered to appear for the Railway recruitment exams. Raj demanded that Marathi youths should get preferential treatment in jobs and accused the Railways of not publicising the ads for the recruitment drive in the state.

Complaints of Uddhav's inaccessibility started circulating in Sena circles widely after the Mahabaleshwar conclave. People said, in hushed tones, that even senior Sena leaders were made to wait for hours at Matoshree, often in vain, and that Uddhav's private secretary seemed to have an unhealthy hold over matters: he would deny appointments at the scheduled hour, the complainants said, cancel meetings at random and, in some cases, even decide on appointments of Sena office-bearers. An incident that occurred sometime in 2004 began to be mentioned as illustrative of the new order at Matoshree.

A delegation of senior Shiv Sainiks from a remote part of Maharashtra had gone to meet Uddhav, it was reported in the Marathi media. They were first made to wait for long and were later told he could not meet them. 'Saheb's favourite fish, which he had imported, has died, and he's upset about it, so he can't meet you,' the delegation was apparently told.

The criticism grew more fierce after the Sena failed to win the 2004 Assembly election, the campaign for which was spearheaded by Uddhav, Thackeray Sr having withdrawn further from the party's day-to-day functioning.

The sense of drift in the Sena was now all too evident, and its first serious consequence was the exit of senior leader Narayan Rane in mid-2005.

Rane, who was close to Raj Thackeray, first said that though he was leader of Opposition in the Assembly and Sena legislature party leader, he was not being invited to meetings of party leaders. Almost immediately after that, at a party conclave at the Rangsharda auditorium in Bandra, Rane sensationally claimed party tickets were being sold. He was indirectly pointing a finger at Uddhav. When Thackeray Sr promptly expelled him, he said, 'I spoke out at the convention and was victimised by Uddhav. I will present workers who had paid money for tickets in the last election. Uddhav's PA brokered the deals. The Sena today is not the party of Balasaheb's dreams.'

Clearly, it wasn't. Anyone who had left the Sena earlier had had to take police cover. This time, loyalists of two Sena leaders (one of them Rane) came to blows in Rane's stronghold, Chembur, in north-east Mumbai and smashed each other's offices. He even posed a question to Balasaheb about his 'love for the son' and reiterated his charge of 'moneybag politics'.

With the party in disarray, Rane had decided to take his chance. Given his strong mass base in the Konkan, unlike some Sena leaders such as Manohar Joshi, Subhash Desai, Pramod Navalkar and Dattaji Nalavade, he had sent across the message that he was not fine with simply shifting from being in Balasaheb's shadow to Uddhav's shadow.

Rane thus became the third leader with a mass base and with a good following among the party cadre to quit the Sena − after Chhagan Bhujbal and Ganesh Naik.

The Sena suffered a humiliating defeat in the by-election in Malvan necessitated by Rane's resignation. The party's candidate, Parshuram Uparkar, lost his deposit against the rebel Sainik.

Days after the by-poll defeat, it was the turn of the man within the family to suggest he was breaking away. On Sunday, 27 November 2005, Raj Thackeray addressed an impromptu meeting of his followers outside his residence at Krishna Kunj building, Shivaji Park, and said he was resigning from all Sena posts (Sena leader and president of the Sena youth wing). He was still devoted to his *Vithal* (his idol, Thackeray), but the *badwe* (priests) were doing their damnedest to keep him away from the deity, he said. People close to Balasaheb had tried to poison the Sena chief's ears against him and his supporters, Raj claimed, and alleged that a quartet of *karkoons* (clerks) was running the Sena. He did not want to be party to the Sena's destruction, he pointed out, and added that he did not want to embarrass anyone either.

A stunned Thackeray responded the next day in *Saamna* by saying the Sena was 'nobody's private property'. Those who live in the shadow of the Himalayas should not think they are bigger than the mountain, he said. Everyone who stabs the Sena in the back should ponder over where they would have been if not for the Sena, he said, and reminded the nephew and his own followers that even Shivaji had been troubled by conflicts within the family and had wondered how his kingdom would last in the face of such conflicts.

Raj's angry supporters had damaged public property at Shivaji Park after his outburst and had even smashed the car of *Saamna*'s executive editor, Sanjay Raut, who had gone to Raj's house to pacify him. Referring to that, Thackeray Sr said, 'This *josh* (energy) is absent whenever the Sena is in crisis or when opponents attack the party. We'd have appreciated if this *josh* had been shown against Rane in the Malvan by-poll.'

Raj had come back half-way from his journey to the Konkan for the poll campaign. He would later claim he came back because he was informed of a conspiracy to 'finish him off'. This, again, was not an allegation against Rane but against others in the Sena.

Even after all the drama that unfolded outside Raj's house, most political observers ruled out the possibility of Raj leaving the Sena, especially in the wake of Thackeray's statement a day after the *Saamna* comment that 'Raj will listen only to me'.

Here I must say that I made the right prediction – and I am saying it only because that was one of the very, very few times I have got things right. Like all political animals and observers, I like to make predictions, and I get them wrong almost invariably. Normally, one has to weigh various possibilities, but this time, I had no doubt that Raj would quit the Sena. Many pundits argued that there was no way Raj would quit till Bal Thackeray was around. He was, after all, part of the family, and his case was significantly different from that of Bhujbal or Rane.

My theory went like this. We were in 2005. The Sena had not only lost power but much of its appeal, even for its own support base. It was quickly losing ground even in its strongholds, Mumbai, Thane and the Konkan. It had failed to win the 2004 Assembly poll, it had lost Rane, and with Bal Thackeray, around whom the party revolves, announcing in the midst of the Malvan by-poll campaign that he was going into semi-retirement and would only work on the party's advisory board, the crowd-puller was no longer very active. If there was anyone who could revive the Sena, it was Thackeray himself. That was indeed how he had constructed his outfit. Uddhav's image as a quiet organiser and a low-profile administrator had taken a serious beating, and it was now a question of whether the party would be able to keep its flock together.

I did not think Raj would wait for the party's base to erode further and for a greater number of Sena followers to go to other parties. If he moved away immediately, he could take away a chunk of the Sena's constituency with him. After three-four years more, there would perhaps be not such a huge chunk left for him to take away; they – party activists as well as voters – would have already sought and taken other political options by then. It would then perhaps even be a little late to invoke memories of his own leadership within the Sena, as his position within the party would have weakened further.

There was no doubt that the Sena's constituency was up for grabs; and if there was a time for Raj to make his move, it was in 2005.

Three weeks after his outburst, Raj quit the Sena and formed his own party. He called it the Maharashtra Navnirman Sena (MNS) and, hoping to draw in Sena followers anyway, sought to make it broad-based. He said he would welcome all communities into its fold and stressed that he envisioned Maharashtra as a progressive, forward-looking state. 'I want farmers in this state wearing jeans,' he said at the party's inaugural rally early in 2006.

Raj's party won seven seats in the 2007 Mumbai municipal elections which the Sena won again – thanks once more to the electoral logic mentioned earlier and to Sharad Pawar's last-minute decision not to enter into an alliance with the Congress. However, the MNS did not have any USP that would help distinguish it from other parties in the state. If it claimed to be inclusive, it did not win over all communities, and it was still not hardcore Maharashtrian enough to be able to sway the Sena's followers. If it wanted to be an umbrella organisation that would attract people from all backgrounds, then India's Grand Old Party was going to be a stiff competitor. People with left, centrist and right-wing ideologies all gathered under the Congress's shadow; the NCP was a shadow of the Congress itself; and then there was the BJP, which in Maharashtra had done adequate social engineering to attract people from various castes.

So early in 2008, Raj reworked his strategy in order to wean away the most vulnerable constituency, the constituency he originally had on his mind: the Sena's. The Sena was also the party that attracted plenty of first-time voters, so if it could become an option to that party, it would win over a significant percentage of Marathi youth, the MNS figured.

Opening up a campaign against North Indians, Raj first attacked actor Amitabh Bachchan, saying he loved Uttar Pradesh more than Maharashtra though he had become successful after he came to Mumbai. He said Amitabh had chosen Barabanki in Uttar Pradesh to open a girls' school but had not opened any school in Mumbai. Amitabh's wife, actor Jaya Bachchan, responded by saying they would surely start a school in the city if Raj gave them land for it. 'I heard he has a lot of land in Mumbai, at Kohinoor Mills,' she said. Raj, along with Sena leader Manohar Joshi's son Unmesh, had in 2004 bought the mill property in Dadar for Rs 421 crore (they have since sold it).

In February 2008, MNS activists first clashed with Samajwadi Party workers and then attacked taxi drivers from North India in Dadar and other parts of Mumbai. Commuters were attacked on the Western Railway, mainly in the suburbs beyond Borivli, and Raj accused North Indians of organising chhat puja in Mumbai as a show of political muscle.

Raj was soon arrested for creating public disharmony. With the arrest, he effectively anointed himself as the 'next Thackeray' and created an identity crisis for the officially anointed successor. Bal Thackeray was first arrested in 1969 as Sainiks went on the rampage in Mumbai over the Maharashtra-Karnataka border dispute. This was three years after the Shiv Sena was formed. Raj was held two years after his party's founding, and under the same section his uncle had been booked several times.

His identification with his uncle's identity – aggressive Maharashtrianism, anti-migrant denunciations, the cult of violence – was almost complete. He had Thackeray Sr's looks, mannerisms and the voice; now he had firm beginnings of a similar track record. This was what he wanted.

At the time Raj launched his anti-North Indian drive, Uddhav was working on building a multi-community identity for the Sena by trying to woo North Indians by holding Uttar Bharatiya Sammelans. They, after all, would comprise one-fourth of voters in Mumbai and Thane in the Lok Sabha and Assembly elections due in 2009. He was also working for the 2009 Assembly polls by holding rallies on power and farmers' issues. Raj obfuscated all the issues Uddhav was trying to raise and changed the subject of debate across Maharashtra. For the Sena-BJP to start the anti-incumbency rhetoric all over again and gain the same momentum would not be easy, given the limited time on hand. He also ensured that the North Indians who were slowly beginning to take a positive view of the Sena would now stay away from it – because he had reminded them of the Sena's past.

The Sena's positioning on Maharashtrianism had become confused, and it had ceded ground on the issue fast; Raj had stepped in to take that space. While giving Sena voters an option, he had sent North Indian voters into the arms of the Congress and NCP.

Raj's verbal attacks on North Indians and demand for preferential treatment for Maharashtrians continued in the run-up to the May 2009 Lok Sabha elections. The result: the MNS put up candidates in just 12 of Maharashtra's 48 constituencies – 9 in Mumbai-Thane and three others in Pune, Nashik and Aurangabad respectively – and polled over one lakh votes in all except one. In south Mumbai, where 26/11 had happened, it emerged number two, and in most other seats, a close number three, bagging a total of 8,68,000 votes in Mumbai alone as against 15,72,000 of the Congress-NCP and 11,48,000 of the Sena-BJP; and its combined tally in Mumbai and Thane was 21 per cent of total votes polled, as against 29 per cent for the Sena-BJP. Cause enough for concern for all major parties in the state.

The fight within the family proved costlier for the Sena in the Assembly elections in October 2009. While the MNS won 13 seats on debut, the Sena, for the first time in two decades, was relegated to fourth position in the state and even lost the post of leader of Opposition to the BJP, which had been its junior partner in the state all along. The defeat was remarkable because the performance of the Congress-NCP alliance government in the past one decade had been far from impressive, but the voters had rejected the principal opposition – the Sena – emphatically.

Raj had targeted Bachchan as he knew full well that the actor was close to the Sena and to Bal Thackeray and had released a book of poems written by Aditya Thackeray, Uddhav's son. (Aditya, aged 21 in 2012, has since emerged as the newest Thackeray on the block. He was appointed head of the Yuva Sena in 2010, and his first political act was to force the University of Mumbai to take Rohinton Mistry's novel *Such a Long Journey* off the arts syllabus because it contained uncomplimentary references to the Shiv Sena. In March 2012, in the wake of a series of goof-ups by the university, he led a raucous but unsuccessful campaign for the removal of University Vice-Chancellor Rajan Welukar. The Yuva Sena members led by Aditya created a ruckus in the University Senate over the issue and were suspended.) After its defeat in the Assembly polls, the older Sena picked cricketer Sachin Tendulkar as its target, knowing that he and Raj were on good terms.

Tendulkar was asked by a reporter, in the midst of the 'Marathi-non-Marathi' controversy following MNS violence, if he considered himself an Indian first or a Maharashtrian. 'I am a Maharashtrian, and am proud to be Maharashtrian, but I am an Indian first,' Tendulkar said.

Bal Thackeray criticised him sharply, saying he should stick to the cricket field and not try to enter the political arena. This criticism did not go down well even with the Sena's constituency, which felt the attack on Tendulkar was unwarranted.

The two sides have since continued to pick on each other and on people perceived to be close to the other camp, regardless of whether such closeness is for real or not or is simply social acquaintance.

Late in 2011, Raj criticised those opposed to the construction of the Peddar Road flyover. This includes the Mangeshkar sisters, who had at one point threatened to leave Mumbai if the flyover was built (the Mangeshkars live at Prabhu Kunj on Peddar Road). Now, both Lata Mangeshkar and Asha Bhosle have had excellent relations with Raj, but their brother, the music composer Hridaynath, had joined the Shiv Sena in 2009. The older Sena responded by saying that those who had defended Sachin Tendulkar's demand for extra FSI for his new home in Bandra (Raj had done that) had no right to criticise the Mangeshkar family, which was full of icons.

As I was concluding this chapter on the Raj-Uddhav conflict, the Shiv Sena, against all expectations, won the Mumbai civic elections in February 2012. The polls were key to the Sena's future. It had done badly in the previous decade, had lost an assembly post and was left number four in the state. If it had lost the BMC, whose budget is bigger than that of many states in India, there would have been a serious question mark over its future.

Defeat looked certain when the Congress and NCP formed an alliance for the polls; Maharashtra's Chief Minister Prithviraj Chavan even went to the extent of saying that Thackeray and his Shiv Sena would be rendered irrelevant when the poll results came out. But the Shiv Sena won 75 seats, its partner BJP 32, and the Sena recaptured power in the BMC comfortably.

The win has given new wind to the Sena, raising its hopes for the 2014 Assembly elections, but the results were equally encouraging for Raj Thackeray's party.

The MNS secured 28 seats, a major improvement over its 7 seats in the previous elections, and worryingly for the Shiv Sena, the MNS was Number 2 in 56 constituencies.

In a column I wrote for the *Hindustan Times* (19 February 2012), I explained what the results meant for both parties. I had pointed that the Shiv Sena owes its victory in the Mumbai civic polls not so much to its deft handling of the poll candidatures and campaigns by its Gen Now and Gen Next, but to the party-organisational network built up by Bal Thackeray over the last four decades. And to its excellent civic and neighbourhood links in the city which made its task of convincing voters easier.

Speculation began soon after the impressive performance of the two Senas in the Mumbai elections on whether they would tie up in future to keep the Congress–NCP out of power. There was even talk of an eventual merger when Raj Thackeray ensured the victory of the Shiv Sena in the Thane mayoral polls on a request made to him by three local Sena functionaries who had called on him at his residence. It was expected that the older Sena would, in return, support the MNS's attempt to get its own mayor in Nashik, where it was falling short of the required number and would have won with the Sena's support. Uddhav, however, refused to extend that support. The Sena's partner BJP nevertheless supported the MNS in the Nashik mayoral poll, sparking speculation of an altogether new alliance that might take shape in Maharashtra in the future, with or without the Shiv Sena. Ever since, talk of a Sena–MNS merger, or at least a tie-up between the two parties, has gained further momentum. The chief reason for this is the truce in the Thackeray clan that came about in the wake of Uddhav Thackeray's hospitalisation in July 2012. Raj, on his way to Alibaug for a party meet, rushed to Mumbai on knowing that Uddhav had been admitted to Bandra's Lilavati Hospital following complaints of breathlessness. Raj was by Uddhav's side as an angiography was conducted on him, and on Uddhav's discharge, drove him to Matoshree and spent more than an hour with Bal Thackeray and other family members. When Balasaheb was admitted to Lilavati soon after because of gastro-intestinal problems, Raj visited him at the hospital, inquired after his health and spent quite some time with him, as Uddhav was then at home, recuperating. On his discharge from hospital, Bal Thackeray hinted in an interview to *Saamna* that Raj and Uddhav had a lot in common and supported Raj's act of organising a morcha to protest against the violence at Azad Maidan following a Raza Academy meeting on 11 August 2012. He also said the media should not spread canards or disrupt the reconciliation process. Then, in his video-recorded speech played out to Sena cadres at the party's Dussehra rally in October 2012, an ailing Thackeray asked his Sainiks to back his son and grandson. In the same speech, he expressed concern that in Dadar, where the Shiv Sena was born, there were now two Senas. 'It's time to introspect. Marathis should come together and throw out the Congress.' So will the cousins come together? It would suit them politically in view of the 2014 Assembly and Parliamentary elections. But the one question to which there is still no answer is the question of leadership. One leader does not want to play second fiddle to the other. In such a situation, will a tie-up happen, and if it does, will it last? The least we can do is not rule anything out. Politics, after all, is the art of the possible.

BAL THACKERAY = SHIV SENA

B al Thackeray created a party-organisation which took shape almost as a ghetto of the Marathi *manoos*, and he introduced the Shiv Sena to the *manoos* as the modern-day army of Shivaji which would gather all Marathi-speaking people in its fold to correct wrongs done to them.

He quickly identified an enemy, the South Indians, whom he called the '*yandugundus*', as responsible for most of the wrongs. Those who inflicted these wrongs were to be resisted, he said, giving young Maharashtrians the go-ahead for a full-fledged assault on the alleged doers of injustice. 'You must demand that which is yours,' the Thackeray chant to Maharashtrian youth went. 'And if someone refuses to give it to you, you must snatch it.'

No non-violence, please, we're inheritors of the warrior tradition, he told Maharashtrians, many of whom added their rage to his and went about thrashing South Indians, 'International' Communists and just about any establishment purportedly discriminating against sons of the soil. Later, he told the Hindu community that they were second-class citizens in their own country and roused much the same level of anger, and the same bitter reaction, against 'pro-Pak Muslims'.

Having always exhorted his followers to pursue the path of '*thokshahi*', that is, rule by force and 'constructive violence', he has prided himself on every act perpetrated by his Sainiks, no matter how reprehensible some of their violent deeds have appeared to the rest of society.

Sainiks have forcibly shut down the whole of Mumbai any number of times over the last four decades, for one reason or another. Sometimes, the bandh has been a protest against some terrorist act; at other times, it has been part of an agitation against rising prices, or a show of solidarity with some aggrieved section of society, factory workers who have not got their dues or mill workers in the city who have not got the homes they were promised. All of these bandhs have been coercive in nature, though they have invariably been labelled 'spontaneous' by the Sena, and they have seen wanton violence and destruction of property by Sainiks, resulting in the loss of crores of rupees to the Indian economy. But every time the Sainiks have crippled Mumbai, Thackeray has held it up as a badge of honour for his party and as proof of its continuing hold over India's financial nerve-centre. He has encouraged Sainiks to deal physically with those who stand in the Sena's way and has publicly stood behind partymen who have followed his word to the T.

In 1967, he claimed he was proud of the Shiv Sainiks who destroyed the Communist Party's office in Lalbaug in central Mumbai; in 1991, he praised his band of followers – Shishir Shinde in particular, who has since shifted to Raj Thackeray's party – who dug up the Wankhede pitch in Mumbai to protest against India–Pak cricket; in 1992, he said that if the men who pulled down the Babri Masjid were indeed his, he was proud of them; and in 1999, he again patted the backs of Sainiks who dug up the Ferozshah Kotla ground in New Delhi to protest against Pakistan's proposed tour to India.

If there has been one refrain in Bal Thackeray's speeches and writings over the years, it has been 'My Shiv Sainik', with a pronounced emphasis on 'my'. Look at his oft-repeated assertions:

> 'My Shiv Sainik is my strength.'
> 'As long as my Shiv Sainik is with me, I don't care for anybody in the world.'
> 'I don't want any official post, because I consider the post of Shiv Sena pramukh given to me by my boys to be the greatest on earth.'
> 'I live only for my Sainiks. They are the highest authority for me.'

He has thus created a strong bond between himself and his men, in much the same way that the leader of any monolithic outfit establishes an emotional and psychological connect between him and his followers. Whenever he has been faced with a rebellion in the party or a crushing poll defeat, he has threatened to resign owning responsibility and given his larger-than-life image among Sainiks a boost; and in the event of a significant victory, he has genuflected before his followers on-stage to let them know how grateful he has been to them.

And yet, in doing all this, he has not forgotten to project himself as some sort of a messiah who is out to set right all the wrongs done to his people. He has consistently portrayed himself as saviour and benevolent dictator who would restore the rule of Shivaji and has swayed the masses with his fiery talk and fervent appeals. And he has rewritten slogans in the form of firmans and, by proving his threats real, has ensured that he is never ignored by well-wishers and haters alike.

In fact, so successful has Thackeray been in expanding his band of loyal followers that those who attended his speeches as youths in the 1960s now have their grandsons attending his rallies.

In 1966, the Sena chief could attract a crowd of two lakh youngsters for his rallies. Now, in his eighties, he commands the presence of at least a lakh listeners, no matter where he performs his verbal pyrotechnics.

He is an engaging speaker who holds their attention, builds up a wave of enthusiasm, even frenzy, on which he carries them, creates a mood that is as important as the speech itself, and, furthering the impression that it is the audience itself, with its cheers and bursts of applause, that is helping him carry himself from sentence to sentence, builds the crowd up into one single mass that is then willing to do anything for him.

Thackeray has, in addition, had an uncanny sense of the public pulse, something even his bitterest political adversaries acknowledge, and an ability to speak the language of the people. His line in oratory has often been dismissed as vulgar and distasteful by critics, but it has been his tempestuous terminology free of political platitudes that has made him the phenomenon he has turned out to be.

He has never written his speeches, has demonstrated disdain for intellectual gymnastics and has said that he hates hypocrisy. This purported dislike for hypocrisy is carefully cultivated in an era in which Indian politics has become synonymous with double standards. Thackeray's strength is to appear apolitical and to often react to a situation against the grain of a run-of-the-mill politician.

We'll take the example of a youngster's encounter with him sometime in 1973. Ajit Nadkarni, a 16-year-old from Dombivli moved by Thackeray's speeches, goes to meet him at his Matoshree residence in Bandra. 'I have just cleared my SSC exams, and I have a desire to work for the Shiv Sena full-time. I have earlier worked for the RSS, and in the RSS tradition of a full-time pracharak, I want to devote all my time to the Sena,' he tells the Sena chief.

Nadkarni, who later went on to become standing committee chairman in the Kalyan-Dombivli Municipal Corporation (KDMC), remembers:

> He (Thackeray) asked me to work for the Shiv Sena, but not full-time. He said: "You have just cleared your SSC exams. You must pursue your studies and become financially independent. Stand on your own feet. You must not be dependent on anyone for money, and do not just think of getting a job. Think of setting up your own business. Marathi youths must compete with others in the world of enterprise. If you work full-time for the Sena, your studies will be affected."

Nadkarni came out of the Thackeray home surprised.

The year we are talking about is 1973. The Sena is still not such a big organisation. It is confined to Mumbai, and it is still in need of expanding its network and attracting more youths into its fold. The conventionally smart thing would have been to get the young boy to work 24 hours for the party. But Bal Thackeray sent across a message to the teenager that he was not prepared to sacrifice his future for the Sena. In so doing, he won greater loyalty from the 16-year-old than he would otherwise have got.

Each of these so-called apolitical acts has been aimed at improving his political standing among the youth.

For instance, unlike the average Indian politician, Thackeray has not cared to be seen and heard in the properly newsworthy and photogenic context. He has never cultivated the media. And he has turned the exigencies of the politician's trade on their head by smoothly playing the role of a caricaturist: he can indulge in self-deprecating wit, though he and his Sainiks do not countenance criticism otherwise, can compare his political rivals to members of the animal kingdom, can deliberately add more than a touch of sexual innuendo to his political talk, and he has used Bollywood idiom effectively in order to attract crowds and once even danced to *Jumma Chumma De De* at one of his rallies.

Thackeray has even admitted what politicians consider the inadmissible: 'Yes, I do get money, but see how it is being distributed.

A heart patient comes, asks for ₹ 10,000, I help him. Some Sainik comes, needs money for bypass surgery, I help him. I have distributed more than ₹ 1 crore as Shiv Sena pramukh.'[157] Such admissions are intended to impress upon the people a dislike for the pretence of piety, and they have worked well in making many youngsters feel the man is anything but a *dhongi* (hypocrite).

Thus, Thackeray has defied the stereotype: he will eschew political theories, offer quick and easy solutions to problems and make emotional appeals.

There are other ways, too, in which he has aroused curiosity, attracted attention and proven to be something of an enigma.

He has threatened violent upheavals a number of times, but he is very well-organised in his personal life. He likes big celebratory fests in his honour, yet his tastes are simple, a glass of warm lager beer and a pipe (which he stopped smoking a few years ago) being minor indulgences. In public, he may freely use words considered offensive, but he is well-read, and a brilliant mimic. He plays the role of a dictator in his party and advocates violence, but at home, he is a family man who remembers the birthdays of his close ones and is dead against the idea of beating up children. He asks his Sainiks to dig up cricket pitches but counts Bapu Nadkarni and many of Mumbai's, and India's, old-time cricketers among his friends (Bapu and he used to take the train together to work from Dadar). And he rubbishes the Marathi novel, saying he does not approve of the form, and sharply attacked the famous writer Pu La Deshpande for his criticism of the Sena government – he even called a Marathi literary meet a '*bail* bazaar' (a gathering of bullocks) when writers there spoke disapprovingly of his words for Deshpande – but among his favourite recreations is listening to Pu La's CDs.

What does one say of a newspaper owner and editor who lambasts journalists in public and even suggests that they be thrashed? Or of a leader who denounces Bollywood icon Dev Anand one day for selecting a Pakistani girl as female lead in his film and, on realising it's a case of mistaken identity, instantly makes peace the next morning? Or of a politician who condemns the Mandal Commission report even though his party's support base consists largely of OBCs? Or one who routinely attacks his alliance partner, the BJP, without compunctions? Or a Hindutva protagonist who takes the most hardline stance on the demolition of the Babri Masjid and, some years later, suggests that a national monument for Hindus and Muslims be built at the Ayodhya site? Or a 'remote control' who, on realising that one of the ministers in his own government has committed an embarrassing blunder at a function by calling a dead actor on-stage, says "these are the illiterate rulers we have"?

Nobody believed, in the first place, that the heavy-throated slogans of Shiv Sainiks and the appeal of Bal Thackeray would ever go beyond the back alleys of Mumbai. When that happened and the Sena conquered Mumbai's civic body, it was said that Thackeray's charm was restricted to the metropolis and would never work anywhere else in the state. When the Sena started making inroads into rural areas and Thackeray claimed he would overthrow the Congress regime in Maharashtra, nobody believed him again. This last task was too tough and bordered on the impossible, it was argued not only by his foes but also by some friends and many of his partymen. Yet he succeeded, by conducting whirlwind campaigns across the length and breadth of Maharashtra, in unfurling the saffron flag atop Mantralaya.

Thackeray's strongest detractor will admit, in an undertone of course, that the Sena chief has, with his personality cult, brought the Sena where it is today, and what has indeed drawn so many to the party is his magnetism. He continues to hold sway over Mumbai, India's financial powerhouse, the multi-crore Hindi film industry (though Raj Thackeray is emerging a competitor in this regard), and the minds of so many.

A poll once conducted by *Mid Day* showed he was one of the three best known Indians in Pakistan, and a survey done by *Outlook* marked him among the three Mumbaikars that Delhiites would most like to have in the capital. For Bal Keshav Thackeray, that is a long way indeed, and testimony to his staying power.

To paraphrase what *Sunday* magazine once said about Thackeray, when he and his Shiv Sena first emerged on the Mumbai scene in 1966, when Indira Gandhi had been prime minister for a year; V.P. Naik was chief minister of Maharashtra; S.K. Patil was the Congress boss in Mumbai; and Dr Zakir Hussain was president of India.

Sunday said, in its issue published in the 1990s, that all those people had faded away from the national scene years later, but Thackeray and his Shiv Sena were still around.

I write this in 2012, when things have changed immeasurably even from the decade of the 1990s. Indira Gandhi's grandson, Rahul, has by now already spent quite a few years in politics and is being spoken of as a possible contender for the prime minister's post in the future. V.P. Naik died long ago, and has long been forgotten. S.K. Patil died in 1980, and today, he is hardly ever remembered in the city he once ruled. And the president today is Pranab Mukherjee.

When Thackeray started out in politics, Raj Kapoor was the leading star in Bollywood, and Amitabh Bachchan was a boxwallah in a Calcutta company. Sharad Pawar was a political non-entity. Nobody had even heard of V.P. Singh or P.V. Narasimha Rao. Tiger Pataudi was captain of the Indian cricket team, and Sunil Gavaskar was yet to play his first Test.

Today, Thackeray, at the age of 86, sits down to chat with Raj Kapoor's grandson, Ranbir, and has Amitabh Bachchan and his children and even grand-children over to dinner. Sharad Pawar treats him as a foe sometimes, and sometimes as a friend. V.P. Singh, Narasimha Rao and Tiger Pataudi have passed away, and Sunil Gavaskar retired a long time ago.

But Bal Thackeray has been the one constant, unchanging factor in Mumbai and Maharashtra's politics.

Thackeray, of course, has had numerous ups and downs. He has been abused by his political opponents and the media as fascist and Hitlerian (he has more than once spoken of his admiration of Hitler as an artist, orator and mass organiser, though he has said that the killing of Jews was wrong). He has been embraced by the Congress and by Sharad Pawar, he has been attacked by the Congress and Sharad Pawar. He has been arrested once by the Congress government for violence over the Maharashtra-Karnataka border dispute, and once again by the Congress-NCP government, in the year 2000, on the orders of then deputy chief minister, home minister and former Thackeray acolyte Chhagan Bhujbal (the court threw out the case, registered for inflammatory writing in the early 1990s, saying the state government had come to the court too late). He has been embraced by George Fernandes, he has been attacked by George Fernandes. He has been attacked by the BJP, he has been embraced by the BJP. He has been worshipped by his nephew, first from within the party fold, and then from the platform of a rival Sena. He has been written off as a spent force. News-wise, he has been controversial and therefore among the first choices of the media, though it has seen him as an anti-hero.

Through it all, Bal Thackeray has refused to go away.

The word Shiv Sena is synonymous with him. The party is woven too closely around him and is identified too much with its maverick Senapati to make way for anyone else as its unquestioned leader after him. Succession may be easy; success is what the heirs will have to work really hard for.

For the Shiv Sena, Bal Thackeray has been one of a kind. And therewith: irreplacable.

NOTES

1 *Marmik Mehfil*, 25 May 1997.
2 Ibid.
3 Ibid.
4 Ibid.
5 Ibid.
6 Ibid.
7 Mary Fainsod Katzenstein, *Ethnicity and Equality: The Shiv Sena Party and Preferential Policies in Bombay,* Cornhill University Press, 1978.
8 *Saamna*, 23 January 1997.
9 *Bal Thackeray: A Photo-Biography*, Raj Thackeray, UBSPD, 2005.
10 Thackeray's interview with Sudhir Gadgil, mid-2009, ahead of Assembly polls in Maharashtra in October 2009.
11 Ibid.
12 Ibid.
13 Ibid.
14 *Gathoda*, a collection of Pu La Deshpande's largely unpublished work, published by Parchure Prakashan Mandir in March 2012.
15 Thackeray's interview with Sudhir Gadgil, mid-2009, ahead of Assembly polls in Maharashtra in October 2009.
16 Ibid.
17 Ibid.
18 Ibid.
19 Ibid.
20 K.C. Zachariah, *Migrants in Greater Bombay*.

21 Ibid.
22 Census of India, Maharashtra, 1961 (published in 1964).
23 Census of India, Maharashtra, 1961, and Census of India, Mumbai, 1951 (published in 1953).
24 Census of India, Migration Tables, 1961.
25 'Origins of Nativism: The Emergence of Shiv Sena in Bombay', *Asian Survey*, 13 April 1973.
26 Mary Fainsod Katzenstein, *Ethnicity and Equality: The Shiv Sena Party & Preferential Policies in Bombay*, Cornhill University Press, 1978.
27 Edwardes, *The Gazetteer of Bombay*.
28 Shanti Patel, *Twin City Bombay*.
29 Mary Fainsod Katzenstein, *Ethnicity and Equality: The Shiv Sena Party & Preferential Policies in Bombay*, Cornhill University Press, 1978.
30 University of Mumbai Annual Reports.
31 Government of Maharashtra Education Department, Educational Development in Maharashtra State, 1950–51 to 1965–66, Mumbai, Government Central Press, 1968.
32 'The Endangering Tiger', *The Times of India*, 21 December 1997.
33 'What after Thackeray', *Outlook*, 25 September 1996.
34 Ibid.
35 V.S. Naipaul, *India, A Million Mutinies Now*, Minerva, 1990.
36 *Marmik Mehfil*, 25 May 1997.
37 Ibid.
38 Ibid.
39 V.S. Naipaul, *A Million Mutinies*.
40 *Marmik*, 19 July 1966.
41 Interview.
42 Interview.
43 *Marmik Mehfil*, 25 May 1997.
44 *Nava Kaal*, 31 October 1966.
45 Ibid.
46 'The face of a lumpen state', *The Pioneer*, 21 September 1997.
47 Interview.
48 *Marmik Mehfil*, 25 May 1997.
49 Thackeray's interview with Sudhir Gadgil, mid-2009, ahead of Assembly polls in Maharashtra in October 2009.

50 Katzenstein, *Ethnicity and Equality*.

51 Interview.

52 A total of 105 people demanding a Samyukta Maharashtra were shot on the orders of then Mumbai Chief Minister Morarji Desai.

53 Interview.

54 *The Times of India*, special supplement on Bal Thackeray, 23 January 1997.

55 Katzenstein, *Ethnicity and Equality*.

56 Jnyanesh Maharav, *Thackeray Family*, Prabhat Prakashan, 1995.

57 Ibid.

58 Katzenstein, *Ethnicity and Equality*.

59 His brothers are Shrikant and Ramesh, and his five sisters are Sudha Sule, Pama Tipnis, Sushila Gupte, Sarla Gadkari and Sanjeevani Karandikar. Prabodhankar also had an adopted son, Ram Harne.

60 When Menon was defence minister in 1962, India had suffered an ignominious defeat against the Chinese, and Menon's Communist leanings were cited by many as the chief reason for the ill-preparedness of India's forces.

61 Prakash Akolkar, *Jai Maharashtra*, Prabhat Prakashan, 1998.

62 Interview.

63 *Marmik,* 13 March 1968.

64 Ibid.

65 19 April 1968.

66 Girija Keer, *Balasaheb*, Madhavi Prakashan, Pune, 1996.

67 *The New York Review of Books*.

68 Dipankar Gupta, *Nativism in a Metropolis, The Shiv Sena in Bombay*, Manohar Publications, 1982.

69 Katzenstein, *Ethnicity and Equality*.

70 Ibid.

71 Interview.

72 *Marmik*, 11 August 1968.

73 Interview.

74 Interview.

75 Interview.

76 Gupta, *Nativism in a Metropolis*

77 Ibid.

78 Interview.

79 *Hindutva: Saar Aani Dhaar*, Dimple Publications, 1991.

80 The Mahajan Commission was set up by the Centre to look up into the border dispute. It upheld the merger of the border areas with Mysore.

81 *Nava Kaal*, 23 January 1969.

82 *Nava Kaal*, 28 January 1969.

83 Girija Keer, *Balasaheb*.

84 Ibid.

85 *Nava Kaal*, 2 February 1969.

86 *Marmik*, June 1991.

87 *Nava Kaal*, 18 February 1969.

88 Ibid.

89 *Nava Kaal*, 20 February 1969.

90 *Nava Kaal*, 21 February 1969.

91 *Nava Kaal*, 13 March 1969.

92 *Chavan, A Biography*, Somaiya Publications, Mumbai.

93 Interview.

94 *Balasaheb*, Girija Keer, 1991.

95 Interview.

96 *Nava Kaal*, 2 February 1970.

97 Sena rally at Bhoiwada Maidan, 9 February 1970.

98 *Maratha*, 8 June 1970.

99 *Nava Kaal*, 5 July 1970.

100 Interview.

101 Katzenstein, *Ethnicity and Equality*.

102 Interview.

103 Interview.

104 *Shiv Sena Speaks*, by Kapilacharya, Limaye Printing Works, 1967.

105 Sena's Dussehra rally at Shivaji Park, 27 October 1982.

106 Antulay was forced to resign on 12 January 1982, after the Bombay High Court found him guilty of using cement permits in return for gifts to the Indira Gandhi Pratibha Pratishthan, a trust managed by him.

107 Interview.

108 Jnyanesh Maharav, *Thackeray Family*.

109 Sena-BJP rally, Girgaum Chowpatty, 1 January 1998.

110 *Saamna*, 23 January 1998.

111 Mohammad Ahmad Khan of Indore had filed an appeal in the Supreme

Court against a Madhya Pradesh High Court judgement to his divorced wife, Shah Bano. The Supreme Court, on 23 April 1985, upheld the High Court ruling and said Section 125 of the Criminal Procedure Code, which made it compulsory for husbands to make provisions for their divorced wives if they had no other means of sustenance, would also apply to Muslim husbands. The intervener in the case, the Muslim Personal Law Board, called the judgement an interference in Muslim personal law. The Supreme Court had also consulted the text of the Koran, and the MPLB held it had no business to do so.

112 *Marmik*, 13 October 1985.

113 *The Shah Bano Controversy*, edited by Asghar Ali Engineer.

114 *Marmik*, 1 December 1985.

115 Interview.

116 *The Free Press Journal*, 6 September 1988.

117 Ibid.

118 October 13, 1988.

119 *The Daily*, 31 January 1988.

120 *Mainstream*, 3 September 1988.

121 *The Indian Express*, 8 February 1988.

122 Ibid

123 *The Indian Post*, 20 September 1988.

124 *The Hindu*, 6 March 1988.

125 *The Telegraph*, 6 March 1988.

126 *The Indian Post*, 18 March 1988.

127 *The Sunday Observer*, 24 April 1988.

128 Ibid.

129 *The Times of India*, 26 May 1988.

130 21 April 1988.

131 *The Indian Post*, 6 July 1988.

132 *The Statesman*, 22 October 1988.

133 *The Times of India*, 12 October 1988.

134 1 January 1989.

135 *The Sunday Observer*, 24 April 1988.

136 22 May 1989.

137 Interview

138 *The Indian Post*, 22 May 1989.

139 *The Indian Express*, 7 October 1990.

140 *The Times of India*, 23 March 1991.

141 *The Sunday Observer*, 2 February 1992.

142 *The Independent*, 26 October 1991.

143 *Politics in Maharashtra*, Himalaya Publications, 1995.

144 Ibid.

145 *The Afternoon on Sunday*, 15 February 1995.

146 *The Indian Express*, 8 October 1998.

147 The Puranik committee report was placed before the Assembly by the then chief minister, Manohar Joshi on 24 April 1997.

148 The Dudhat committee report was placed before the Assembly on 15 April 1998.

149 *Saamna*, 21 March 1998.

150 Here it is pertinent to note that for all the noise it makes on the issue of Marathi, the Sena has mostly sent non-Marathi-speaking to the Rajya Sabha: Chandrika Keniya, Mukesh Patel, Pritish Nandy and Sanjay Nirupam among them.

151 *The Indian Express*, 29 July 1998.

152 Ibid.

153 *The Times of India*, 3 May 1998.

154 *The Indian Express*

155 The strictures were passed by a division bench of Justice Srikrishna and Justice S.S. Parkar on 12 March 1999.

156 The Congress and NCP came together after the poll results to form an alliance government.

157 Public rally in Dombivli, 6 November 1989.

BIBLIOGRAPHY

Gupta, Dipankar, *Nativism in a Metropolis: The Shiv Sena in Bombay*, Manohar Publications, New Delhi, 1982

Kapilacharya, *Shiv Sena Speaks*, published by Bal Thackeray, VD Limaye Printing Works, 1967.

Katzenstein, Mary Fainsod, *Ethnicity and Equality: The Shiv Sena Party and Preferential Policies in Bombay*, Cornell University Press, Ithaca and London, 1979.

Krishnan, T.V. Kunhi, *Chavan: A Biography*, Somaiya Publications, Mumbai, 1971.

Lakdawala, D.T. *Work, Wages and Well-Being in an Indian Metropolis*, Bombay University Press, Mumbai, 1963.

Naipaul, V.S., *India: A Million Mutinies Now*, Minerva, 1990

Patel, Sujata and Alice Thorner (ed.), *Bombay – Metaphor for Modern India*, Oxford University Press, Mumbai, 1995.

Thackeray, Raj, *Bal Thackeray: A Photo-Biography*, UBSPD, New Delhi, 2005.

Thakkar, Usha, and Mangesh Kulkarni (eds), *Politics in Maharashtra*, Himalaya Publishing House, Mumbai, 1995

The Bombay Civic Election of 1968 (Bombay: All-India Institute of Local Self-Government)

Marathi
Akolkar, Prakash, *Jai Maharashtra*, Prabhat Prakashan, 1998.

Deshpande, Pu La, *Gathoda*, Parchure Prakashan Mandir, 2012.

Keer, Girija, *Balasaheb*, Madhavi Prakashan, Pune, 1996.

Maharao, Jnyanesh, *Thackeray Family*, Prabhat Prakashan, 1995.

Musle, Anil, *Shiv Sena: Apaprachar aani Vastavta*, Satej Prakashan, Navi Mumbai.

Thackeray, Bal, *Hindutva: Saar aani Dhaar*, Dimple Publications, 1991.

Newspapers
Marathi
Saamna, Maratha, Nava Kaal, Loksatta, Maharashtra Times
English
The Times of India, The Indian Express, The Telegraph, The Pioneer, The Asian Age, The Indian Post, Mid Day, The Afternoon Despatch and Courier, The Hindu, The Independent, The Sunday Observer

Periodicals
Marathi
Marmik, Lokprabha
English
The Illustrated Weekly of India, India Today, Outlook, Frontline, Onlooker, The New York Review of Books

INDEX

Advani, L.K., 15, 32, 177, 193, 197, 215, 225

Ambedkar, Bhimrao, 96, 191
  Writings and Speeches

Atre, Acharya, 11, 13, 26, 49, 50, 115
  Rally at Thane's Gamdevi
  Maidan - 115

Athawale, Ramdas, 116

Babri demolition, 193, 196, 206, 212

Bambi, 9

Ban on screening of Hindi films in Madras, 53-55

Bardhan, A.B., 92

Barve, S.G., 49, 50, 52

Behere, G.V., 115

Bhartiya Janata Party (BJP), 32, 34, 44, 45, 128, 135, 138, 139, 140, 142, 147, 149, 150, 162, 165, 166, 169, 170, 173, 176, 177, 178, 179, 180, 181, 182, 183, 184, 185, 187, 194, 197, 208, 214, 215, 216, 217, 218, 219, 220, 221, 223, 226, 227, 237, 238, 239, 240, 241, 247, 249, 254.

Bhujbal, Chagan, 18, 20, 96, 97, 140, 145, 146, 147, 148, 150, 153, 155, 160, 161, 162, 163, 169, 184, 185, 186, 187, 189, 191, 206, 219, 220, 221, 230, 235, 236, 249
  Quit Shiv Sena, 184-92

Cariappa, Lt. Gen., 99, 100.

Cartoonist, 1, 3, 7, 8, 10, 11, 13, 15, 23, 25, 46, 181.

Chafekar, Achyut (Barrister), xi, 23, 53, 86

Chavan, S.B., 151, 160, 164, 170

Chavan, Y.B., 14, 31, 56, 73, 74, 80, 81, 82, 83, 95, 96.

Dandavate, Madhu, 44, 56, 157

Dange, S.A., 11, 26, 30, 49, 68, 92, 98, 130

Dassera Rally, xiii, 24, 47, 129, 242

Desai, Krishna Death, 89, 91

Desai, Morarji, 12, 75

Desai, Ramakant, 41

Deshmukh, Vilasrao, 169

Deshpande, Bani, 58, 130

Deshpande, Madhav, 28, 96, 189

Deshpande, Roza, xi, 30, 63, 104, 117, 157

Dhale, Raja, 116, 161
Dhanurdhari, 13
Dhasal, Namdeo, 116, 161
Dhavan, Sadakant, 90

Emergency, 114, 118, 119, 135

Fernandes, George, 28, 43, 49, 50,
51, 98, 127, 166, 172, 249
Free Press Journal, 1, 2, 3, 11, 170

Gadkari, Nitin, xv, 217
Gandhi, Indira, ii, 12, 71, 80, 81,
92, 98, 102, 117, 118, 119, 122,
128, 132, 134, 135, 138, 181,
248, 249
Gaonkar, Vijay, xi, 24, 82, 94, 95,
95
Giri, V.V., 98
Gupta, Dipankar, 60, 67

Hazare, Anna, 220
Hindu Mahasangh, 131, 132
Hindutva, xix, 32, 39, 46, 68, 70,
86, 87, 93, 99, 115, 129, 131,
132, 133, 135, 137, 138, 139,
141, 142, 145, 150, 156, 161,
165, 166, 170, 172, 174, 176,
177, 179, 182, 190, 193, 208,
209, 210, 229, 247.
Hitler, 216, 249

Janata Dal, 61, 97, 165, 166, 173,
176, 177, 178, 179, 184
Jatra, Ravivarchi, 23
Joshi, Manohar, 28, 53, 57, 69, 75,
76, 77, 83, 84, 96, 97, 99, 100,
102, 120, 123, 125, 153, 161,
162, 184, 185, 193, 214, 215,
218, 219, 227, 234, 237
Joshi, Murli Manohar, 194
Kamath, M.V., 12

Katzenstein, Mary Fainsod, 4, 5, 18.
29, 34, 60, 92, 110
Ethinicity and Equality: The Shiv
Sena Party and Preferential
Policies in Bombay, 4, 18
Kesri, 13
Ketkar, Kumar, 20, 26
Khambete, D.P., 13, 14
Khandilkar, Nilkanth, 129
Practical Socialism, 129
Khopkar, Shridhar, 174
Krishnaji Madhav 'Appasaheb', 7
Kumar, Dilip, xv, 40, 225

Labour unrest, 124

Mahadik, Wamanrao, 28, 29, 84,
92, 93, 96, 97, 123, 153
Mahajan, Pramod, 138, 177, 226
Maharashtra Girni Kamgar Union,
124
Maharashtra Navnirman Sena, xiv,
237, 238, 239, 240, 241, 247
Mahatma Phule, 8, 94, 162
Malkani, K.R., 177, 178
Mantri, Madhav, 41
Maratha, 13, 14, 26, 51
Marathi Manoos, 4, 22, 23, 25, 26,
32, 57, 67, 92, 99, 103, 138, 190,
218, 243
Marmik, ii, 1, 3, 4, 5, 6, 10, 13, 14,
15, 16, 18, 20, 21, 23, 24, 27, 43,
50, 51, 54, 55, 57, 59, 70, 90,
101, 118, 135, 143, 153, 165, 172
Matoshree, xv, xviii, xix, 8, 40, 43,
190, 218, 223, 228, 231, 233,
234, 241, 245
Mehta, Arun, 62, 78
Menon, V.K. Krishna, 49
Migrants in Bombay, 16–27
Modak, Emmanuel (Police
Commissioner, Mumbai), 75

Munde, Gopinath, xvii, 45, 185, 215, 223
Murder of Ramesh Kini, 230
Muslim League, 44, 105, 106, 169, 178

Nadkarni, Bapu, 41, 247
Nagarkar, Kiran, 116
  Bedtime Story, 116
  Saat Sakkam Trechalis, 116
Naik, Vasantrao, 14, 57, 72, 115
Naipual, V.S., India: A Million Mutinies Now, 21
Nationalist Congress Party, xiv, 217, 224, 227, 237, 238, 239, 240, 241, 249
Nava Kaal, 25, 27, 129
Navalkar, Pramod, 6, 57, 67, 79, 84, 96, 97, 102, 106, 123, 153, 199, 219, 234
Nehru, Jawaharlal, xiv
News Day, 12, 13
Nirupam, Sanjay, 226

Padhye, Bhau, 116
Paper Tiger, 3, 172
Patil, S.K., 2, 14, 49, 51, 52, 57, 98, 101, 248, 249
Pawar, Sharad, xiv, xv, 43, 45, 122, 127, 139, 160, 170, 176, 182, 203, 207, 215, 218, 221, 227, 237, 249
Peasants and Worker's Party, 57, 148, 158
Pradhan, Satish, 97, 174

Rane, Narayan, 234
Rangnekar, Ahilya, xi, 32, 63, 91
Rashtriya Mill Mazdoor Sangh, 62, 126
Riots 1992-93, 193-206
RSS, 32, 34, 35, 72, 92, 93, 96, 115, 116, 147, 162, 166, 171, 176, 179, 194, 208, 246

Saamna, 11, 138, 172, 189, 190, 193, 196, 197, 201, 204, 205, 210, 211, 219, 221, 229, 230, 235, 236, 241
Salvi, Dattaji, 28, 62, 69, 77, 84, 96, 97, 126, 153, 210
Samant, Dr Datta, 124, 166, 188
Sampoorna Maharashtra Samiti, 49, 56, 70
Samyukta Maharashtra, 1, 11, 12, 13, 14, 20, 26, 31, 49, 57, 58, 70, 130, 163
Sarabhai, Kartikeya, 110
Satya Shodhak movement, 8
Shinde, Sushilkumar, 43
Shiv Sena
  Alliance with BJP, 175-183
  Anti-price rise agitation, 94-95
  Attack on Ganesh Talkies, 54
  Banning publication of Marathi novel Raada, 116
  Banning publication of play Bedtime Story, 116
  Birth of Saamna , 172
  BMC poll in 1973, 102
  Boycott of Sikhs, 166-68
  Call for bandh in Bombay in 1973, 114
  Campaign Against 'Yandugundus' (south Indians), 53-55
  Campaign to employ Maharashtrians, 109-10
  Comparison with RSS, 34-38
  Criticism of Communists, 59-61
  Damage to Wankhede stadium, 187
  Enron issue (Rebecca Mark), 218

Entry in Maharashtra Legislative assembly, 91-93
First public meeting in Shivaji Park, 23-27
Formation, 19-22
Guidelines set for Bhartiya Kamgar Sena, 63
Hindu nationalism, 68-69
In power (1995 – 1999), 217-27
In praise of Nathuran Godse, 186-87
Loss in BMC election, 1992, 186
Maharashtra Dharma, 32
Mobilization of Sainiks, 24-29
Network of mandals and gymnasium, 24
Protest against the play Ghasiram Kotwal, 115
Protest in 1969, 72-77
Pune Convention, 17172
Riots in Bhiwandi, 85-87
Role of Sena shakhas, 36-38
Saffron Guard, 88-89
Shiv Sena Speaks, 53
Sons-of-the-soil movement, 4, 29, 70
Statement of Oath, 22-27
Stopped screening of Hindi films made in South, 53-55
Support to Congress in 1967, 101
Thane municipal corporation election 1967, 52-53
Tie-up with Congress, 101-02
Tie-up with Praja Socialist Party, 56-61
Win in Aurangabad, 168-70

Shivaji Jayanti 1970, 85
Shivaji Park, xiii, xv, xix, 8, 23, 24, 25, 27, 41, 51, 54, 55, 72, 73, 74, 76, 93, 99, 121, 128, 131, 167, 180, 214, 215, 220, 235
Shrikrishna Commission report, 223

Tendulkar, Vijay, 115, 118
    Ghasiram Kotwal, 115
Thackeray, Bal
    Appeal to Shiv Sainiks from Yerwada Jail, 79
    Arrest in 1969, 78
    Arrest in 1969, 78-83
    Birth, 7
    Children, 43
    Death of eldest son, 43
    Established Bhartiya Kamgar Sena, 62
    Estrangement with brother, 44
    Estrangement with son Jaidev, 43
    Felicitation by Bombay Film Industry, 55
    First speech, 25-27
    Formed Shiv Sena, 21
    Joined Free Press Journal, 11
    Konkan tour in 1970, 83-84
    Love for cricket, 41
    Love for gardening, 42-43
    Love for Hindi movies, 41-42
    Marriage, 43
    Oratorical skills, 15
    Organised first rally in Shivaji Park, 23-27
    Relationship with media, 187-88
    Sense of public pulse, 245-250
    Setting up of an employment bureau, 67
    Slogan 'Bury the five demons', 49
    Stand on Karnataka-Maharashtra border dispute, 70-77

Started *Marmik*, 1
Theory of '*thokshahi*', 94
Theory of constructive
   violence, 94–95

Thackeray, 'Parbodhankar' Keshav,
   1, 3, 4, 7, 8, 9, 11, 13, 14, 15, 21,
   22, 25, 31, 35, 51, 97, 228
Thackeray, Raj, xiv, xix, 19, 40, 43,
   44, 188–90, 219–20, 228–42
   Bal Thackeray's influence, 229
   Childhood, 228–29
   Death of Ramesh Kini
      controversy, 230
   Formation of Maharashtra
      Navnirman Sena, 237
   Michael Jackson concert
      controversy, 230–31
   President, Bhartiya Vidyarthi
      Sena, 189

Resignation from all Sena posts,
   235
Thackeray, Smita, 231
Thackeray, Uddhav, xiii, xiv, xviii,
   xix, 40, 43, 44, 45, 188–90, 225,
   226, 228–42
   Appointment as executive
      president, 233
   Interest in photography, 229
   Mee Mumbaikar campaign, 233

Vajpayee, Atal Bihari, 139

Wagle, Nikhil, 187, 210
   *Work, wages and well-being in an
      Indian metropolis*, 18

Yerwada Jail, 42, 79, 82

PHOTO CREDITS

1. Frontispiece (pg. i) *Fatkare* by Bal Thakeray, 2012
2. Frontispiece (pg. ii) *Fatkare* by Bal Thakeray, 2012
3. Page: xvi-xvii Picture copyright: Getty Images

Pictures as they appear in the insert:
3. *Fatkare,* by Bal Keshav Thackeray, 2012
4. *Fatkare,* by Bal Keshav Thackeray, 2012
5. *Bal Keshav Thackeray,* Photobiography, Chinar Publishers
6. *Bal Keshav Thackeray,* Photobiography, Chinar Publishers
7. *Fatkare* by Bal Keshav Thackeray, 2012
8. *Fatkare* by Bal Keshav Thackeray, 2012
9. *Bal Keshav Thackeray,* Photobiography, Chinar Publishers
10. *Bal Keshav Thackeray,* Photobiography, Chinar Publishers
11. Copyright: MID-DAY
12. *Bal Keshav Thackeray,* Photobiography, Chinar Publishers
13. *Bal Keshav Thackeray,* Photobiography, Chinar Publishers
14. *Bal Keshav Thackeray,* Photobiography, Chinar Publishers
15. *Bal Keshav Thackeray,* Photobiography, Chinar Publishers
16. Copyright: Getty Images
17. Copyright: Getty Images
18. Copyright: Getty Images